THE GR
WHIT

The Life an

Alan 'Howling La d' Hope

Leader of the Official Monster Raving Loony Party

Rock 'n' Roller and Country Music Vocalist

Hotelier

And for the very first time

The untold story of what really happened in December 1961

when The Beatles visited Aldershot

Written by

Alan 'Howling Laud' Hope

with 'Prince Rex of Fleet'

ISBN-13: 9798640657746

This book is dedicated to:

John Anthony Hope (14th February 1947 to 19th October 2017)
Mary Hands – my sister
Norma Hope (13th April 1949 – 29th April 2007)
To my parents – George and Eleanor
And to my children: Mark, Angela, Gina and Helen.

For my good friend
Dean

'Welcome to the Station'

'Fleet'

Best wishes

[illegible signature]

A disclaimer …

In writing this, I have done my best to be accurate in terms of time and place, and in describing events. But memories do fade, and stories get embellished over the years. History is the past we have each invented for ourselves.

If there are errors or inaccuracies, I sincerely apologise. But these are my memories, honestly and truthfully re-told.

So enjoy! I'm looking forward to writing volume 2 when I hit 100!

Alan Hope

CONTENTS

Welcome …

Greetings, dear reader!

Well, this is it. This is me! All 77 years of me!

This is my story as I remember it … and I have a good memory.

I've tried – I've really tried – to be as open and honest in the telling of my story as I can be. Some things are easy to talk about; some are more difficult. But hopefully, you will enjoy the tale and that it will entertain and amuse. That's really all I can ask for. That I have entertained you as you read. At the end of it all, I am just a Showman – always have been, and always will be!

I've presented this in seven main parts, reflecting the different stages of my life:

Part 1 looks at (more or less) the first 20 years – my journey from birth to adulthood;

Part 2 describes my years in the music business, and my alter-ego Kerry Rapid;

Part 3 focuses on my time as a hotelier and publican;

Parts 4 and 5 deal with my political career with the Official Monster Raving Loony Party;

Part 6 focuses on some other major interests and achievements; and

Part 7 wraps the whole thing up.

These stages in my life-journey overlap so the story is not completely chronological. But in a sense, I have had several distinct 'lives' and it just seems right to tell the tale that way. And I've tried to make this read as if we are just having a chat over a pint in the pub. What better way is there to tell a story?

Creating this book has been an interesting and enjoyable experience. Retrieving sometimes hazy memories, sometimes crystal-clear images. It made me think. Made me think about who I am, and importantly, how I became the person I am today. A voyage of self-discovery. Not all of it was easy. Talking about the good times is fine, but I am naturally quite a private person, so the more difficult times are harder to reveal. But I hope I have not just described the 'external' Alan, but the 'internal' Alan too. You will be the judge of that.

Despite the highs and the lows, the good and the bad, I would simply say:

"It's all been GREAT FUN."

I truly hope you enjoy the journey too!

PART 1

BEGINNINGS

In this Part:

Chapter 1: How I was born in the middle of World War II, and some background on the post-war environment; my family; and my upbringing.

Chapter 2: My schooldays and all the stuff you get up to as a kid.

Chapter 3: The abolition of National Service just in time, and that first generation of teenagers, of which I was part.

Chapter 4: My first girlfriends, my first wife and the birth of my son.

CHAPTER 1

Family life …

I was born – as they say – at a very early age. Specifically, on the 16th of June 1942 at 61 Colefordbridge Road in Mytchett, Surrey.

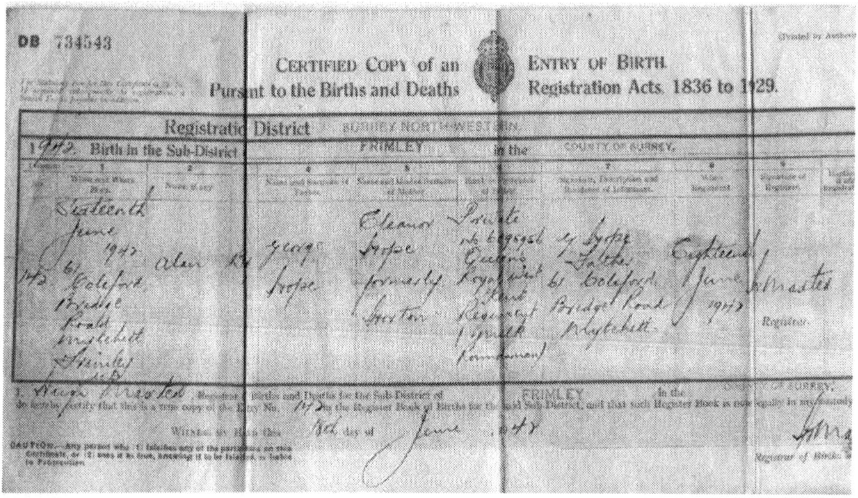

My birth certificate. (My private collection)

I am the eldest of three children: my brother John was born in 1947, and my sister Mary in 1954. But more about them in due course.

So let me take you back a few years and set out the story of how I came to be …

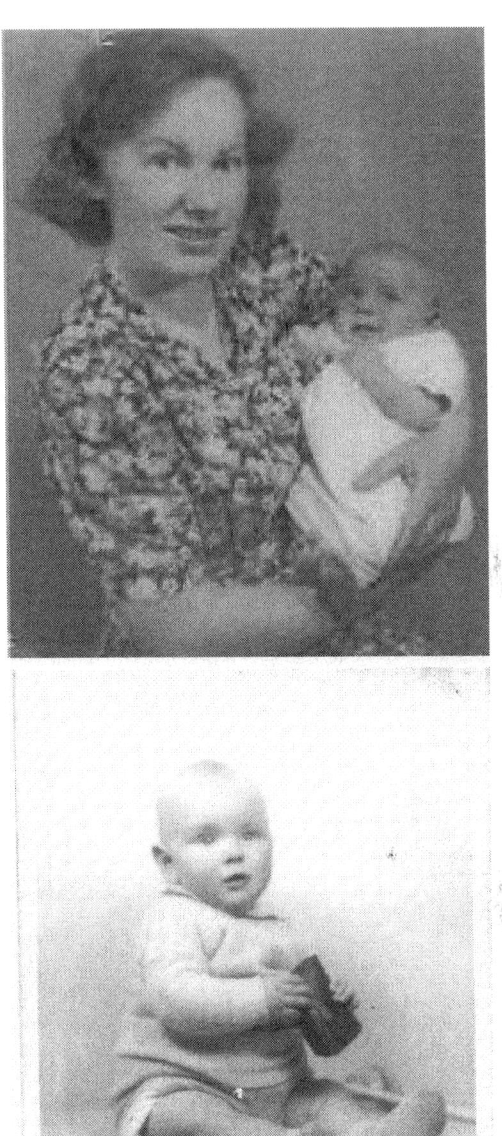

Ain't I cute? (My private collection)

Meet the ancestors …

My father, George, was a Geordie – George the Geordie! He was from the Benwell/Scotswood Road area of Newcastle. He knew all the verses of the 'Blaydon Races' at any rate. It would be romantic to say that my father came south with the Jarrow March, and simply stayed put – but that's not really true.

I'm pretty sure his family were what we would call today 'Economic Migrants'. We're going back to the Depression of the 1930s. Work was hard to find, and of course, the North suffered more than the South.

But my father's family were not without a bob or two. I was told that his father had owned a chain of fish and chip shops in Newcastle, so they were not penniless. The whole family came south on a coal barge: his parents; my father; his step-brothers Tom and John (Jack) Archibald; and his sister Caroline Hope. No-one really spoke about that side of the family much. I got the impression it was all very secretive. I don't know if my grandmother had been married before, and perhaps her husband had died. There was a story – or a rumour in the family – that he'd disappeared to Australia. We never really knew the real truth. But in those days, if you did something naughty, you were transported to Australia. He was never seen again. It's all a bit of mystery. I can't say if it's true or not.

There were some more children in the family too – James Hope, Elsie Hope, and Marion Hope. They were all born in Cove after the family came down here. They've all passed away since of course, which makes me the oldest Hope. My father would have turned 104 on the 11th November (2019) if he was still alive.

My father wasn't a big man – quite small and skinny. I haven't really turned out like him at all. I don't know if he had a particular trade, but he was very good with his hands. He did some delicate veneering and was great at that style of painting (stippling, I think it's called) where you apply a thick coat of paint and then make patterns through it. It was all the rage at that time. He was very good at sewing too – I remember he treasured his Singer sewing machine. He suffered very badly every summer with eczema on the hands, and he had to wear white gloves. He'd fill the fingers full of cream to coat his hands when he put the gloves on. But it cleared up in the winter. I never knew what caused that.

The family settled in Cove, and one way or another, my father met my mother …

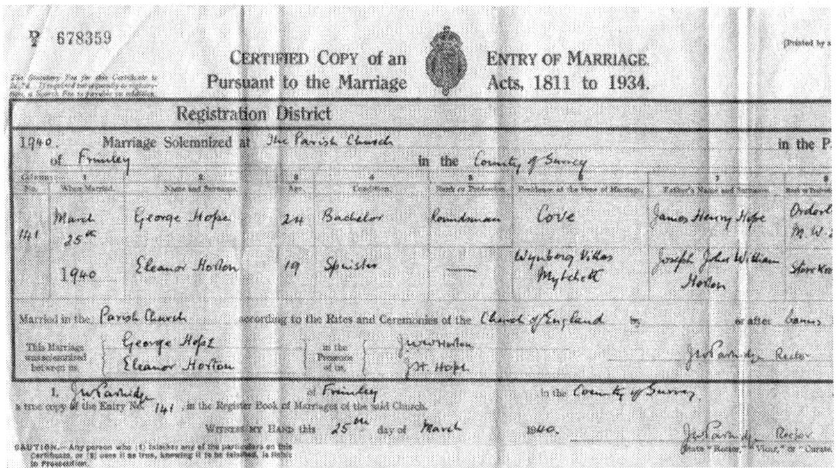

678359

CERTIFIED COPY of an ENTRY OF MARRIAGE.
Pursuant to the Marriage Acts, 1811 to 1934.

Registration District

1940. Marriage Solemnized at The Parish Church in the P
of Frimley in the County of Surrey

No.	When Married.	Name and Surname.	Age.	Condition.	Rank or Profession.	Residence at the time of Marriage.	Father's Name and Surname.	
141	March 25th 1940	George Hope	24	Bachelor	Roundsman	Cove	James Henry Hope	Orderl[illegible] M. W.
		Eleanor Horton	19	Spinster	—	Wynberg Villas Mytchett	Joseph John William Horton	Storeke[illegible]

Married in the Parish Church according to the Rites and Ceremonies of the Church of England by or after Banns

This Marriage was solemnized between us, George Hope, Eleanor Horton, in the Presence of us, J. W. W. Horton, J. H. Hope. J. W. Partridge Rector

I, J. W. Partridge of Frimley in the County of Surrey, a true copy of the Entry No. 141, in the Register Book of Marriages of the said Church.

Witness my Hand this 25th day of March 1940. J. W. Partridge Rector

Marriage certificate for Mum and Dad. (My private collection)

My doting parents. (My private collection)

My mother – Eleanor Horton – was living nearby in Mytchett (I'll describe these places in a bit). She lived with her parents in the house where I was born – Colefordbridge Road.

My maternal grandfather (Joseph John William Horton) was born in Grimsby in 1894. My maternal grandmother (Eleanor Drew) was born in Durham in 1892. They married in Wynberg, South Africa, in 1912. Joseph was serving with 2nd Battalion East Lancashire Regiment. There is a memorial stone commemorating the presence of the Regiment near the old Military Hospital in Wynberg which is still there. The house I was born in (their house) was called Wynberg Villa because of the South African connection … although it is only a bungalow.

My grandparents must have been OK for money as they owned that house. That was quite rare in the 1930s.

Wynberg Villa pictured in 2018. (Courtesy of Barry Toms)

So now it's 1940. World War 2 is in progress, and my mother and father decide to get married – on the 25th March 1940. My dad was 24 and my mother just 19. Father moved in with my mother and her parents. I don't know whether or not my father had been called up at this time, or whether he had already enlisted, but getting married made sense. These were uncertain times, and, although it sounds quite mercenary, a wife could get a War Widow's Pension if the worst happened – so there was something of a glut of marriages at that time. They were a happy, contented couple, and deeply in love, so that wouldn't have been the primary motivation. But why wouldn't you?

My father served with the 8th Army in North Africa – Montgomery's Desert Rats. I think that he must have come home on leave in September 1941, and that led to me being conceived.

My dad in uniform. (My private collection)

He never talked much about the war, and didn't really answer any questions. Once, when I was about seven or eight, I asked him: "Dad. How many Germans did you kill in the war?"

"Don't you ever ask me that again!" he said. And that was that.

About the first thing I remember is lying in the cot one night, and somebody came in, dressed in what I now recognise as a khaki uniform, and placed a wooden tank on my chest. I must have been only eight or nine months old. People say you couldn't remember that, but I do. I assume my dad had made that tank for me.

But my birthday was important for another reason. Rudolph Hess was third in command in Hitler's Germany. In 1941, he made an ill-fated flight to Scotland with the aim of trying to negotiate a peace treaty (without Hitler's consent). He crash-landed and was immediately arrested. He was kept prisoner at Mytchett Place, very close to where my family lived. On the day I was born, Hess made a futile attempt to commit suicide by jumping down a stairwell. As a result, he was transferred to a secure hospital in Wales. It's odd to think that just I was drawing my first breaths at the start of my life, Hess was trying to end his own. You might think that's just coincidence, but I like to think there's a link there! Maybe it's because my initials are 'AH' – as in Adolf!

The early years …

Now I think we should come forward a few years – starting at the end of the war. It was all a long time ago, so for my younger readers – and that will be all of you – a bit more scene-setting.

Mytchett was not then what it is today. It's perhaps best described then as a village to the east of Farnborough, but quite separate. The same can be said of Cove, just to the west of Farnborough. But the whole area had, and still has, a strong military influence. Farnborough Airfield (sometimes called the home of the RAF) was just a few miles away, and Aldershot, a few miles to the south, is the home of the British Army. We were surrounded by military land, barracks and what have you. I wouldn't say the area was war-ravaged, but you couldn't escape that military presence. That was our normality.

I remember those early years in Mytchett. Up until the early 1950s, there was still wartime rationing. I can remember having to go to shops with coupons for butter, or sugar or whatever. You had to spend the whole coupon. You couldn't get change. I remember my grandmother sometimes getting me a few sweets as a treat, if she had anything left from her sugar ration. It's odd to think of that now – that you couldn't just walk into the shop and buy whatever you wanted.

I often used to play around Mytchett Lake – we could fish there of course. I used to love coarse fishing (not sea fishing). I used to go down to Mytchett Lake with my Uncle Tom. My love of fishing lasted for many years. When we were in our late teens, three of us had booked up to go on a week's fishing holiday on the Norfolk Broads – my brother John and Raymond Hemmings. I got taken ill with pneumonia, which was terrible timing and probably the first time I was ever really ill. Sixty years on they still remind me of that and how good a time they had without me.

Life at home was very, very good. My grandparents were still living in the house, and all my aunts and uncles lived nearby. There was always lots of family around. And I can remember playing football in the garden with my Uncle Tom, with a football stuffed with newspapers. We couldn't afford a bladder!

My father passed his driving test while he was in the Army. He could drive anything, anywhere. In those days, not many people had a driving licence, so my father could find work quite easily. He was a baker's roundsman for a while and later a butcher's roundsman. My mum worked as well – various jobs. She worked in the 'Toni Perms/Gillette' factory for some while as did most of the females on Hawley Estate. That made the area quite affluent. My mother also did some child-minding – she was always good with children. We weren't well off, but with both of them working, there was enough money.

A little while after my father was demobbed, and while he was working for the butcher, the small flat behind the shop became available to rent, so my mother, father and I moved there. This was at the back of Hill's Butchers in Victoria Road, Cove. Now, it's the motorbike shop opposite St. Christopher's Church, opposite what was Instone's garage. I guess they felt they needed to have a place of their own.

Our flat was out the back! (Courtesy of Barry Toms)

The flat behind the butcher's was very small – two rooms, a scullery and a toilet. I've been back quite recently, and the flat's still there, although it's just used as a storeroom-cum-workshop now. That's where my brother John was born in 1947. It was quite cramped in the flat, but we can't have been there very long. At that time there was a massive programme of house-building all over the country – part of the recovery from the war – much of this was Council Housing. The basic rule was that if you had two or more children, you would have some priority for a house. In that sense, John did us a great favour. Because of him we were able to move into a brand-new, three-bedroomed, semi-detached in Hawley Estate – No. 3 Ley Road. Luxury!! And we managed to move in there just in time for Christmas 1947. That house was part of our family for many years, and that's really where I grew up.

The family home in Ley Road pictured in 2018. (Courtesy of Barry Toms)

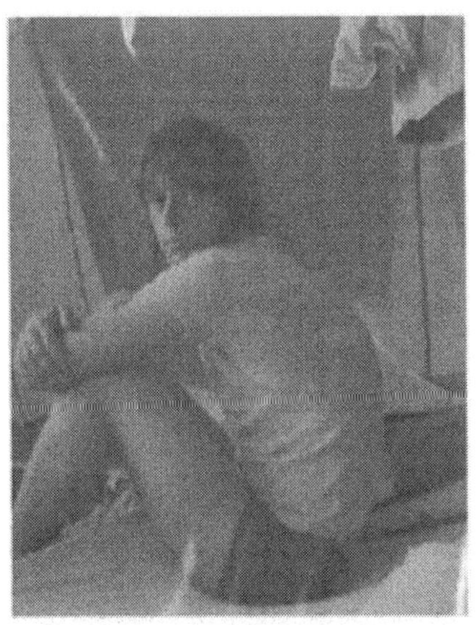

Brother John as a young lad. (My private collection)

I remember the February of 1947 when John was born. He was actually born on St. Valentine's Day. There was talk of calling him Valentine, but it seems good sense prevailed. While the midwife was tending to my mother, I was banned from the house. I was in a flat across the road, and I remember thick snow everywhere that seemed to me to be hundreds of feet deep. It wasn't, of course. But that's how I remember it. It was a bad winter.

Being a kid …

My parents were only as strict as they needed to be. I had a good upbringing, really. My father would sometimes give me a clip around the ear – but only if I deserved it – which I frequently did! But you learn from that. They were never cruel. They were always caring. We did lots together as a family, and I certainly remember spending a lot of time with my father.

Although we were by no means well-off, we always used to go on holiday to Hayling Island. To the same caravan called 'Step-in-side'. One year, my brother John had come down with chicken pox just before our planned holiday. There was a bit of debate about whether to go or not. I remember my father saying: "Look. We've paid the money. We've got to go." So we just kept away from everybody else. I've actually got photographs at home of me, my mother, father and John, sitting on a beach all by ourselves.

It's odd the way your parents can pass on their habits. I sometimes think my mother had some kind of OCD. The bus stop was just across the road. If we were waiting for the bus, my mother would keep popping back to the house to check she'd turned the gas off. She would go perhaps half a dozen times. And now, whenever I go out, I have to go round and check everything is turned off. Just a habit, but I can't shake it!

My mother was a strong woman really. I particularly remember a running joke she would share with other women in the street. As they passed, one would shout: "Lately?"

And the reply would be: "Yes, last night." Or, "Last Tuesday." It was years before I understood what they meant!

I always got my shilling a week pocket money (5p in today's money!), then it went up to two shillings, might have got to half a crown at one time. I used to do a milk-round and a paper-round as well. So I got 7 shillings a week for the milk-round – one shilling a day – and about 4 or 5 shillings for the paper-round. That was both rounds every morning before school. It was hard work. I gave up the milk-round after a few years, and I got promoted on the paper-round. I started making up the rounds, writing the addresses on the top of the papers. I got paid more for that – I think 7/6d a week. If you were getting that, and your pocket money, you were a bit better off than most of the other kids.

I used to have a great time as a kid with the old I-SPY books. I-SPY on the Farm, I-SPY on the Road. I used to spend hours watching butterflies, or looking for flowers. You may remember (if you are old enough), that if you filled up the book and sent it off, they sent you a Red Indian feather. I only ever completed one, and only then because I cheated, I must admit. I-SPY Aeroplanes. By this time my father worked for the Royal Aircraft Establishment at Farnborough and he would tell me all the aeroplanes that were there that were in the book. So I marked up that I'd seen them, although technically I hadn't. Anyway, I remember one Saturday morning, I was sitting in bed, my mother shouted up the stairs: "Come on down, my little Indian." And I got my first feather. I had great fun doing that.

Stamp collecting. I used to be a very avid philatelist. My Uncle Joe, my mother's brother, got me into that. We used to play lots of games: marbles, collected cigarette cards, even hopscotch. Kids don't do those things now, do they?

So Hawley Estate was really where I grew up. People now tell me that it was a tough estate and a difficult place to grow up, but it didn't seem like that to me back then – we were all just kids. But I do remember getting into a scrap with a kid called David Smith. I can't remember what it was about. It was down by the river, and the only reason I won was because I managed to fall on top of him. But when it got around the estate that I was the victor and I'd won, a lot of the other kids wanted to fight me. I kept asking what they wanted to fight me for. We were best friends. "Yeah. But you beat David Smith, so we want to beat you." But I always talked them out of it. I remember that one was called Denis Rossiter and another was Clive Slater. David Smith died quite young, but he was in Rock 'n' Roll bands later, as I was.

We became very friendly after the fight. But when David went home, his dad asked him what had happened. "This big bloke down the road beat me up," he claimed. So George Smith (his father) and David came round and knocked on my door with all of David's gang of friends. My father answered.

George Smith: "Your son beat my son up."

My father: "Alan. Come here."

So I came to the door. George Smith took one look at me and said to his son: "You little bugger. I thought you told me he was bigger than you!" and gave him a clip round the ear and sent him home. I enjoyed seeing that. I became good friends with George Smith in later years.

I really don't like swearing. I try not to myself, and I can get upset with people if they are swearing too much, but I can remember the first time I swore in front of my mother. I would have been about 11 or 12. She said: "I'll tell your father when he gets home."

"Oh Mum, please don't tell him. Please don't. I won't do it again. I won't. Please don't tell him." I was pretty scared about what he would say. This was a Thursday. He got home from work, nothing happened. Friday and Saturday, nothing happened. I was now quite worried.

But my father knew I loved Lonnie Donegan, and he was top of the bill on Sunday Night at the London Palladium this particular Sunday. We were all watching TV – waiting for him to come on, and the compere says: "And now it's time for the top of the bill, here he is, Lonnie Donegan."

My father turned to me and said: "Right, son. Off to bed."

I said: "What for?"

He said: "You swore in front of your mum." And that hurt me more than anything else.

Always a singer …

I was in love with music from my early days. I think it must be in my blood. My father was a musician. He could play the harmonica and the piano accordion. And when we used to go on coach trips from Hawley Estate, I'm pretty sure my father got a free ticket as long as he took his accordion with him. We always had a sing-song on the way back.

My mother used to be a singer in the Wally Goodman Band. Not Benny Goodman, Wally, a locally-based big-band. She was lead singer for him for a little while. She had to give up when she became pregnant. She always blamed me for her not becoming famous. She told me this one day, and I said: "You can't blame me, Mother, it was your fault." I always pulled her leg about that for the rest of her life.

And my Uncle John used to sing for the Bob Potter Band and that's how I first got to hear of Bob Potter, but we'll talk more about that later.

I didn't really have to learn to sing. I just sang along to the radio. If you weren't sure of the words, you could often find the sheet music to fill in the gaps. Singing ran in the family, so it was just natural. And there was a small book published monthly that gave the lyrics for hits.

We couldn't afford a television in those days – but the Collins family next door, did have one. And my mother and father used to go round, because they liked the Sunday Night at the London Palladium, and it seemed to me that every week, Liberace was on. Obviously that's not true, but it certainly felt like that. I used to sit at home and listen to the Top Twenty on Radio Luxemburg. And it became a game, who was going up, coming down, who's no. 3, no. 2, no. 1 … and that's where I picked up my music. I loved that early Rock 'n' Roll.

Radio was 'always' in the house. His insurance paid for our first carpets – previously we just had lino. But my father bought our first record player as a birthday present for me. It was second-hand. It plugged into a light fitting, and you had to connect it to the radio as it had no amplifier or speakers of its own. It came with one record – 'My Dixie Darling' with 'I'm Just a Rolling Stone' on the B side – Lonnie Donegan.

I can remember the first three records I bought for myself: 'That'll be the Day' – Buddy Holly; 'All I Have to do is Dream' – Everly Brothers; 'Please Don't Touch' – Johnny Kidd. Great records!

But I had a number of favourite songs that I never owned on record: Sea Cruise – Frankie Ford; Splish Splash – Bobby Darin; Johnny B Goode (1958) – Chuck Berry. There was so much great music back then.

As I said, my mother and father never had a lot of money, so I never got what I really wanted for Christmas, although I did in a way. If I wanted something special, like a pair of ball-bearing roller-skates, like all the other boys and girls had, I didn't. I got drum wheels, cheaper ones. When I was about 13 or 14, I said: "I want a guitar for Christmas, Dad. I want a guitar for Christmas." And I kept on and on.

Then on Christmas Day: "Here you are, son. Here's your guitar."

"Oh. Thanks Dad." But when I opened it up it wasn't a guitar at all, it was a ukulele. It came with an instruction book, and I fiddled around with it a bit, but I couldn't really master it.

I must have been sitting on the front step one day trying to get a tune out of it, when Mr Reynolds from across the road came over: "Do you want to learn to play the ukulele? I can play the ukulele." He showed me a few things he thought I could do, but I wasn't really interested.

About three or four months later, my father said to me: "Son, I don't see you trying to play your guitar."

I said: "Father, it's not a guitar. It's a ukulele."

He had a quick reply: "If it's good enough for George Formby, it's good enough for you."

So that's why I never learned to play guitar, or the ukulele. I reckon if I had got a guitar back in those days, I'd be better than Jeff Beck, better than Jimmy Page, or any of those guys by now. But I'm not.

John Hope recalls...

Alan and two of his friends used to gather in the dining room. My brother with his ukulele which he could never play. One friend had a washboard; and the other had a tea-chest, with a broomstick and a bit of string. That was their skiffle group. And that must have been in the days of Lonnie Donegan, and all those. I don't know how long that carried on for, but it seemed quite a regular thing.

I never had any musical training, it's all by ear. I knew I wasn't tone deaf, because I knew I could sing in tune, and I was a good whistler as well. I wanted to be like Lonnie Donegan. I wanted to be a singer. My father hated Lonnie Donegan. "He can't sing to save his life," he said to me. "Unless you can sing like Nat King Cole, Bing Crosby, and Slim Whitman, son, you'll never get anywhere." And George Formby of course. He loved George Formby.

My brother John wasn't really into Rock 'n' Roll – he was a Beatles fan. I used to tell him they were rubbish – not as good as the real Rock 'n' Roll. But he wouldn't have it. He was a member of the Beatles fan-club and everything. He was always my kid brother. When he met a girl on holiday (Jane), then got married and had children, I was quite surprised. He'd grown up all of a sudden. My friend Peter Collins had a younger brother called Kenny. He was about the same age as John – so they were the best of friends. And a sister, Judy Collins. She married the boy at the bottom of the garden, so to speak. Well, in the house at the back!

And then there was Mary ...

Apart from my brother John, I have a sister called Mary. She's 12 years younger than me. She lives up in Crewe at the moment. I go and see her as often as I can. As we move on, I'll tell you a lot more about Mary. Certain things happened in her life that affected me as well. In those early years, I wasn't around that much. I was out with bands and stuff. I didn't see a lot of her really, not that I remember. I remember the day she was born. I was still at school. I rushed into school after she was born and said: "Oh. I've just had a little sister this morning." And the first time I saw her, she was all blue. I remember saying that at school. All the kids laughed.

When Mary was a child, I don't really remember seeing much of her. I do remember my friend Micky Rooney coming round soon after she was born. She had blonde hair, and Micky said in front of my father: "Cor. She's going to grow up into a lovely blonde, isn't she?" I was quite embarrassed by that – even at 12. I felt that didn't sound right. Well she grew up anyway. She was a naturally clever girl and very well educated at school. But I remember that she got very ill when she was in her late teens and was in hospital for a while. The side effects of the illness and also her treatment made her very confused for a while. One time when we visited, I remember her saying: "Hello. It's good here, isn't it?" She thought we were all in Heaven. I was very upset by all of that and very worried for her. Then later on after she was out of hospital, I moved her and my mother down to Devon and gave them a flat at the back of my hotel. She got better in the end, and she married a local lad from there called Paul Hands. They've had a long and very happy marriage. She was very bright, perhaps even a genius. She's fine now, which makes me very happy.

Mary, John and me. (My private collection)

Crash!

6th September 1952 is a day I will always remember. The Farnborough Airshow was on, and it was the day of the main flying display – a Saturday. My father was working at the airfield at that time, driving a fuel tanker for the planes, so of course, he was busy at work.

In the afternoon, some of us kids were playing football out the back. This plane came over us so low we had to duck – well, at least we thought we had to. We stood there transfixed as it broke up into pieces over the aerodrome. That was the DH110 flown by John Derry. He was killed, along with his co-pilot and 29 spectators, when it crashed in the crowd. Of course, ordinary people like us didn't have telephones in those days. We heard about it on the radio. My father would normally have been home at 5 o'clock. Well, 5, 6, 7 o'clock all came and went and he wasn't home. My mother knew he could have been killed. She was very worried, and crying. Now, my father owned a little push-bike. On the back was a little 2-stroke engine. You had to pedal it to get it going. It must have got to about 10 o'clock. My mother had the window open and she was listening for any sound in the road. All of a sudden, she heard this *putt-putt-putt*. He was back! He said he been seconded – against his will – into picking up body parts and putting them into bags. Pretty gruesome work!

That was bad enough, but a few years later – in 1958 when I was 16 – there was a real disaster that changed all our lives forever ... my father died!

My father had survived all the way through the war – in North Africa, Tripoli, Alexandria, Egypt, Sicily and into Italy. He died of kidney stones on 30th October – he was only 42. I can remember quite soon after he died, we were watching 'Tomorrow's World' and they were explaining how they could scatter kidney stones with laser beams. That was really hard for my mother – for all of us. He died too early. Mother ended up drinking a bit, I think it affected her – but I can't really say how she felt exactly. But I do think that's why she started to drink. I had to go and buy a bottle of RSVP Sherry for her every day. It must have been awful for her – she was only 38.

John was very quiet when my father died. My mother and I were very upset and crying. Then about 6 weeks later, he just started screaming. He was inconsolable for a week or so. It certainly affected all of us, it was a horrible time. Fortunately, my sister Mary was just a little too young to understand what had happened. She was only four.

I don't know what money my mother might have got from the government. I was working by this time and giving her half my money, and we managed. We always had the cheap cuts of meat, but there was always food. My mother was a very good cook. She used to cook stuffed hearts and pig's trotters – and, of course, lots of stews. I would often be sent to the butcher's: "Mother would like a nice piece of skirt please!" *(Skirt is a cheap cut of beef underbelly. Tasty, but tricky to cook – Rex)*

My father didn't leave a will. I don't think he thought it necessary – he probably thought he had another 40 years to go. It took a while to sort out his estate – not that there was much to sort out. In

January 1959, his estate was valued at just £510 16s 11d.

His death came as a real shock. It made me sad rather than angry. Of course, there were a lot of kids around who'd lost their fathers in the war, and for the first few years, I only saw him when he was on leave as he was still serving with the Army.

On the day he died, I had to go up to the shops. It was a nice sunny day and everyone was laughing and joking. I was quite upset that everyone was so jolly, and I was so sad. But of course, the next time I had to go the shop it was quite different. Everyone had heard and they were full of sympathy.

The one regret I still have, is that I was never old enough to go the pub and have a drink with him. And it changed my life forever. When I left school, I had every intention of joining the Navy – some of my friends were signing up, and it seemed like a good idea. But when my father died, I just couldn't. I felt I had to stay and support my mother, very much so. I can remember going to see father shortly before he died in Farnham Hospital. I felt a bit awkward as I'd cut my hand at work and I didn't want him to know, so I kept trying to hide it behind my back. But it was the last time I saw him and I think he knew he was going to die. He took my hand and he said: "Son, whatever happens to me, look after your mother."

I had to stay. What else could I have done?

CHAPTER 2

Schooling …

We were still living in the flat at the back of the butcher's shop when I started school – Tower Hill Infant School in Cove. I must only have gone there for a few months before we moved to Hawley Estate.

Tower Hill pictured in 2018. (Courtesy of Barry Toms)

Most of my primary education was at St. Peter's School in Priory Road, Farnborough Street. It was split into two sections: the infant school up to age seven; and the junior school up to age eleven. I played football for the team. We didn't play cricket or rugby, just football. Just as well – I only liked football. At that time. I always got my football boots, studs and shin pads from Johnny Berry's Sports Shop in Farnborough. Johnny Berry played football for Manchester United and England. He was a survivor of the Munich Air Crash in 1958. In that crash 23 of the 44 people on board were killed, including eight players and three staff of Manchester United.

St. Peter's in 2018. (Courtesy of Barry Toms)

I got up to all the usual kids' tricks – and giving a bit of cheek here and there. I had an angelic face, so they tell me. When I left, I was known as the Angel of St. Peter's, but I was a naughty little imp.

I had a bit of a stutter in those days – although people find that hard to believe today. It used to annoy me when the teachers at school used to make me stand up and say my two times table. "T … T … T…" I could say three, four, five, but not two. I'm sure it was deliberate, and all the class would start laughing. I was quite embarrassed about that. But I got over it. And even my father took me to task about it. I couldn't say Dad: "D … D … D … Dad." I could say "Father". And he used to say: "Call me Dad," but I couldn't.

I started singing very young. I joined the choir at school, and I found that when I sang, I didn't stutter. That's a known trait though, isn't it? I suppose the stutter went away when I was about 16. Sometimes I still stutter, but basically it just went away. I don't bite my nails anymore either.

Cove School …

I sat my 11+ while at St. Peter's, although the examination hall was actually at Cove Junior School – I didn't pass. I didn't really want to pass. I deliberately gave wrong answers. If I had passed, I would have gone to Farnborough Grammar, and I would have had to play cricket and rugby. I didn't want to. I wanted to play football. And at Cove School, I knew the sports master was Charlie Mortimore who was captain of the Woking side, and also played for Aldershot (my local team) at one stage. And I knew that Cove School was very, very renowned for football. So I wanted to go to that school, and once again, me being the mischievous kid that I was, I didn't get on well with Charlie. When I did see him years later, and he said he remembered me, I knew I must have done something wrong!

Sadly, Charlie Mortimore MBE has recently passed away at the grand old age of 91 (September 2019). I went to the funeral and there must have been around 100 people there. Quite a big turn-out really. During the time I was at Cove School, Charlie Mortimore played for the England Amateur Football team and was captain of Woking FC when they won the FA Amateur Cup Final at Wembley in 1958 in front of 71,000 spectators.

Charlie's brother John Mortimore, who was also a teacher at Cove School for a while, played 279 games for Chelsea and managed Benfica, the famous Portuguese team, when they won the League twice and the Cup twice. John served Southampton FC for over 30 years in various different capacities and became President of the Club.

Cove School pictured in 2018. (Courtesy of Barry Toms)

I enjoyed school. I didn't mind it at all. I did well at first. I was top of the class the first year I was there; then 3rd the following year; then 7th; and ended up 32nd. That says something about my interests over those years. I was always good at reading and arithmetic, but I couldn't see the point of trigonometry. I had no qualifications when I left. It didn't seem important.

And of course, back in those days, people would say to you: "Look after your schooldays. They're the best days of your life."

And you'd say: "Yeah, yeah, yeah."

But now you realise that they were right. And of course, when I was at school it always seemed to be summer. But the key phrase is 'seemed to be'. You only remember the good bits.

I was very good at the three Rs – Reading, Writing and Rock 'n' Roll. But really the four Rs: Reading, Writing, Arithmetic and Rock 'n' Roll. But I think I was only really interested in the last of those.

I can remember the music teacher who taught us when we were 13 or 14. We'd just listened to Bill Haley, and the music teacher was trying to teach us Strauss Waltzes, and Fingal's Cave, the Trout, and that sort of thing. "We wanna hear Rock Around the Clock." We led the teacher a merry dance. His name was Samuel F. Woolway. I remember one time, he got fined 10 shillings for having no reflector on his push-bike. This made the newspapers and of course we all read it. His nickname was Sammy, so we made up this song: "Poor old Sammy – oh, fined 10 bob – oh, he had no reflector, couldn't afford to buy one." And we sang it to him in a line-up in the class. He went ballistic – to put it mildly.

By this time, I'm well into pop music. I was in the choir, I think we just sang hymns, but I wasn't in it for long. Although I could sing, I got chucked out. The lady who used to run the choir at school was called Mrs Redgrave, and she was the headmistress of St. Peter's. We were rehearsing one day, and something went wrong. She was angry: "Come on. Own up. Who was that? Who was that?"

Nobody was owning up, but because I was so interested and wanted to get on with it, I said: "It was me, Miss."

"Right," she said. "Get out!" It wasn't me at all. I was trying to get on with it. So I got chucked out and the other boy never owned up, but I know who it was. He was called John …

I didn't bother with the choir at Cove Secondary School. But I remember at one assembly the headmaster, Mr Chappell, saying: "If anyone wants to join the choir at St. John's Church in Cove, you can miss the first lesson on Monday mornings." Of course, we thought that was a good idea. We'll do that. We weren't wanting to sing at all really, just to miss the first lesson.

Well, we didn't get away with that for very long. What changed our minds was that the school either bought time, or was allowed time, for swimming lessons at the Aldershot Command Baths on Mondays. I much preferred to go swimming than go to church. We still missed a lesson – we had a swimming lesson instead. I was quite a good swimmer, and I can still swim now. In fact, I first learned to swim under water. One day, at the 'Puddle' in Farnborough (as we called the local swimming baths), somebody said to me: "If you try swimming on top of the water, as soon as your head goes under, you'll panic. But if you take a deep breath and start doing the breast-stroke under water, you'll find when you come up you can just carry on." And that's dead right. I spent a lot of time swimming. Not just at the Puddle, but Aldershot Lido and the Camberley Blue Pool. I really enjoyed it.

While I was at Cove School, I joined the Army Cadets. Clive Taylor, one of our teachers, our biology teacher, was an instructor for the Cadets. He got quite a few of us to join. And we liked that, the little gang of us, so we also joined the ATC in Farnborough. But that didn't last. We were just really interested in girls and Rock 'n' Roll by then.

Charlie Mortimore's brother, John, was also a teacher at Cove School. He used to play for Chelsea and he was 2nd in command at Southampton under Lawrie McMenemy. That explains why Cove School was renowned for its football. I did play as an amateur for Frimley United for some years – up until around 1968 when I came down with that bout of pneumonia I mentioned before. I was pretty nimble on the right wing, and not bad in goal. I carried on as manager for the reserve team for a while, but by then, my life was getting pretty busy and I didn't really have the time.

But my schooling was fairly 'normal' and pretty uneventful although …

I remember a new school music teacher started after Mr Woolway left. Her name was Miss Knight. She was doing something on the blackboard and I saw a bit of chalk on the floor. I couldn't resist – I picked it up and threw it at her. It missed her but hit the blackboard. "Who did that?"

I jumped up and said: "Tony Knight." It wasn't him at all, but he couldn't talk his way out of it. And the same thing happened with the goldfish in the tadpole tank.

"Who put the goldfish in with the tadpoles?"

"It was Alan Hope."

"No I didn't, it was Arnold Slater." But no-one believed me. Once you start saying no, you just seemed to dig yourself in deeper. Just schoolboy fun.

But I must tell you about the garden fork incident! Mickey – I've already mentioned him – and me always entered the gardening competitions at school, and we always won. We were there one day, probably not paying attention, and I stuck this garden fork straight through my foot – right between the toes. It didn't touch the bones, just the flesh, but there I was pinned to the ground – I couldn't move. I was taken to Park Prewett Hospital in Basingstoke, which was mainly a mental hospital in those days. I was there for a couple of weeks. It was really painful. I had to sleep with my leg tied up in the air. They said that was because so much dirt had got in the wound. I think it was a bit of a concern for a while. If gangrene had set in, I would have been in trouble. But it didn't. I was lucky!

Boyhood fun …

I always had lots of friends. Loads of them. I could give you a list, but you probably wouldn't care. I didn't really have a best friend. Just the boys and girls. But I have to mention the boy from next door. Peter Collins, he lives up in Barnsley now. When I'm up that way I try to pop in and see him. I'll tell you a story about him in just a minute, but first …

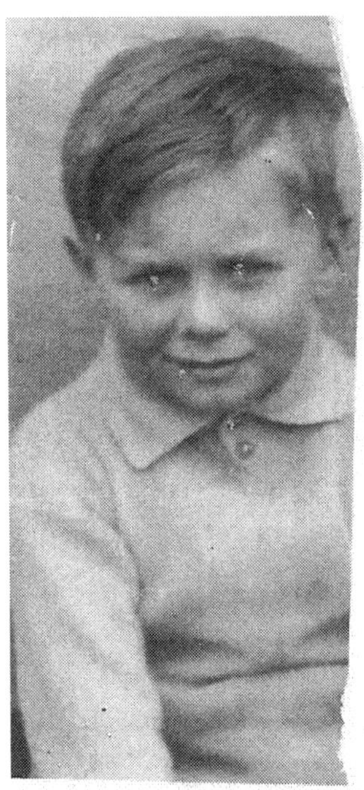

Me as a young boy – looking a bit annoyed!

(My private collection)

Younger brothers get in the way …

John was five years younger than me, and of course he always wanted to hang around with his Big Brother. He was really too young to come out with me and my friends. I had to think of a ploy: "Let's play 'tying-up'." It was a little game I'd invented and he always fell for it. He would go first and tie me to the chair. But I knew if I held my hands a certain way, I'd be able to wriggle out of it. He couldn't fathom it. Once I'd got free it was my turn! I'd tie him up really hard and just leave him. He might be there two or three hours before someone came home. And of course, I'd pretend to dribble on his face – things like that. But I never did really hurt him. I felt a bit protective of him, but he had his own friends. I never really had to go to his rescue or anything.

I have a great story of John when he was about 7½, and I would have been about 13. He always wanted to play with his older brother. And my mother said: "No. You're not going out. They've got bows and arrows. You'll get an arrow in your eye."

And one day he snuck over the back fence, and joined me and Peter. Peter had a bow and arrow. He fired this arrow up in the air, and my brother stood there watching it, watching it come down, and it hit him straight in the eye. And I said: "Tell Mum you fell over. Don't tell her you were hit with an arrow." It actually happened, although these were toy arrows with rubber tips. She was dead right.

My mother also had a reputation as the 'tooth-puller'. You know, when your milk teeth start to come loose. She was the best at getting them out without causing too much pain. We often had kids with 'wobbly' teeth knocking on the door!

John Hope recalls …

We used to have an old WW2 gas mask. Don't know where it came from. Anyway, Alan was at the back door, and he put this gas mask on and looked through the window. I was about 6 or 7 years old, and I started screaming that there was an octopus at the door, because of all the tubing. He used to blow pepper in my face. He was a little sod. He used to steal my toys and take them to school to sell them to buy sweets. One in particular was a big red London bus. He's denied it ever since – well he might admit it now – but he'll be grinning when he denies it.

We used to have these coach trips arranged locally by a Mr Dillon – to the beach on a Sunday. I always got the impression that we got free tickets because my father took his accordion. He could play all the sing-along songs: 'One man went to mow'; '10 green bottles'. But before we could go on the trip, I had to go up to the shop to get the papers for my paper-round. Sometimes I'd take John and give him a ride on the crossbar of my bike down the hill. It wasn't that far, but all the way I'd be digging my chin in back of his head. Typical sibling rivalry, I suppose.

I was great friends with Peter. We were next-door neighbours. We lived at no. 3, he was at no. 1. They were semi-detached houses, so we were attached from the beginning, as it were.

He's a little bit older than I am, probably about 18 months, something like that. He shared the same birthday as my father. That meant I could go round to his birthday party while my father had his party at home. Being with my friends was much more fun. We grew up on the estate, and there were between five and ten of us of the same sort of age who would run around playing havoc in the fields that surrounded the estate. Like lots of boys of that age at that time, we'd go to Saturday morning pictures, and then come home for the afternoon and play Robin Hood, or cowboys and Indians, or whatever. I vaguely remember doing things like that. We quite enjoyed playing around together.

I had a real Teddy-Boy jacket. It was grey with a velvet collar. It was a great jacket and I was beginning to like clothes and fashion. My mother ran a Gratton's (mail order) catalogue. That was a bit like using the internet today, except it was a real catalogue and everything had to be done by post. One day, I ordered an Italian suit from the catalogue. My mother always hated the Teddy-Boy jacket, and on the day the suit arrived, my mother ripped my Teddy-Boy jacket to shreds. To say we had a row would be an understatement. She might have had 'one too many' sherries. She tried to throw a chair at me but I warded it off. Ever after, our larder door had four holes in it where the chair legs had landed.

Peter recalls …

We were just a little local gang. I don't remember it now, but we had our own special whistle. So if you wanted someone to come out and play, you stood outside and you whistled. We didn't have to go round knocking on doors. We must have picked that up from Saturday morning pictures or somewhere.

Alan had a good singing voice and we used to go carol singing – I was tone deaf. So we'd go around singing. He had a good voice, so I more or less mimed and we got away with it. We earned what we thought were nice little tips.

Cows and acorns …

We used to walk home from school along the Fernhill Road past Hawley Manor. Two old ladies owned it. The Northcote sisters – Sybil and Olive. They owned the fields across the road too. There was a cow in this field. Sometimes we'd take a short-cut across the field and along the river – doing a bit of bird's-nesting or whatever. One day, the gate had been left open, and the cow got knocked over in the road. I got blamed for leaving the gate open, but it wasn't me. In those days when you were at school and somebody accused you of something, you had one hell of a job to talk your way out of it.

One of my favourite stories involves my friend Micky Rooney. We were doing things that kids do. We climbed up an oak tree, and we were dropping acorns on the cars as they went by. *Ping! Ping!* Someone passing by must have seen a policeman. Next thing we knew was a policeman parked under the tree on his bike. He said: "Oi, you two. Come down out of that tree." He said: "You've been dropping acorns on cars, haven't you?"

We said: "No, no, no. It wasn't us. We know who it was, but it wasn't us." Typical schoolboys, eh?

He said to my mate: "What's your name?"

He replied: "Micky Rooney."

He looked at me, and he said: "Ha, ha. I suppose your name's Bob Hope is it?"

I said: "No. It's Alan."

"Alan what?"

"Alan Hope." He thought I was taking the piss. He asked where I lived and he marched me round there and knocked on the door. My father answered. The policeman told him what had happened and that I'd been cheeky to a policeman. My dad said: "He's not being cheeky at all. My name's George Hope, and he's my son Alan."

Peter recalls…

I can remember that there was some waste scrub land at the back of the estate. Bits of bushes and old building, a sawdust pit, a bit of a lake, and so on. It was a real adventure playground for us.

We used to start fires on the deadwood and brush. Normally they would just flare up and burn out. It was good fun. But of course, there were a couple of times when we couldn't contain the flames and it caught on. And we suddenly realised that we weren't in control anymore so we ran away, and called the Fire Brigade anonymously. Then we'd listen out for the approaching sirens with bated breath. I think that happened on a couple of occasions. We got away with it. I don't think anyone knew it was us.

Mother's revenge …

There was always some rivalry between Peter's mum and my mother. When I was a Teddy-Boy, I made sure I had all the right gear; the drainpipes and the brothel-creeper shoes, the hairstyle, and the velvet collar and everything. And I remember Peter's mother saying to my mother: "Look at your son. I'd never let my son walk around like that."

Well, when Peter left school he went to college, he went to university. And when he came home one day from university, he was walking down the hill from the railway station or the bus. He'd turned into a Beatnik. He was wearing a long smock, flowers all round his neck, a beard, sandals on. I remember my mother saying to his mum: "Look at your son. I'd never let my son walk around looking like that." He'll remember that story. My mother got her own back. but it was good natured, I often used to remind Peter's mum of that, and we'd have a smile about that story.

CHAPTER 3

Teenagers are born!

Ah. The late 1950s! What a time to be young!

It seemed that we had everything. Britain had won the war; the NHS had been born; rationing was over; we were rebuilding and modernising the country; there were jobs aplenty and…

We had ROCK 'N' ROLL!!!!!!

I can remember going to bed one night listening to Dickie Valentine, or whoever, singing: "Mister Sandman; Bring me a dream; They go together like peaches and cream." And then next morning hearing: "One, two, three o' clock, four o' clock rock."

"Wow, what was that?" That was the start.

'Rock Around the Clock' was a massive hit. It was used in the film 'Blackboard Jungle' which caused riots up and down the country when it was released. Because of that, Bill Haley became the first real Rock Star.

Bill Haley came to the UK to do some shows. He travelled by ocean liner to Southampton. We knew that the Daily Mirror had sponsored a train called 'Haley's Comet' to bring him to Waterloo. So we skived off school and stood on the mainline bridge at Farnborough. But we never really saw the train … we just got smothered by all the smoke. By the time the smoke cleared, he was gone!

I think my first hero in Rock 'n' Roll was Gene Vincent, and then of course, Chuck Berry. But it started before that, listening to the hit parade as a seven-, eight-, nine-year-old. I knew all the words of Davy Crockett. I knew all the words of Robin Hood riding through the glen. All that sort of thing. And the Yellow Rose of Texas, I knew all those words. I used to sing to all the kids as school at play-time. I knew all the words and I stood on a low wall, and I'd sing Rock Island Line. That used to impress them: "Come and listen to this, he knows ALL the words to Rock Island Line." Those were really my first performances. I could sing a few other Lonnie Donegan songs. I'd sing while riding my bike. People would ride alongside listening to me singing them.

Earning a living ...

Before I left school, my father taught me how to clean my boots, press my trousers, and darn my socks: "You need to know these things, because when you leave school you'll be called-up. You'll join the army, navy or air-force, where you'll get a good apprenticeship."

So, when I left school, Father said: "Son, don't worry about getting a good job as you'll be called up. Just get a job and try and earn some money for your mum." My first job was at a place called 'Plasticables' on Frimley Road towards Camberley. A little turn-off down Bridge Road. I was getting 1/6d an hour (that's 7½p in today's money). I was 15. I left that job after about 6 months to go and work for an engineering firm called Eastmeads for 1/6½d an hour. Wow – what a pay rise!

These were just unskilled jobs. I was tea-boy in the first one. I did a bit of rubbing down and stuff, but mainly the tea-boy. I used to go up the sandwich shop to get food for everyone. One day, this woman said to me: "Get me a half-pound of mints please."

"OK," I said. But I must have misheard, so I went to the butcher's and got her mince.

"Oh no," she said. "Barker and Dobson mint sweets, you silly boy." She laughed and said: "Well I know what I'm having for my tea tonight."

It was a job that gave me a bit of money. I was still living at home. 1/6d an hour doesn't sound a lot now, but in those days, you could get by. You could only afford to go out one night a week though. The great thing about those days was if you had a pound note, and you changed it, you might tuck the old brown 10-shilling note (50p) in your shirt pocket. You might forget where you put it, and then by Wednesday and you're raking through your jacket and you find that note, you were rich again!

I never even thought about learning to drive when I was younger. I could always find someone to give me a lift or go by bus. I did have a provisional motorbike licence for a couple of years. I had a little motorbike (Triumph Tina) for a couple of years in my teens, but it wouldn't do more than 20 mph downhill. When I was 16, I was sitting on the back of a distinctive black and white Lambretta belonging to my friend Gary Camm. He'd taken his L-plates off so he could give me a ride. Then a policeman gave us a good staring at as he rode past on his bike. About two hours later, he rode around Hawley Estate on his bicycle, and spotted the motor-bike. Gary had gone back home and replaced the L-plate, and had to own up. That led to the policeman knocking on my door. I had to go to court for aiding and abetting. I was banned from having a driving licence until I was 18. Of course, Gary got a ban too.

The rise of the teenagers …

On 1st October 1958, the government announced there would be no more call-up, or the end of National Service to be more correct. Up until that time, teenagers were required to do two years' service with one of the forces. I was one of the first batch not to be conscripted. I think my mother and father were quite happy about that, but I wouldn't have minded going in. I knew a bit about army life being brought up in the Aldershot and Farnborough area. I never had any first-hand experience of it. But the boys two or three years older than me did. You had to have been born by 1939 to be called up. If you were born in the last quarter, you missed it. If I'd been called up all those many, many years ago, would I have been writing this book now? Of course not.

We really were the first Teenagers, in the way we think of them today. Before that, we didn't really exist. You were a school-kid; then you did your National Service; then you got a job; you retired; and then you died!

But not us. We were young, I was 16, and the threat of conscription had gone forever. We had our freedom, and we had money. It was a time of great optimism … a time of hope. In that sense, I really am "The Great White Hope."

I knew about the 2i's coffee bar in Soho. I used to get on the train at Frimley, and stay there all night. If my mother and father ever knew that, they'd turn in their grave. I was quite shy, I think, when I wasn't on stage. But I wasn't scared of talking to people or going anywhere. I suppose I was shy because I was mixing with people who were a bit older, and seemed to me much more grown-up.

A classic shot of the 2i's. (My private collection)

The 2i's was just how you imagine it. It was the birthplace of British Rock 'n' Roll. If you go there now there's a plaque on the door saying: 'This is where British Rock 'n' Roll was born'. But the people who own it now, know nothing about it. The 2i's was named after the Irani brothers who were the first owners. But in the time I used to go there, it was owned by Paul Lincoln (aka Doctor Death, the masked wrestler) and Ray Hunter.

I became friends with Tom Littlewood who worked behind the bar and was the manager of the place. I was always a bit wary because he used to call me 'Baby Face'. I heard a few stories – well, more rumours really – and I don't know if they were right or not. But I was always a bit wary of him. We'll say no more than that. I can remember seeing a very young Cliff Richard. Not on stage, just outside the door. I had some good times. They were good days. I did actually play there once.

Yes. We really were the first teenagers. That's really what made that decade from 1955 – 1965 so wonderful. When you consider that I'm two days older than Paul McCartney, a year older than Mick Jagger, and Cliff Richard is a year older than me. Just that little gang, and everybody else. If call-up had carried on we wouldn't have had the Beatles, the Rolling Stones, the Kinks, the Animals. All that would never have happened. They would never have met. And I was part of that.

I used to go up the 2i's. Didn't tell my parents. I'd go up to London's Soho and come back on the last train around midnight. But then I found there was a mail train that left at about 2 in the morning. As long as you bought the guard a bacon sandwich at the station, he'd let you on there. So I would catch that train from Waterloo to Frimley, walk back to Hawley Estate, and maybe get home about 4am. Nobody bothered me.

I did that quite a bit. At this time, my Uncle George lived in Tooting. My father had gone by this time. I think my mother must have known what I was doing, because one day my Uncle George said: "If you ever get stuck in London, give me a ring and we'll put you up." The London Underground ran pretty late and he didn't live far from Tooting station – Gorringe Park Avenue.

One day, I took him up on that. I turned up at his house around midnight, told him I was stuck, and asked if I could stay the night. He hesitated a bit, but eventually asked me in. My Auntie Meg, his wife, was sleeping in one room, and he was sleeping in another room in a double bed with his son. Auntie Meg was rather unwell, and I think that's why he hesitated. I had to top and tail them in that bed!

In the morning, I thanked him and came home. In the post a couple of days later, my mother got a very snotty letter from her brother George saying: "How dare you let your son of 16 roam the streets of London this late at night?" It upset my mum, but she sided with me. She knew about all the Rock 'n' Roll stuff, and she encouraged me in singing. My father not so much – he didn't think I was that good.

I used to talk to her about all the guys I'd met at the 2i's – they were always on programmes like 'Oh Boy!' and others. They were all 2i's boys. They were on Drumbeat too, a BBC version of Oh Boy. The resident band on Drumbeat was Bob Miller and the Millermen, and the band on Oh Boy was Lord Rockingham's XI. They had a female keyboard player called Cherry Wainer. I met her daughter in Malta recently. She often claimed to be the band leader, but I don't think she was really. Harry Robinson was the leader, although Rory Blackwell will tell you that he was the original Lord Rockingham. That's his story. I spoke to Rory on the phone just a couple of weeks ago. He lives down in Devon. I think he has gone pretty deaf: "I can't hear yer. I can't hear yer." I don't think he even knew who he was talking to. We'd been great friends for years. Again, he was a 2i's boy. He had a band called Rory Blackwell and the Blackjacks. If you look at the history, he is credited with recording the first ever British Rock 'n' Roll record – a version of 'Wake up Little Susie' – the Everly Brothers' song.

CHAPTER 4

Oh My Dear!

While I was still at school, we sometimes had a gypsy camp close to Hawley Estate. For a while, I got quite friendly with a gypsy girl called Eliza. We used to play around together quite a bit. One day, I was up in the camp, when this voice rang out: "Eliza. Come here. Stay away from him. He's not one of us!" I was a bit upset about that, but it was years later when I finally understood what lay behind those words. Now I understand that they simply didn't want their children getting friendly with those outside their community. That's awful. It still makes me angry now.

My most embarrassing story happened in the first part of 1957. I was still at school, and only 14. Like all kids of that era, Saturday morning pictures was a must. I had been doing that for maybe nine or ten years by now, so I was pretty well known amongst the management and other kids of that time. As a result, I was invited to join the Saturday Morning Picture Club Committee. All we had to do was keep the children in an orderly queue and make sure there was no mad rush as soon as the doors opened. The bonus of this was that every Monday you attended a meeting up in the manager's office. When it was over, you were allowed upstairs to watch the film that was on, whether it was over 18, an X film or whatever.

I knew all the kids and they knew me. One day I noticed this particular young lady kept looking my way and smiling; she was a very well-endowed young lady for her age. I didn't recognise her, but I knew the girl she was with. I kept looking away making out I wasn't aware, but I was. Later, when we were all sitting down, I noticed I wasn't too far from where they were. Next thing I know, her friend came over and said that her friend would like to come and sit next to me. So she did, we got chatting, her name was Shirley. She told me that she lived on Hawley Estate.

I said: "Well so do I but I've never seen you before."

"Oh no," said she, "we have just moved there, we live in Sand Hill."

So now a friendship had struck up, I said, well, why don't we meet up by the shops on the hill, about halfway between where we both lived, about 3 o'clock next day on the Sunday, and that I would show her around. OK, a date was set.

I got there at three on the dot, waited and waited and waited, then gave up, was just about to walk on back home when I heard a voice calling, "Alan, Alan." It was her. "Sorry I'm late," she said, "but I forgot it was my father's birthday, I told him I was meeting you so he said to bring you back as well."

So we were walking down Sand Hill; all of a sudden she turns left into the Church of the Good Shepherd. I was suddenly made aware that Shirley was the daughter of the new vicar. So there I am in the front room of the vicarage, being introduced to Uncle Cecil and Aunt Amelia, Uncle Hubert and Aunt Hilda among others, and of course her parents. I can hear them muttering amongst themselves, saying: "That seems to be a nice young man that Shirley has brought home."

Shirley all of a sudden says: "Excuse me if I go upstairs and change, then I'll come down and help Mummy lay up the birthday party food." Things were going fine. Now she was out of the way for a while, they all wanted to talk to me, I suppose to make me feel at home or not feel out of it. Now bear in mind my earlier remark, Shirley was 'very well endowed'. She came down stairs wearing an immaculate strapless green dress, showing all her curves and so forth. She sets about helping her mum carry food in from the kitchen, puts down a plate of sandwiches, goes back, brings out a bowl of trifle. On reaching over the sandwiches the seam at the back of her dress opened up just like a zip. You could hear it, 'riiiip'. Her boobs fell out all over the table. To save her any further embarrassment I shouted, "Quick, quick, everybody look out of the window!" and there were two dogs knotted together on the lawn.

Don't remember leaving the house, don't remember walking home. Don't ever remember seeing that girl again.

Around this time, newspapers were beginning to publish photos of topless models, giving rise to the 'Page 3 Girl' label in due course. But the first 'Page 3 Girl' was actually in The Times. The model was called Vivienne Neve and she became quite famous as a result. Before that, I had been very friendly with a local girl also called 'Vivienne' – and she looked very much like Vivienne Neve. My friends always noticed the similarity and pulled my leg. We were only 15 or 16 then and we both used to go Frimley Green Youth Club. I'd like to say she was my girlfriend, but that wasn't really true. I never got my hands on her assets either!

My first real girlfriend, was Maureen Smith. She lived in London, and we met down on the beach at Littlehampton. We stayed in contact for perhaps a year or so. We met up a few times, and she took me home to meet her parents. But then I suddenly got the 'Dear John' letter, or 'Dear Alan' letter.

I met my wife, my first wife, in the Il Primo coffee bar in Camberley. My band and I were playing there.

In the 60s there was a Rock 'n' Roll tour of the West Country – North Devon and Bristol – and the three singers on the show were Kerry Rapid (that's me), Nelson Keene and Julian X. We were all local lads. Julian X was going out with my wife to be before I was. I was going out with a girl called Brenda. We ended up swapping girlfriends and marrying them. Julian's real name was Julian Lee. So when Brenda married Julian she became Brenda Lee. She's still around and I see her from time to time. I was quite friendly with her sister Moira as well!

I actually got married two days after my 18th birthday. My wife was only 16. We'd been naughty together, if you get my drift! When her father found out she was pregnant, he went mad. He said: "Young man, you're very, very lucky. I've worked out that you were within the law by 3 months." I can't say whether I really loved her, these things just happen. And I don't know if she loved me. She was pretty, and a lively girl, and I enjoyed her company.

But I don't think her father really knew the full truth. We had been 'naughty' more than once. The first time, and this was when I lost my virginity, was behind a rhododendron bush in the grounds of Sandhurst Military College. My son was conceived, maybe, under an oak tree on the A30. The tree is still there. Maybe I should get a 'blue plaque' for it!

Our marriage was at Aldershot Registry Office and we spent our honeymoon in West Wittering. After that, we moved into her parents' house on Old Dean estate in Highland Road, Camberley. We moved in there free-of-charge. That was probably the worst thing that ever happened to us because it was all so easy.

Her father worked at Blackbushe – he was a trained pilot and had his own plane. He got himself a job at Flight Recording in Wimborne. They moved down there, and just left the house for us – we didn't have to pay rent or anything.

I think that was the beginning of our problems. We were just too young and we probably both felt a bit trapped. By this time, I was working in the band, and I was away, some of the time, on tour. I wasn't a professional singer then so I still had my day-jobs. But I really enjoyed the tours. In fact, in the first Rock 'n' Roll tour booked in the Midlands by Bob Potter, I was the star act. I'd wear a bit of make-up and do my stage act, and all the girls would go crazy. I enjoyed that! But I don't think any of that helped our marriage.

Our son is called Mark – Mark Vincent Hope – Vincent from Gene Vincent. Mark was christened at St. Michael's Church in Camberley, and Bob Potter and his wife Daphne, were his Godparents.

Bob Potter recalls …

My wife Daphne and I were delighted when Alan asked us to be Godparents to Mark. We'd known the Hope family for many years, and they were like family to us.

The whole relationship with my wife lasted no more than a year and a half. I moved out because I found out she was having an affair with somebody else. We had a lot of friends in common, so I soon got to know who it was. The chappie lived in North Camp. His name was Brian. I went and knocked on his door. A lady answered, so I asked: "Does Brian live here?"

"Yes, he does."

"OK. Can I have a word with him for a minute?"

She called for him. I explained who I was looking for and asked if he knew her.

He replied: "Yes I do. I met her at Farnborough Town Hall."

I said: "She's my wife."

He was taken aback. "Is she? Wait a minute." He came back with a photograph: "Is this her?"

"Yes. That's her." It was a photo of me and her which we had had taken at the Agincourt Ballroom. It was my favourite photograph of us together. But the photo that he had, had me torn off. He didn't know she was married. He was an innocent party to all this. When I went home and confronted her with this, she went berserk. I don't really know why she had the affair, but remember she was barely 17 by this time.

So I moved back home – to my mum in Ley Road. I can remember coming home one day from work, and Mother was holding a baby in her arms. I said: "You look a bit odd."

She said: "You can look odd. This is your son Mark. I found him dumped on the doorstep."

I suppose I was quite angry at the time, but my mother was quite happy to have a child to look after again. She loved it … changing nappies and all that. Mark was only a few months old when that happened, so he never really knew his real mother. My mum brought him up, along with my sister Mary who was only about 8 at that time.

It seemed to work. Mary didn't get jealous and my mother was a kind-hearted, caring woman who loved kids, and just got on with whatever needed to be done. The only complication there was that my mother had by now taken in a lodger called Paddy. She'd known him for years, and he was more of a family friend, and company for my mother, but they never married. I would say now that I was just angry that he had 'replaced' my father. It was all still too soon.

I don't have any contact now with my first wife. Neither does my son. She doesn't want to see him. It breaks his heart really because she's got grandchildren and she doesn't want anything to do with them. It's a sad story.

It was one of those happy coincidences that my mum was still young enough to look after Mark, and that she was delighted to do it. It could all so easily have gone so very wrong.

It's now 1962, and we had to sort out custody. You can imagine that back in those days – and even today – it's very difficult for the father to get custody. But that is what we wanted. We had to go to court to settle the matter.

It was more or less a joint decision with my mum to apply for custody; we just felt we had to do it. By this time, Mark had been living with us for over a year. My mother was still only 38, and that I think really helped our case.

I don't remember much of the court hearing. It only took perhaps 20-30 minutes. It was quite formal and calm. No shouting or whatever.

But what would the court decide? I was nervous and excited at the same time.

Can you imagine how I felt when I walked out of that courtroom?

I had the Custody Order in MY HAND!

PART 2

KERRY RAPID AND …

In this Part:

Chapter 5: The beginnings of my rock and roll singing career and my first band, Kerry Rapid and the Blue Stars.

Chapter 6: Freelancing as a guest singer for many different bands including the Bandits, the Nightriders, and Screaming Lord Sutch.

Chapter 7: My second band – Kerry Rapid and the Soultones.

Chapter 8: My personal life. My second wife Pamela, and my three beautiful daughters.

Chapter 9: Joining Threewheel and the eight years of success on the Country and Western circuit.

Addendum: The full story of how I saw off the Beatles in Aldershot in 1961.

CHAPTER 5

Getting started

Some context …

Ah, those early, heady days of Rock 'n' Roll.

It just seemed to explode into our lives. It truly was a 'youth revolution'. But the trouble was that none of us knew what we were doing!

I'm no social historian, but I need to explain a bit about how things were back then. As I mentioned in the previous part, in the late 1950s the UK was emerging from the post-war blues. The economy was growing, National Service had ended, and there were plenty of jobs for us 'kids'. That meant we had free time and money. There was a general feel-good factor and we wanted to enjoy ourselves free from the constraints of our parents' generation. As Harold McMillan (the British Prime Minister at the time) was quoted as saying: "You've never had it so good." Rock 'n' Roll was the answer!

The Rock 'n' Roll business was nothing like the multi-billion-dollar business it is today. There were no big stadium gigs; no well-oiled management and publicity firms; no real tour managers or sound and light engineers; equipment was basic and unreliable; and it was very much DIY.

For the bigger stars there were essentially only two circuits of performance venues: there were what we used to call 'one-night stand' tours. This would be maybe 5 or 6 acts, touring on a bus, playing a different town every night (often two shows a night), for perhaps two or three months. OK, so each act would only play for perhaps 20 minutes, but the schedules were punishing.

Buddy Holly's first and only tour of Britain in 1958 was like that. Two and half months non-stop, and poor old Des O'Connor as compere trying to manage the crowd who were there for one reason only and were getting impatient.

This type of tour carried on till the mid-60s. The Beatles, Rolling Stones, and even Jimi Hendrix starred on such tours (although Jimi was in support – not yet a star).

But there was a second, club-based circuit. Mainly focused on old dance halls, town halls and some new music clubs. But these were not big venues, and you could get up close and personal with your heroes.

Then for local lads like me, there seemed to be venues everywhere that you could get a gig (and sometimes get paid): church halls; village halls; clubs; pubs – all sorts of places.

The other key point is that we all thought we could be stars. Our heroes – or at least the British ones – were just ordinary boys and girls from ordinary backgrounds. They were just like us. If they could do it, so could we. Why not?

But it was tough. We all had to learn from our friends, by ear. There were no places you could go to learn Rock 'n' Roll. You had to imbibe it. It was all trial and error – mainly error. You used whatever equipment you could borrow, beg or steal. Anyone with a van became indispensable. But there were no motorways or fast roads. Travel was slow, and you slept when and where you could.

So it was grubby, messy, poorly paid; and all quite seedy. But it was glamorous to us. After all, we were going to be stars next week – weren't we?

But enough of that. Let's get back to me!

...the Blue Stars

I suppose my very first foray into music with a group, although I don't think we ever played in front of anybody, was with a tea-chest bass and a guitar with two strings. It was our skiffle group. There was Ronnie Saywood, Brian Garner and me. We just used to perform in people's front rooms, and make up words as we went along. But we had great fun doing it. It was Lonnie Donegan who showed all us young boys that we could do that. Good old Lonnie has got a lot to answer for. We loved him, we really did.

The beginnings in music were very amateurish. I was at a youth club one day in Camberley, Surrey, called the Red Ridge Youth Club. At the time, what is in my opinion the best British Rock 'n' Roll record ever made, 'Move It' by Cliff Richard, was all the rage. There was a band on this particular night, and they were singing things like 'Charlie Brown' and stuff like that.

People were shouting out: "Move It. Move It. Let's hear Move It." One of the lads in the band said: "We know the song, but we don't know the words. If anyone knows the words, they can come up and sing it."

So I shouted: "I do!" and I was up there in a flash. They played it pretty well. I don't know how they learned it without anyone actually singing it, but they did.

Then at the end of the night they said: "We're looking for a singer. Would you consider joining our band?"

I said: "Yeah. Why not?" So I did. I can't remember the name of the band, although it might have been 'The Charlie Browns'.

That was back in 1958, and it was all beginning to kick off in the music business.

When we were rehearsing one time, one of the lads said: "Cor. We wrecked that song, didn't we?" We were wondering what to call ourselves, so our first name was 'Alan Hope and the Wreckers'.

After a couple of rehearsals, we played our first gig under that name, at the Il Primo coffee bar in Camberley. In was in the cellar underneath the coffee bar, next door to the Duke of York, which isn't there any longer, and neither is the Il Primo coffee bar.

We ended up playing there quite often – Saturday and Sunday for the princely sum of £4 for the two gigs between five of us. That meant that each of us got 8s (40p) a night – 16s (80p) for the weekend. We were quite rich kids then, I suppose. We had a little bit of extra money. All my mates, if they wanted to borrow a shilling or sixpence, they'd come and see me, because I had that little bit extra, added on to my work money, which was £3 2s 6d per week. So now I was rich. I was earning about £5!

What's in a name?

Then eventually the band said they didn't like the name, so they called themselves 'The Blue Stars'. I thought I should change my name – Alan Hope didn't seem to have quite the right ring to it. At the time, there were all these names like Johnny Gentle, Dickie Pride, Adam Faith, Marty Wilde, Billy Fury, Vince Eager, Lance Fortune. One day I was in the kitchen. The TV was on in the front room. I wasn't really listening, but I thought I heard the name 'Kerry Rapid'. I thought, *That's a good name.* but of course, I'd heard it wrong. But I thought I'd keep it. Lots of people used to say to me: "Did you work for Larry Parnes? That's a Parnes' name, isn't it?" It could have been one of his names, but it wasn't. Larry Parnes managed many of the singers listed above, and he always tried to give them catchy stage names. One of the few artists who resisted was Joe Brown. Parnes would have liked to change that, but Joe stuck to his guns, and it didn't do him any harm. Well I never said whether Kerry Rapid was or was not a Parnes name. I had met Larry Parnes a couple of times at the 2i's coffee bar in Soho. I was well aware that he was a renowned 'talent spotter', but I didn't care for him very much – just something I didn't like about him. He never came up with a name for me, nor did he offer to add me to his stable.

Before I decided on Kerry Rapid, I was considering calling myself Frankie Fable, or Danny Coral. Even to this day I think they are both good names. But you can't keep good ideas to yourself – someone always steals them. I had a schoolfriend by the name of Malcolm Holland. He was a singer too. He liked the name Danny Coral and worked with it for a while. Later he had some fame as Nelson Keene – another Larry Parnes invention. We never really worked together despite being the same age and at the same school. We used to compete in a friendly way at the local talent contests, but there were a number of times I had to help him out by writing out lyrics for him.

At a talent competition at the Plaza Ballroom in Guildford, Surrey, I sang 'Please Don't Touch'. I asked the band to play it in E but they thought I'd said A. All wrong for me, and I was rubbish. Malcolm was on the same show and he sang 'Danny'. He won. Bunny Lewis – a well-known Rock and Roll promoter was in the audience, and that's how it started for Malcolm. I might have won it if the band had played in the right key.

I wasn't really jealous when Malcolm had a Top 10 hit with 'Image of a Girl'. I thought well done – but it could have been me. He never had any significant success afterwards. He was a pretty boy like me!

Cover for Nelson Keene. (My private collection)

The photo below is a 'promo' that was taken professionally at a session arranged by Bob Potter. I look rather like a young Adam Faith!

Posing in a 'thoughtful' way, and learning a song lyric. (My private collection)

And while I'm talking about ideas being stolen …

Look at that publicity shot of mine from 1960 where I'm sitting on the amplifier at the Aldershot Palais. I'm wearing my silver lamé jacket, cerise trousers and white shoes. We worked with Paul Raven; he used to marvel at my silver jacket and proclaimed: "I must get one like that. I must get myself a silver jacket." Paul Raven had some success for a few years but just seemed to fade away.

Early promo taken at Aldershot Palais. (My private collection)

I never heard much more of him until 1972, and there he was on Top of the Pops now re-born as Gary Glitter, singing 'Rock 'n' Roll – oll, Rock 'n' Roll' all dressed in silver glitter. He copied my idea. I'd love to see him again to mention that story to him. He couldn't deny it.

John Hope remembers …

I clearly remember the Blue Stars, Alan had married his first wife and I remember her making Alan's silver jacket. This was before his son was born.

I think the first semi-professional gig we did away from the Il Primo, was at Frogmore Village Hall, just a short way from Camberley – opposite the Bell Pub that's still there now. The Village Hall was just a tin shack, and we got £8 for the evening between us. That was big money in 1958/9. Getting ourselves there was quite a challenge. Our drummer came from Aldershot. He got on the bus in Aldershot, putting his drums in the well under the stairs, came up to Camberley, unloaded his drums and there was a van there to take him up to Frogmore. That's how it was in those days. No-one had transport, we'd go everywhere on the bus.

Hey! We're booked at the Agincourt

Around this time a new Rock 'n' Roll venue opened in Camberley, at The Agincourt, run by Reg Calvert. He would have acts the like of 'Buddy Britten and the Regents' – 'Danny Storm and The Strollers' – 'Freddy Weir and the Werewolves', plus many more. These were really the first Rock 'n' Roll acts to come to Camberley, and we were all in awe of them. Every week there would be a talent competition, and of course I would enter, how could I resist? For the first three weeks I won singing 'Teenager in Love', but then I was asked not to enter any more to give the others a chance. In return, I could have 3 bottles of Pepsi Cola on the house.

So, when I got the chance I told Reg that I had my own band 'Kerry Rapid and The Blue Stars'. He said: "OK. You're on next week." That came as a bit of a shock, but that's how things happened back then. We rehearsed a couple of times that week and we thought we had got to quite a good standard. Along came the big night. We were pretty excited, and we had told all and sundry that we would be on. All the girls were screaming, the curtain opens and we are on – Kerry Rapid and the Blue Stars. We opened up with 'Lawdy Miss Clawdy'. You had never heard such a diabolical row in all your life, we started in the wrong key, stuff was out of tune. We died a death after one number, I don't even think we finished it.

Did we leave that stage with our tails between our legs? Of course we did. What a complete let-down. Had we still been Alan Hope and the Wreckers we might have got away with it, taking the piss as it were, but we weren't, we were Kerry Rapid and the Blue Stars, Britain's future No.1 Top of the Pops, we thought. The only good thing to come out of that night was the fact that Reg Calvert wasn't actually there, he never heard us, and a good job too! Reg Calvert was an important man in the local music scene. Had we messed up in front of him, that would probably have been the end for us.

Agincourt 1950s

Then we learnt about the Aldershot Palais in Aldershot, Hampshire, and their regular Sunday afternoons gigs. We popped along there one afternoon and there was a band playing called 'Dean Rich and the Ricochets'. They were a local band from around Aldershot, Farnborough, Camberley. I knew a couple of the boys in the band, and we got talking. They introduced us to Bob Potter who was running those gigs, and so we started playing the Aldershot Palais every couple of weeks.

This is where all the big stars played. The Agincourt in the late 1950s (above) and in 2018. (Courtesy Barry Toms)

What was the Aldershot Palais as it is in 2018. (Courtesy of Barry Toms)

Bob Potter OBE remembers …

We first met at Aldershot Palais. Later, I would pick Alan up at his mother's house: "Look after him," she'd tell me. I knew Alan's mum pretty well. He'd be all dressed up – Jack the Lad.

John Hope remembers …

My mother had reservations about Bob Potter. She called him a shyster. But he's been very good to Alan over the years and he is a very philanthropic person. He donates lots and lots of money to Frimley Park Hospital. I know he's got his Rolls Royce with the BP 1 number plate. He can be ostentatious. But you shouldn't put him down too much.

Sue Glover – session singer and formerly a member of Brotherhood of Man remembers…

I often went to the Agincourt in Camberley to see Kerry Rapid and the Blue Stars. I wanted to get into the music industry and went along to listen and learn from the master. I have to say not only I, but loads of girls found him gorgeous, you couldn't get near the stage as the girls would rush to the front just to get near him. He was and always will be one of my closest friends.

Beating the Beatles

The Palais was a regular gig for a while. But one day, Bob Potter told us: "That weekend in December that you're playing. Take the time off because there's a thing going on called 'Battle of the Bands'. A band being arranged by somebody else." It was being arranged by Sam Leach from Liverpool.

Mike Burton, who had the Central Ballroom round the corner, knew we had the weekend off. Brian Ford, our drummer, had told Mike we had the weekend free, so Mike asked us to play round there. We agreed. In those days, we knew our audience pretty well. They were all the kids we'd grown up and worked with. Our drummer lived in Aldershot so he let all the Aldershot boys and girls know. I let the Farnborough people know. The other guys lived in Camberley, so they put the word round Camberley.

Everyone got to know we were playing at the Central Ballroom this time, so they all came round there. The gig at the Palais went ahead, but it seems only about 11 people turned up. We still didn't know who was on. We found out about six weeks later that the band that was on was the Beatles. So I suppose you could say that our local heroes had beaten the Beatles for a day, if you like. We didn't know who they were anyway, and nor did anyone else. The other band that was supposed to be on was Ivor Jay and the Jaywalkers, but they never turned up.

It seems odd that the Beatles came all the way down from Liverpool to play one gig on a Saturday night in Aldershot. It was really down to their manager at the time, Sam Leach. It seems he thought Aldershot was part of London and he could get a good crowd. Ivor Jay and the Jaywalkers were pretty popular, so he would expect them to bring a good audience with them. Obviously, they decided that Aldershot not worth the travel for them – or maybe they heard we were playing around the corner and got cold feet!!

Extract of emails between Alan and Sam Leach

From Alan to Sam

Back in the early 60s, I was lead singer with a band called Kerry Rapid and the Blue Stars, operating around Aldershot and we were very popular. Resident band at the Aldershot Palais every weekend. Owner Bob Potter stood us down one weekend as he said he had hired out the venue to someone who wanted to stage a 'battle of the bands' featuring Ivor Jay and Jaywalkers, and a band from Liverpool whose name he couldn't remember.

Local booking agent Mike Burton, heard we'd been cancelled and asked us to play at the Central Ballroom, just around the corner.

Our regulars from the Palais followed us to the Central, Ivor Jay was a no-show, so just the Beatles.

Reply from Sam

Well that explains a few things, and shows the failed gig wasn't all down to me.

You are an interesting guy, and I think you and Screaming Lord Sutch did a gig for me at the Tower Ballroom New Brighton in 1964.

The Beatles Aldershot gig was Dec 9 1961 – and their lowest ever gate.

I got to meet Sam Leach in 2014, although he died a few years later in 2016. A friend of mine in Fleet called Ron Stevenson retired and moved back to Liverpool. I went to stay with him and he asked: "Here. Have you ever heard of Sam Leach?"

"Yes. He's the chap who booked the Beatles in Aldershot."

"So do you know him?"

"Yes, I do. And he will know me. I'd like to meet him."

"Well, my friend Dickie is his cousin. I'll get in touch with him and see if it's alright to go round there." So that got sorted, and Sam knows I'm coming.

We get round there and Sam opens the door: "Oh, it's you, you bastard. I've always wanted to meet you," he said with a smile on his face. He blamed me for pulling down all the posters advertising the Battle of the Bands. I protested my innocence, but he didn't want to believe me. I found out later that there had been some mix-up over payment to the newspaper so the Aldershot News never publicised the gig. But he actually blamed me for being the reason why the Beatles left him, and went with Brian Epstein. I've got his obituary at home and it says that after the Aldershot gig, John and Paul called him in for a meeting. They told him they had a new backer with lots of money – Brian Epstein – and the rest is history.

Ron Stevenson remembers …

Alan wanted to meet Sam. Sam had promoted the Beatles gig in Aldershot and blamed Alan for its failure: in part because Alan's band 'stole' the audience; in part because he always believed that Alan had taken down posters in the area advertising the gig. Alan maintains he is innocent of this.

"When we went round to see Sam, he immediately invited me in: 'Hello Ron. Come on in.' and turning to Alan: 'You'd better come in too you ***!'"

But actually they had a pretty friendly conversation lasting about 1.5 hours. But it was impossible to get Sam to believe Alan, and he maintained it was all Alan's doing up until he died.

(There is a much fuller telling of this episode, which can be found as an Addendum to this Part of the book – Rex)

Rolling with the Stones ...

Another gig I particularly remember was the Plaza in Guildford on a Sunday afternoon. The guy running the venue said: "We've got another band on this afternoon, so just do half a show. You'll still get the same money."

"OK. Fair enough."

So we did our bit, came off and this other band came on. I didn't think much of them – just another band who eventually became the very famous Rolling Stones!

But people seemed to love them. We were doing our stuff at the Agincourt one day when some guy came over to us: "All this Chuck Berry and Bo Diddley stuff you do. There's a band up in London does all that. You ought to go up and see them." Off we went up there and of course it was the Rolling Stones. That was at the Station Hotel in Richmond, south of London - the original home of the Crawdaddy Club. They were the House Band. The next time I saw them, they were playing the Wooden Bridge in Guildford, Surrey, in 1963. They'd just brought out their first single, a Chuck Berry song called 'Come On'. I thought it was a bit of a shambles really. A few weeks later it was in the hit parade, and they had a nationwide tour supporting Ike and Tina Turner. But there you are. They made it. We didn't.

We used to play at the Roaring 20s Club in London. I think it was our second visit when we noticed a group of guys sat at the bar having a nice time. They said: "We want you to sing 'Whole Lotta Shakin' and 'Johnny B Goode' tonight. You sang them quite well last time. If you do, we'll buy you all Cokes." I was only about 16, so underage. Maybe I shouldn't have been in there at all. So we made sure we sang those songs, and the Cokes duly arrived. I didn't know who they were. They just seemed to be three wannabes in the audience. But when the Kray story broke a few years later, I realised it was Ronnie and Reggie Kray together with Ronnie Knight (at one time Barbara Windsor's husband). I was surprised as they just seemed like three nice guys. Anyway, years later, Norma and I were on holiday in the Costa del Sol, and we drove to a small village called Mihas. We went into a typical English tourist café. We were the only two in there. In walks this guy. I said: "That's Ronnie Knight."

"Don't be silly," she said. But I was sure it was. Anyway he looked at us, and I said: "Hello. How are you?"

"Cor," he said. "Why do you know it's me? How did you find me?" He didn't have a lot to say.

The Blue Stars didn't last all that long, we split in early 1962. We all went our separate ways over the years. Our drummer Brian is in South Africa; Jimmy on lead guitar is in America; the bass player lives in Gibraltar. So that just leaves me and Mick Fry. At least he's still about!

Bands just come and go I suppose, a bit like relationships. The birth and demise of the Blue Stars roughly ties up with my first marriage, and the break-up that followed pretty soon after. I don't think there's a link – just coincidence.

CHAPTER 6

Guesting …

… Nightriders and Bandits

One door closes, and another door opens. I still KNEW I would be a famous Rock 'n' Roll singer. It was just a matter of time, wasn't it?

I became a freelance singer after the Blue Stars broke up. Bob Potter was both a friend and my manager and he kept me in work. There was a local band at the time called 'Johnny Arkel and the Nightriders'. Johnny Arkel left, so they needed a singer and I teamed up with them. But I was never really the singer of their band, I was just the singer who used to sing with them. A little later the Nightriders re-named themselves The Emeralds. We did OK and we did once get to play at the 2i's. But we were told our lead guitarist sounded too much like Hank Marvin, so that was the end of that!

In fact, in 1960, we actually recorded 'Come Outside' at Holland Park studio.

Bob Potter took me with The Emeralds to Tin Pan Alley – to KPM Music in Denmark Street in London. We met Bill Jones who was an A&R (Artists and Repetoire) man. He liked my demo – 'Hush-a-bye Little Guitar' (originally by Paul Evans). Bill gave me the sheet music for 'Come Outside', written by Charles Blackwell – a well-known songsmith. We didn't think that much of the song, but later Mike Sarne released his own version with Wendy Richards doing the answer-backs. When we heard that, we knew it was a winner, and in 1962 it got to No. 1. Was I annoyed? You bet. It was our song! On the B-side, we did a song called 'It's You'. In 1962, Tommy Bruce got a hit, and the B-side was the same song – 'It's You'. I'm still convinced to this day that Mike Sarne used my recording as a demo. I'd love to meet him again to see if he's still got it. We didn't make any money out of that record – but he did!

On stage with the Nightriders. (My private collection)

There was some time left at the end of the session, so The Emeralds recorded 'The Kerry Dancers', and a track called 'Little White Lies' – both instrumentals. That session was in 1961, but the song was not released until 1963. In that sense, I might have been the first person to have a tribute record made about him, although they might have meant Kerry in Ireland. But I had been their singer after all, so it could have been about me. You can decide!

There seemed to be quite a demand for freelance singers (if you were any good – and I was). In 1964 I joined up with the Peppermint Men. They had six weeks' worth of work in and around Stoke-on-Trent and their singer, Ray Anton, had just left. It was good solid work, but it didn't lead anywhere.

I teamed up with the Bandits as well. They were one of Bob Potter's backing bands. They were pretty good, and I was happy to work with them when they needed me.

A poster from a Bob Potter tour. (My private collection)

We used to do a lot of the American bases for Bob Potter. We used to go to Welford and Greenham Common. And of course, Aldershot. Bob was tied up with the Officers' Messes and so on, and we used to do some good work. We really did. And we did pretty well out of it.

Bob Potter OBE remembers …

We hired the rooms, and got the audience in. We had no wage – just what we could make on the night. It would be the Bandits and three or four singers. We were on hard times then – maybe making 30 bob (£1.50 today). Sometimes we got nothing. Maybe a small audience, or our posters were ripped down, or whatever.

And we got better and better as we went. In those early days we were a bit green. We learnt as we worked. In this business, the more you work, the better you get. You need that experience.

We used lots of old Army and Air Force coaches for transport. We were all chasing a dream. Alan worked with all of my bands. I varied the line-up to keep everything fresh.

I was still semi-pro at this stage, and working quite a bit with the Bandits. They never had a permanent singer. They just used back-up singers from whoever Bob was putting on the tour. One day in 1962 we were playing at the Civic Hall in Wallingford, Oxfordshire. There was a young lad there with his guitar, and he kept asking if he could come up and sing and play. Well, we let him up and he was pretty good. He ended up joining the band and stayed with us through the summer of 1962. That was none other than Jeff Beck, later of the Yardbirds and voted one of the best 5 guitarists of all time!

He called himself Jeff Mason in those days; he didn't like the name Beck. He and I hit it off pretty well. He was a Galloping Cliff Gallop fan. Cliff Gallop was the lead guitarist of Gene Vincent's Bluecaps. He had this unique sound – great sound. You ask any guitarist who's old enough, and they'll all know Cliff Gallop.

I toured with the Bandits lots of time and there was another chappie who used to come along called Mel Turner; then there was Cal Danger; Baby Bubbly. Another guy around at the time – we backed him quite a lot – was Paul Raven. He morphed in later years into Gary Glitter (and 'stole' my silver jacket idea). I must admit that all the time we worked with him, we got on very well. We never had an inkling of what the end product would be.

Yes, you get to meet a lot of people on the road, but do you ever really know them?

We were playing at Southampton Guild Hall around 1964 and we were supporting Manfred Mann. Paul Jones, their lead singer at the time and now a respected blues expert as well as a great performer, remarked that I sounded so much like George Melly. I didn't think I did, but over the years, a number of other people have said that, so maybe I did, or do. I look like him a bit now.

Another time, we'd just finished a Bob Potter tour of the Midlands. We came back home, but I had no job to go to. It was four weeks before the next tour – to the West Country. So Bob got me a job with his demolition firm who were pulling down one of the barracks at Aldershot – I was only a young lad then. Mr Carroll the boss, gave me the job of going to each billet and taking the mirrors off the wall. I was working on my own, no-one ever saw me. After three weeks or so, he accused me of not being there. He obviously told Bob, as when it came time for the next tour of the West Country, Bob wouldn't let me on the bus. He had forgotten that he'd promised me a place in the show. Anyway, one way or another I managed to sneak onto the bus.

Bob Potter remembers …

He'd been on some of the tours before, but he gate-crashed this one. He climbed out from amongst the kit at the back. I did let him sing, but told him he wasn't going to get paid.

Alan comments: But he did pay me afterwards!

One time when I was touring with the Bandits, we were staying at an old Victorian block of flats in Fishpond Drive in Nottingham. That was our base for the area – Doncaster, Alfreton. Places within a 50-mile radius. One day the landlady seemed to be a bit annoyed, demanding: "I want to see Bob. I need to see Bob." It turned out that someone had broken into the gas meter and stolen all the shilling pieces. It's not fair to name names. All I will say was that he was a great sax player! Bob was pretty mad when he found out. He paid her back though, and another 10s on top for the inconvenience. It was just around the corner from a famous pub called 'The Trip to Jerusalem'. It's dug into the rocks below Nottingham Castle – an interesting old pub!

Privacy? What privacy?

Life on the road then was pretty basic. We had to find our own digs. I can remember doing a tour of the West Country, with a Rock 'n' Roll singer from the 2i's called Keith Kelly. We didn't mind sharing a room if there were twin beds – you could get a room then for 9/6d or perhaps 10s. The next year it was 12/6d and we could hardly afford it. Once we ended up in a room with a double bed. We were stuck and had to make up our minds whether to sleep in the same bed or not. So we did. Never really mentioned it after. When we met up a year or so later, I mentioned this story. "Yeah," he said, "I was a bit curious about you suggesting that."

We always found reasonable B&Bs. We never ever slept in the van. Some landladies didn't like making a late breakfast. One time in Bude, breakfast had been cooked early and kept warm, it was all hard and dried up, but she had tried so we couldn't complain. When we got there the night before she had some fresh mackerel for us that had been caught that very day – lovely. There were ups and downs, but it wasn't really seedy. We had a good time. It was good fun.

All this touring is probably why my first marriage broke up. It's more than likely. I hadn't got married again yet. So I was really just a happy-go-lucky freelance singer for a while. I was living back at home with my mother and son, on the Hawley Estate in Farnborough. My mother brought my son up, until I got married again, when he moved in with me and Pamela. He still calls my mother his mum to this day.

When Bob Potter did his first Rock 'n' Roll tour of the Midlands. I was top of the bill. This would be about 1961. Dean Rich, who I mentioned earlier, was on the bill. And there was another singer, who I think was Tony Angelo … but I'm not sure. Back at the Aldershot Palais, Bob used to put on a guy called Mel Turner – originally from

Jamaica. He was a good act. He became part of the touring Rock 'n' Roll show. I got him on the show. It might have been the worst thing I ever did, because he took over and became the star.

Back to the Nightriders (now The Emeralds). That fizzled out. I went on holiday to Wales for an Easter weekend. When I came back they were working with another singer. His name was Daniel Boone – Daniel Boon and the Renegades. They had been a local band, and I worked with the Renegades from time to time too.

I remember the Renegades knocking at my door midday one day, asking if I could get in the van and go and do a gig in Penzance, down in Cornwall, with them that night. When we got there, the girl on the door remembered me from a gig the previous week – she was quite put out that Daniel Boone wasn't there with the Renegades. In her strong Cornish accent, she said: "You baint be Dan'l Boone. You be Kerry Rapid. You were y'ere lars week."

But I wasn't with the Renegades for long, and I was out on my ear again. Remember I'm still only about 21. I still knew the big-time beckoned. I had the youth and the good looks! But I needed to work and again Bob Potter stepped in to help. "Don't worry about that," he said. "Go and find yourself another band, and then I'll have two good bands and two good singers."

Screaming Lord Sutch

I first met Screaming Lord Sutch at the Agincourt in Camberley, many years before we ever got involved with politics. I wasn't working with him then. He was another 2i's act. I used to go up to the 2i's, mainly on my own, but a couple of times with Bob Potter. Lord Sutch will feature more in the next parts of my story, but it's right to introduce him now.

I think the first gig I did with him was at St. George's Hall in Chichester – but I can't remember the date.

I was never really in the band with Sutch. Bob Potter would book them quite regularly. Sutch was a very visual act. He was only good for perhaps two 45-minute spots. But when the gig ran from 8 till 11 there had to be something else on. So I, as Kerry Rapid, would go along with Screaming Lord Sutch and the Savages and be another singer, and do an act in between his sets with the Savages backing me. It's quite possible that Jimmy Page backed me a couple of times. He was in the Savages for a while, before finding fame with Led Zeppelin. but I can't remember who was and was not in the band at various times, I never took much notice. That's how we got to know each other properly. Travelling in the same van, the same tour bus if you like.

Cal Danger and Baby Bubbly also used to fill in with Sutch from time to time. Cal Danger was a Gene Vincent look-a-like, but he didn't know that many Gene Vincent songs. He was a good act though. He morphed himself into Rip van Winkle, a bit of a novelty act. Kind of a take-off of Screaming Lord Sutch – but no-one could do Screaming Lord Sutch like Sutch himself.

I can remember being up in Nottingham with Sutch. He was a great self-publicist. He had really long hair – all his own hair – that he kept under his top-hat. He would have a leotard on under his shirt. So he went into Woolworths, jumped up on the counter, tore his shirt open, took his hat off and let his hair come down to his waist, and would start screaming and shouting. But it certainly filled the ballroom that night.

Another time, the newspapers got a photo of him pushing a peanut up the middle of the road with his nose. But it got the people in. I learned a lot from him.

There's a great picture of Sutch and me outside No. 10, but it's something of a fake. It was a mock-up for a TV show about something else. I can't remember where that was done. It might have been at Granada in Manchester, or perhaps in some other studio. The giveaway is that the '0' in '10' is wrong. It's the wrong shape. The real one is round. In the photo, it's oval. Can't remember what the programme was about. Something to do with Cyril Smith, and featured Bananarama too. But it never happened.

CHAPTER 7

Kerry Rapid and the Soultones

So the guest work had dried up, and Bob had commanded that I should find a band!

And hey presto! Another door opens!

Late in 1962, Vernon Worsfold, a friend of mine in Bisley, said he knew a band in Bagshot who wanted a singer. That seemed like a good chance so I went to see them. This was in the days when we were doing lots of Chuck Berry stuff, and Bo Diddley, Rhythm and Blues, in the old sense of the term. I sang a couple of songs with them and I was in. They were called the Seltones. Perhaps an odd name, but they all used Selmer amps, hence the name.

John Hope remembers ...

I was unofficial roadie for the Soultones for a while, and I'd often go to their rehearsals. I had an old Phillips reel-to-reel tape recorder. More like a suitcase, and I'd go and record stuff. None of it's left anymore. But they'd keep stopping and doing it again – it was pretty boring – but it was something to do.

We started getting work from Bob Potter as he'd promised me. A couple of the lads in the band didn't want to travel, and that led to a bit of a fall-out. Other people came in and the band carried on. We became quite well-known. I've still got some of our old flyers at home for 'Kerry Rapid and the Seltones'. Then one night, we were playing a theatre in Royal Tunbridge Wells in Kent. When we got there, there was a big banner across the front: "Tonight! The Fabulous Soultones!" They got it wrong, but we thought, *That's a bloody good name. We'll keep that.* We worked with lots and lots of people: Chuck Berry, Sonny Boy Williamson and Long John Baldry; all sorts of people like that. We were on the first show outside of London that Pink Floyd ever did, and of course that was at the Agincourt in Camberley. Lots of London bands came out there. Not so far to travel I suppose. Some good bands too. Who remembers the Herd and Peter Frampton? Everyone, and we played with them!

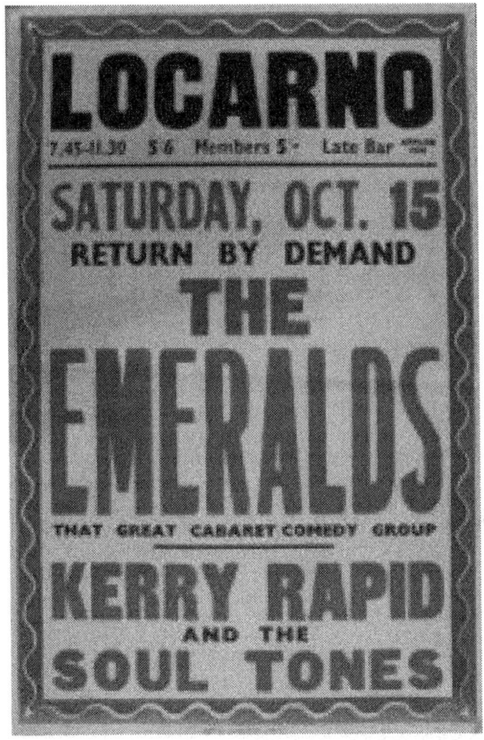

Support for The Emeralds. (My private collection)

We did a gig with Freddy Lennon (John Lennon's father) one time in the Schooner Bar underneath the Atalanta Ballroom in Woking. It was a Bob Potter venue. We were backing Freddy and the only song he knew was 'Only You', but only some of the words. I had to prompt him through the rest. He never really got anywhere though.

Here we are pictured in 2017 – 55 years on!
Bob Webb, Barry Williams, Me, Alan Brinicombe and Brian Cope.
(My private collection)

One time at the Agincourt, we were support to B Bumble and the Stingers from America – they had a No. 1 hit with 'Nutrocker' in 1962. It was really the only tune they knew. Before they went on they were rehearsing things like 'Whole Lotta Shakin' Goin' On' and 'Mean Woman Blues' and songs like that. They weren't going down too well. They started with 'Whole Lotta Shakin', then 'Mean Woman Blues' and so on. As soon as they played 'Nutrocker', that was it, the place became alive. And that's all they played for the rest of the time. People shouting: "Play it again. Play it again." They must have played it about ten times.

Another time, I was working with a chappie called Roy C, he had a No. 1 hit with 'Shotgun Wedding'. I smoked in those days. We were walking along the road to the pub next to the venue before we started, or in the interval, and I was rolling a cigarette – Old Holborn and Rizla Papers, and he said to me: "Hey man. You can't do that over here, can you?"

I said: "What do you mean?"

He said: "You can't do that in America!" Well it was only Old Holborn. He thought I was rolling a spliff.

Hello Chuck …

Classic pose from Mr Berry.

But one of my personal highlights was sharing the stage at the Agincourt with one of my great heroes, Chuck Berry. This was the 26th February 1967, when Chuck was on a pretty busy tour of the UK.

But I didn't really get to meet him apart from a brief chat before we went on. We played a lot of Chuck Berry songs and I was worried he would object to us playing his stuff in our set, so I thought I'd better ask. He was quite relaxed about it: "You go ahead and play whatever you like. I love to hear other people playing my songs."

My brother John did get more of a chat with Chuck. We're on stage doing our set and I could see John sitting and chatting with Chuck in the wings. I was so jealous, but what could I do? Then when we finished our set, he went on to do his. Chuck was never one to hang about. At the end of the set he was whisked away into the night. People tell all sorts of stories about Chuck Berry – that he was aggressive, money-grabbing and so on. I think that was simply because he'd been ripped off so many times in his career. John thought he was a very nice and gentle man – very approachable and friendly. He said that if he ever needed a UK backing band, he'd give me a call – but he never did!

John Hope remembers …

I do remember chatting with Chuck Berry. I was sitting in the wings, watching my brother do his set; and this strange bloke came and sat next to me, and asked me who it was, and what was I there for, and what did I do, and so forth. I knew who it was, but I wasn't really impressed. I wasn't into that sort of music. I was an avid Beatles fan. But now we can see his mark, and the way he changed music. I could see Alan watching me talking to his idol. If looks could kill. He's been eternally jealous that I had a conversation – not about music, not about showbusiness – just ordinary, everyday rubbish, about nothing in particular. Two people just sitting talking.

I think Chuck Berry was booked twice at the Agincourt. But before the gig that I shared with him, I recall that he was booked for a 'Midnight Matinee' – after he played Southampton Gaumont. The place was packed, but he didn't turn up until two in the morning. I remember that quite vividly. Even for the major stars, touring was tough then. Doing two shows a night, perhaps 50 miles apart, is exhausting. That guy sure had some energy.

On the road again …

We were working pretty regularly, but transport was a real problem. A friend of ours had been taking us round, but his old van was really unreliable. I was working with a guy called Keith Smith at Blacknell Buildings, and he had an old Thames van, so I asked him if he would drive them about – become our roadie.

Keith Smith remembers …

I first met Alan when I was about 13, and he lived across the road from a friend of mine. Crew cuts were all the rage at the times, and Alan had got hold of his mum's curtain scissors and cut a great lump of hair off the front. So he had a crew cut sort of at the front, and the rest was his normal long blond hair. That was the first time I ever saw him, my first vision.

Years later, I was working for Blacknell Buildings in Farnborough, and that was where Alan was working. I was actually there when he started, and our first thoughts were: "Oh Christ. We don't want you here, Hope."

Virginia Hill recalls …

I've known Alan since I was 15 years old. We used to work together at Blacknell Buildings in Farnborough, and that was just when he was starting out in the music business. I remember when he was this cute little blond guy. I think he's still inside Alan somewhere!

We did quite a lot of local gigs, mainly for Potter, and up and down the holiday camps, and so on.

And then we did what we called a tour down in Cornwall – but it was only a 4-day trip: Thursday at the Naval Air Station at Culdrose; Friday we were offered a last-minute gig in Exeter. But the job was only worth £15. We turned it down. Instead we went to the Winter Gardens dance hall for a night out where Screaming Lord Sutch was booked. He was mad as a March Hare when he was on stage. To open the show, he was running round the stage with a toilet seat around his neck and swinging a mock axe. He promptly brought all the strip lighting down over the stage.

We were staying at a B&B in Penzance. In the afternoon, we'd gone into Penzance to have a look around. Remember those little spud guns that were also water pistols? Well, Barry, our bass player, Keith and myself had all bought one of these, and a big spud each. Then when we got back to the B&B … God knows what the woman thought the next day. There were bits of spud all over the B&B. We'd had a great night. That's just the sort of crazy stupid little things that we used to get up to.

The five of us had to share just two rooms in that B&B. Brian the drummer and Brinny the guitarist, they shared one room; the other three of us had to share the other room. It had a double-bed and a single bed. I think we must have flipped a coin, and Keith got the single bed, so I and Barry had to share the double bed. They tell me that when Barry woke up I had my arm around him and playing with his nipple. I was still asleep. "Get off, you dirty bugger." They still call me the 'nipple-pincher' today.

We were all in our early 20s. We weren't really doing it for the money. The extra money was useful, but it wasn't much, we did it for the fun. Everything we did was fun. So on the Saturday night of that tour, we went to the Blue Lagoon at Newquay – that was a spectacular place – Sunday night at the Barn Club, and then we travelled home.

On our way back, at some time in the early hours, we came across another band who had broken down at the side of the round. We got some rope and hitched them up. So we had all our kit and the guys in Keith's van, and we were towing this other van full of kit and guys into the nearest town – I think that was the Alan Bown Set who went on to have a number of hits and quite a few TV performances.

Virginia Hill remembers …

Knowing Alan was like having an adventure in life.

He was part of my growing up. I'm proud of him for being who he is. He's an individual. There's nobody much quite like him.

Our drummer was Brian. He was only a young kid and hadn't long passed his test, but he always wanted to drive the van. On the way back from that Cornwall trip, he'd taken over the driving to give Keith a break. I remember we were going down a hill into a town somewhere. At the bottom of the hill was a left-hand bend, and a row of cottages. I think Brian must have dozed off. Keith just had time to reach over his shoulder, grab the wheel, and wake him up. That could have been a nasty accident.

Rodney, Jeff and Freddy …

Long John Baldry, the legendary blues and jazz singer, came to Farnborough Town Hall two or three times. Once with the Brian Auger Trinity. John had this roadie with him called Rod or Stew. He used to do a couple of songs with them now and again. He was neither here nor there really. One time, we were all there together getting set up, and Stew said to Long John Baldry: "Am I going to be able to sing a couple of songs tonight John?"

"Not tonight," he said. "We've got this Julie Driscoll with us and she's got this hit called 'Wheel's on Fire' and it's just bubbling under." So we worked out a little act around her. As we know, that song was a major hit for Julie Driscoll and the Brian Augur Trinity.

Stew asked if he could do a couple of songs with us, and we said: "Yeah. What would you like to do?"

"Whole Lotta Shakin' in C, Johnny B Goode in A."

We already did those numbers so that was fine. I said: "What shall we call you?"

"Call me Stew Stewart." I couldn't call him that because I knew his name was Rodney – Rod.

I had to think fast and when it was time for him to come on, I said: "Here's a young singer who's going to do a couple of songs for you tonight. Ladies and Gentlemen, here he is: Rod 'the Mod' Stewart!" I was the first one to ever call him Rod the Mod, and that was at Farnborough Town Hall. There he was, three years later, famous as Rod the Mod. I like to think that my quick wits created the brand that has made Rod Stewart so successful.

Virginia Hill remembers …

Rod Stewart was almost as good as Alan!

I was still semi-pro, but I was able to get time off. I was working then for Blacknell Buildings in Farnborough. And they knew I was a budding Rock 'n' Roll star, and if I needed a couple of weeks off for a tour, I would just ask. And they were fine. Always kept my job open.

I did two sessions of jury service at Winchester as well as everything else. The first time there, the second case was an alleged rape between a man and his wife. He'd been chasing her round the bed and what have you. We had a break, and I was sitting somewhere near the Judges' Office. The door was slightly open, and I could hear them all laughing and joking about the case we were hearing. Talking about what might have happened and what might come out and so on. But then we went back in, and after a while the girl broke down, and said she'd made it all up, so case dismissed. That would have been about 1972 or so.

Then they asked if I would serve again. I said I would and about four weeks later I was there again. This case was about some old man sat on the toilet – a public toilet in Winchester. All of a sudden the door burst open and there was a young lad with a knife demanding his money. That was the case. The lad's defence was that the story was the wrong way round. He was sat on the toilet when the old man burst in with the knife. He claimed he'd managed to get the knife off him, and sat the old man down on the toilet, and that's why he had the knife when the police arrived. Whether it was true or not I don't know, but the case was thrown out. The only other witness was the person who had phoned the police, but he had only heard a commotion, and of course, what the police saw when they arrived. I don't know the truth, but I feel the young lad might have been right. It's a bit of a far-fetched story to make up.

I remember a particular gig before I joined the Soultones, with the Bandits and Jeff Beck at Newark Corn Exchange. It ended up in a great big fight. No idea what caused the fight – probably just lads getting off their faces on 'Corn Juice' (a local drink). That was the last gig that Jeff Beck ever did with the Bandits. Three years later, now with the Soultones, and we're booked to play Farnborough Tech with the Yardbirds, with Jeff Beck on lead guitar. Jeff and I were back in the dressing room chatting over old times, and I had my song list on the table. Jeff picked up the list and showed it to Keith Relf (Yardbird's Vocalist) and said: "Look at that. There's a song list for you."

"Oh yeah," said Keith, "I wish I knew all those songs."

What links those two gigs is that they both ended up in great big fights. It's in Jeff's biography. He remembers that well. I've got five mentions in that book.

He and I hit it off. We got on pretty well. He was a big fan of Cliff Gallop, Gene Vincent's lead guitarist, and I knew a lot of Gene Vincent songs, and that's how we hit it off together. I didn't just know 'Be-Bop-a-Loo-La' like everyone else, I knew a lot of his rarer stuff too.

The best Rock 'n' Roll band I was saw was Vince Taylor and the Playboys. They were phenomenal. Vince was trying to make out he was American, but he wasn't. He wore all black leather before Gene Vincent.

But probably the best Rock 'n' Roll showmanship I ever saw was Johnny Kidd and the Pirates. I remember working with them in Aldershot – at the NCO's club one time. It was Thursday night, and a radio DJ had said (previously): "Listen in on Thursday and I'll play you a Beatles song you've never heard before." So we listened in and we recorded it on a little Dansette recorder we had. The song was: 'Hey, You Got to Hide Your Love Away.' So we learned this quickly and we finished our first set with this song. People stopped dancing. They were just looking at us. Amazed. Aghast. Of course, they'd all only just heard it earlier in the day.

Even Johnny Kidd and the Pirates came out to see what was going on. So the Pirates played their set, and when we back on for our second set, just like B Bumble and Stingers, we had to play that song another ten times.

It was a shame when Johnny Kidd got killed, he had a lot more to give. His real name was Freddy Heath. You can see why he changed it!

One time I was at the Agincourt and there was a young lad there called Rick Wakeman. Rick's from Camberley. And I can remember years ago, there would be this young lad in the audience. He didn't have much to say for himself, but you could see that he was interested in music. The Agincourt had no bar, just Pepsi-Cola and coffee. Then a few years later there was this big band on stage called 'Yes', and there he was on keyboards. "Hey. That's little Rick who used to be at the Agincourt." I don't know where he lives now, but he must have stayed around for some time, because later on he was Chairman of Camberley Football Club.

Still friends with Rick Wakeman. (My private collection)

I've been on the same bill as Eric Clapton. Farnborough Town Hall with Cream. Cream were playing a series of warm-up gigs in 1966. Clapton had done his stints with The Yardbirds and John Mayall's Bluesbreakers (where he was replaced by Peter Green); and Jack Bruce and Ginger Baker had emerged from the Graham Bond Organisation. All three highly respected musicians even back then. Eric Clapton was still living in Guildford – well, Ripley, actually. But we didn't know in those days that Cream were going to be the big stars that they became. Yeah, they could play a bit, but I didn't think they were miles ahead of anyone else. There were other people just as good. There you are. Some people make it, others don't.

But Ginger Baker on drums always gave 100%. After that gig, we gave him a lift back to Farnborough station. His knuckles were bleeding badly. It must have really hurt.

I worked with Cliff Bennett quite a few times, mainly at the Agincourt. Cliff Bennett and the Rebel Rousers were a musician's band really. When they played, musicians would come along from all over the area. They weren't a pop group. Not a band where young ladies would tear off their knickers and throw them at the stage. They weren't that at all. They were just a fantastic group of great musicians. Mick Green on lead guitar, Frankie Allen on rhythm guitar – he's now with the Searchers. There was Micky Burt on drums, who was the drummer with Chas and Dave. Sid Phillips on sax. Dave Hodges of Chas and Dave on bass.

Bob Potter, Bert Weedon, Cal Danger and me (and that's me again in the picture behind my head!). (My private collection)

Another band we worked quite a lot with was Dave Dee and the Bostons, who became Dave Dee, Dozy, Beaky, Mick and Titch. And the Moody Blues, and Them with Van Morrison – Slough Palais aka Carlton Ballroom. There was an agency in Southampton we used quite a lot run by Len Canham called Avenue Artistes. We still got work through Bob Potter, but we used this agency as well. Bob and this agency teamed up if you like. So, perhaps, the Soultones would go down to Southampton, and the Soul Agents (one of Len's bands) would come up here. I thought the Soul Agents was a pretty good name for a band.

One time we did a show with John Lee Hooker at the Agincourt. But prior to that, we were booked to do a show with him in Portsmouth. We were so pleased to get that gig. But we broke down halfway there and never got there. A sad story!

The van that broke down on the way to the John Lee Hooker gig, was a Commer J2. It was owned by our road manager Stewart Blair, but he'd bought it from Bob Potter and it still had 'Bob Potter Enterprises' on the side of it. After the breakdown we were sat in a pub waiting to be rescued, and this dog came in and pissed all over the brand-new shoes that our lead guitarist – Ken Galloway – was wearing … and they weren't Hush Puppies!

I can remember another time; we were on at Winchester Lido – a regular gig for us – with a band called the Sorrows. They had a minor hit called 'Take a Heart'. Anyway, while we were setting up, I was singing: "All my sorrows, soon be over." Because I was singing that, the chap who'd booked us in just assumed we were the Sorrows. So, he wanted them to go on first, and us to follow as the Sorrows were top of the bill. Don Fardon, who had a hit with Indian Reservation, was their lead singer.

He was put out: "No. We're top of the bill. We're the Sorrows."

The manager said: "No you're not. They are."

"No," we said. "He's right. They are the Sorrows. Why did you think we were?"

"Because you were singing that song."

The Winchester Lido. (My private collection)

A selection of advertised gigs for the Winchester Lido a We are support to The Sorrows and The Paramounts. (My private collection)

We also did a couple of shows with the Paramounts who became Procul Harem. They were at No. 1 for six weeks with "A Whiter Shade of Pale". That band featured Gary Brooker and Matthew Fisher. Matthew used to play with Screaming Lord Sutch, but we'll get to that.

So I've certainly mixed with the rich and famous. But sadly, I'm neither. Well, perhaps a bit famous!

Good morning, Campers!

Many a Saturday night we'd be down in Hayling Island on the Sussex Coast and we'd often go to the bowling alley at Leigh Park in Havant, that was always fun. We didn't have to work on a Sunday so we could stay out a bit. We all had full-time jobs: Keith worked for a timber company in Farnham; Barry Williams was working for a builder in Bagshot; Brian Cope was an apprentice at Vickers; and I think Alan 'Brinny' Brinicombe worked at an electrical shop in Camberley, and I was working in Camberley. Looking back, I don't know how we did it. We worked all day long, and would then go down to a gig AND come back. We might get to bed at maybe two or three in the morning, and then up and off to work. Keith was always last to get home, because he had to drive round to drop us all off.

Sylvia MacMaster recalls …

I remember Kerry Rapid and the Soultones. The blond bombshell. Very good looking. Full of character, great on stage. He used to give me a lift home after the gigs sometimes. Or I might get a lift with any other band that was going Farnham way.

It was good fun back in those days. People played for enjoyment, they weren't really thinking about getting famous. Alan could have been famous (as a singer), just never quite in the right place at the right time.

We did a lot of trips down to Hayling Island. We never got the cream jobs, we always seemed to get the bum ones. There used to be five holiday camps on Hayling Island. I think there's only one now, Sunshine. That was privately owned. There was Sinah Warren which is now part of Warners. So there was Northney, Coronation. We played all of them. The nice thing about playing places like that was that you'd get a different audience each week. That meant you could stick to the same set the whole season!

Keith Smith remembers …

We went to do a birthday party at Holmbury St. Mary – a little village the other side of Guildford. Quite a posh do in the small village hall. There was lots of food there, and by the end of the night there were stacks of cream cakes left. They told us that we could take what we wanted of the leftovers, so we packed up quite a few of these cakes. Meanwhile, I'd got chatting to this girl, and I said I'd take her home after we packed up all the gear.

So we all get round to where she lived, and the lads are waiting in the van as I walk her down this long drive to her front door. Of course, we were having a bit of a snog on the doorstep. Then the door opened, her mother came into full view, but before she could speak, she was hit smack in the face with a cream cake. Pure slapstick. The boys had crept up the drive armed with the cakes.

Once we went down to play at Bristol University at the Students' Union, and the hall was absolutely enormous. We were the supporting band for Georgie Fame. At that time, Georgie Fame had two drummers, so they could make a lot of noise and fill the hall. Well, if you add it up, I don't think we had more than 100 watts between us. You couldn't hear us more than half-way down the hall. Georgie Fame's road crew managed to break the lift while they were getting in. We had to carry our gear up the stairs.

Midsomer Norton was another good job. Just a one off. We stopped off somewhere at a Chinese for a meal. We all rushed to the toilet when we got there, and I found myself at the back of the queue. I couldn't wait, so there I was having to pee in the sink. Of course, Barry being Barry, had to announce this to the restaurant: "Rapid's peeing in the sink."

But we got there, and found a pub. We thought we should try the local Scrumpy and had a pint each, and a game of darts. When we asked for a second pint, the landlord wouldn't serve us: "No. You're not used to it, boys. You can't have two pints of this." We were a bit annoyed about that. We were driving back on the A4 – remember there were no motorways then. We got to the roundabout at Newbury and I think Keith was a bit dozy. He left it a bit late and he had to brake hard. We are all asleep in the back, and Brian's bass drum (in a wooden case), came off the top and landed on top of us. There was a lot of bad language that night.

We were very lucky though. All the miles we did, all tired. We never had an accident. Lots of bands did have accidents. One night, a band called the Canterbury Tales were pushing their van on the A30 when someone ran into the back of them. A couple of the lads were killed.

We did a gig at the Courage Brewery in Alton, Hampshire. We couldn't find a proper power supply. All we could find was one of the old two-amp plugs. So I had to find a way of getting us all plugged into this little socket. I had to stuff the wires in with matchsticks, and wrap the fuse in silver paper – but it worked.

CHAPTER 8

Oh, Pamela!

Sex and drugs and Rock 'n' Roll!

There's a bit more to say about the Rock 'n' Roll, but I want to deal with these other two first.

We didn't really come across drugs in those days. People often say that being in rock and roll, I must know about drugs. I didn't at all. If people were doing it, I was quite oblivious to it. It never affected me at all. I never smoked joints or dropped acid. Lots of musicians did during those times (and probably still do), but it wasn't for me. It wasn't uncommon to come across people smoking 'herbal cigarettes'! Lots of girls – here, there and everywhere. You hear all these stories today of DJs etc being pulled up for girls they met years ago. Well I can tell you now. There were girls of 14 or 15 running around with their skirts up around their ear-holes. They were then, and they still are. It's a fact of life. It never worried me. I remember one day, there was this girl, she seemed interested in me from her eye contact. She got her friend to say to me: "She doesn't want you really. She just wants your surname."

"Why?"

"Her name is Faith."

So I said: "Well, can't we have a sex session and I'll give the money to charity?" I should have recruited them as backing singers – that would have made a great trio.

The problem with being the star on the stage is that girls want to get to know you. When you get together, they always say they don't want to change you … but of course they do. I should have known better, but there you are, and my next relationship began.

Family guy …

I met Pamela when I was about 21 – a little after the marriage to my first wife broke up. I was back at home. Mother was looking after Mark. I was touring a lot with the Soultones and the Bandits, and Pamela moved in with us in Ley Road. And over the next few years we had the three daughters – about two years apart: Angela – 31st August 1964; Georgina – 20th May 1966; and Helen – 15th October 1967.

All the Hope family: Georgina, Pamela, Mark, Angela, Helen and Lil' Ol' Me. (My private collection)

It was like there were two of me: Alan living at home with his partner and children; and Kerry Rapid out on the road doing what Kerry Rapid did. When we finally got our own council house – 20 Oakencopse Crescent. We moved out and into there – Pamela, my three daughters and Mark. My mother was a bit upset that Mark was moving out with us. But it was his choice – we asked him what he wanted to do. This was about 1969, so he was about nine. That was the other side of Hawley Estate. We were there until about 1972, when we moved back to 33 Greatfield Road, which was about 250 yards from 3 Ley Road. We were all quite happy to move back there, and it really pleased my mother. When my mother moved out after the header tank flooded, my brother John bought the house, and moved back in there. That was good for John, but I think it was the worst thing Maggie Thatcher ever did – selling off all the council houses. Big mistake – not just politically – but socially.

Our second house in Hawley Estate pictured in 2018. (Courtesy of Barry Toms)

It was a bit odd having these two lives, but I enjoyed both. I used to take Mark fishing. I'd take him to Aldershot to watch them play football. My daughter Angela used to love going to Aldershot. She'd ask: "When are we going to All-the-Shops again?" But we weren't on tour all the time – perhaps two or three nights at a time. And I would enjoy just going home some nights and just watching TV. I still had day jobs up until 1978, but once again, I would need to get time off. Blacknell's Buildings were very good about that. And also Peppers of Woking, were I was a sheet-metal worker.

I met Pamela at the Agincourt in Camberley – that place has played such a big part in my life. She'd moved up from Wales with her friend Maureen. Maureen teamed up with the drummer Brian Allender, and Pam with the singer (that's me). Pam was two years older than me – I was her toy-boy. I don't know why I fell for Pamela. She seemed a very happy-go-lucky girl. We started doing things together, as you do. And then she became pregnant. Mother was quite happy to have young children around the house. She had worked as a child-minder, and also in a nursery. I used to help out in the nursery on school holidays. It was where Kingsmead in Farnborough is now. I'd do odd jobs. I don't remember getting paid – but I'd get some coffee and bit of bread and dripping – or toast with dripping. I used to love that. Still do today.

Mark seemed to adapt quite well to his new life with Pamela, and then his sisters. But we were only just around the corner from my mother's house in Ley Road. I think Mark used to play one off against the other: telling tales about Pamela; and telling tales about my mother. I'm pretty sure that sometimes he would have a meal at home, then go over to my mother's, complain that he hadn't been fed, and get another meal.

I don't really know why we decided to get married after we'd been together about ten years. We just did. It just seemed to happen. I'm convinced most people in this world decide to get married after a Saturday night piss-up. We got married at Aldershot Registry Office. We went to Wales for our honeymoon – back to where she was from – north of Caerphilly, Hengoed. But it took a while before we could tie the knot. I was still married to my first wife, so we had to track her down and get her agreement for the divorce. It wasn't an easy time for any of us.

If I was doing a local gig, I'd try to take my daughters with me. They always enjoyed music, and it was a way of spending some more time with them.

The daughters remember …

We used to get up on stage with him sometimes – play a tambourine or whatever. If he'd been away for a few days with his band, he'd often get a little toy for each of us. We'd find it at the bottom of the bed when we woke up.

I also made sure I was always the one who would buy their shoes. I'd take them shopping to Clark's. Often they got the same shoes year after year after year – Clark's brown sandals.

But it was really difficult. I would come home from work, eat my tea and then go out with the band. We were normally playing at weekends, so I didn't see much of them then either. And on top of all that there were the mini-tours where I'd be a way perhaps for a week. I was a bit of an absentee father in that way.

The daughters remember …

We didn't think too much about him being a (wannabe) Rock 'n' Roll star. But I do remember when he'd made an album. One day there was a knock at the door and all these records were delivered. Dad was on the front cover. That made it more real. I think everyone on the estate brought one.

After a while, the marriage just seemed to fall apart – despite the three daughters and Mark living with us as well. I think it was me that wanted to walk away. There was just nothing there anymore. Once again, I walked away, and it was up to Mark whether he came with me or not. He decided he would stay with me. I felt very sorry for my three daughters, I really did. And I moved into Norma's house in Blackwater, near Camberley. I already knew Norma. We weren't really having an affair, but we were good friends.

The next evening, I picked the girls up, and took them round to meet Norma, and they all got on like a house on fire. Even today, when you meet my daughters, although Pam is their kids' granny, Norma was the kids' Nanny. I can tell you, she was the best Nanny that anybody could ever have. We all stayed quite friendly. When Norma and I bought the Golden Lion hotel in Ashburton, Devon, the kids would come down and bring Pam with them. In fact, even Pam's mum came down once. Georgina, my daughter, got married down there so the whole family stayed at the hotel – free of charge as well. The break-up with Pamela was quite calm – no smashing of plates – although she could do that – oh, could she! I've had everything thrown at me bar the kitchen sink. It could just be an argument over nothing. Quite scary sometimes. She should have had red hair, really. I would ask why, and she'd start effing and blinding. I'd say: "There's no need for that. What are you swearing for?" I could talk to you for five years without swearing. But some people can't. It all just drifted apart. We stayed the best of friends. She kept my surname. I'm sure she met other people too, while she was working in the pub.

But I admit that I was not the husband she thought she wanted.

But I would think everyone was a bit relieved when I broke up with Pamela. We had been arguing a lot about stupid things. But I think that Pamela did a good job bringing up all the children. It can't have been easy with me away so much of the time. We've stayed in touch as well, although I wouldn't say we are close. But the whole family, my daughters and Mark, still meet up whenever we can and have a drink and a chat.

Mark Hope remembers …

There was an instance when I was about 12 or 13, and I was out with my mates and we were down Fairfax – the old Hawley Lane before all that had been built up. We were climbing trees and that sort of stuff. This little brown mini pulled up. I looked up and thought: "That's my dad." So now I'm hiding in the tree. He walks down – he said he was going to the pub – but I watched him get in the mini and kiss the driver. I suppose we were a bit naïve so when I got home, I told Pam. He denied it, he said it was 'Lofty' in the car. Lofty is about 6ft 8in – he used to play steel guitar in Threewheel. So I said: "Do you normally kiss Lofty when you get in his car, then?"

CHAPTER 9

Threewheel

All things come to pass, and eventually the Soultones decided to call it a day. I was doing some work as a freelance singer again, but I needed something different.

Then on a Sunday afternoon in 1971, there was a knock on my front door, and there was a lad there called Mike Riley. "I'm looking for a singer," he said. "I understand you're the man I'm looking for. Topper Clay told me." Topper Clay was the drummer with Daniel Boone and the Renegades and was well-known locally. "He told me you're good, and you know all the keys you sing your songs in." I agreed. So I joined that band – more or less on trial at first.

My very first gig with Threewheel was at Ripley British Legion; the drummer Mike Riley picked me up from home and off we went. When we got there the band set up and there was a singer with them called Nick Carter, he was very good. I thought to myself, *What do they want me for?* When I asked, I was told that he had his own band and was only filling in till they found someone.

A couple of great pictures of us in our heyday.

(My private collection)

Top pic: Barry; Jet; Me; Brinny; Chuck

Dave; Me; Jet; Mike; Brian

So for the second half of this gig in Ripley, I'm thrown in the deep end, sink or swim! I sang a couple of Don Gibson songs, a couple of Rock 'n' Roll things and it all went well. It must have been a Christmas 'do' at Ripley B L, because my next gig, with me as the main vocalist, was New Year's Eve 1971 at Camberley British Legion. Mike the drummer could sing a few songs, which I very quickly picked up harmonies on. Lofty the lead guitarist could play a few Shadows tunes. I often thought and pulled his leg, that it was he who taught Hank B Marvin how to play. He would amaze the audience with his playing and he sang a couple of songs too. Jet on piano and keyboard could play a couple of instrumentals; Brian the bass player used to stand there looking pretty, and of course myself thrown into the deep end once again, all on my own.

Liz Riley remembers …

My husband, Mike Riley, was the leader of a Country and Western band called Threewheel.

When it was formed, there were three members all of whom sang. By late 1969, two of the originals had left. Their replacements were excellent musicians but not good vocalists, thus Threewheel needed a singer.

Someone suggested Alan Hope might be interested – he was and he joined the band. I have great memories of Alan and Mike together on stage, making music and sharing silly jokes, quick-fire banter and brilliant vocal harmonies.

Alan came to stay with me in 2018 to listen to my collection of Threewheel audio tapes which include a recording of 'Up Country' broadcast on Radio 2 on 31st October 1973.

Fortunately enough they were all very good musicians, I was throwing all sorts at them and we hit it off. Of course, lots of twelve bars, but you can make every twelve-bar sound different. And I knew some of the songs that I heard Nick Carter sing earlier. End of the evening Mike Riley called me over and he said, "We've had a bit of a natter and the job's yours if you want it." Okay, thanks, I took it, and was with that band until New Year's Eve 1977. The line-up was Mike Riley, Drums – Dave 'Lofty' Reng, lead and steel guitar – Richard 'Jet' Hodgins, keyboards – Brian 'Bill' Weller, bass guitar. And of course little ol' me by now. Brian Weller eventually left because he was playing with a radio band called the Alabama Hayriders. So we got Barry Williams on bass from Daniel Boone and the Renegades. Sadly later on Mike Riley had to leave to take up a very high-profile job in Germany, it broke his heart really, it was his band. So we took on The Very Famous Rodney 'Chuck' Pengilly on drums, from a local group called Natural Gas. At this point I would like to point out that the original Threewheel started out in 1968 as a three-piece;

Mike Riley, drums – Denis Collier, lead guitar and Keith Dance, bass Guitar. Threewheel did carry on after I left, but folded in 1980 I believe. But they were still in existence as their own 'tribute band' into the 80s. Mike Riley was back now on keyboards, Chuck Pengilley on drums, Lofty Reng on lead guitar, Brian Weller on bass, and Peter Wilson who was in a band called 'Frisco, but was one of the original Blue Stars.

After Mike left, I more or less became the leader of the band. I'd killed off Kerry Rapid by this time, and was singing under my own name – Kerry Rapid didn't sound right for the music we played. We were really a dance band playing pop and Country and Western. And we could play some pop or rock 'n' roll if that's what the venue wanted. But if we were playing at a dance, we could do some Jim Reeves stuff that people could waltz and foxtrot and quickstep too. We had the best of both worlds. I suppose you could say that if there was ever a Yuppie band, we were the first Yuppie band in Great Britain. We used to do gigs like the Ski Club of Great Britain in London; we used to do the Wimbledon Tennis and Rackets club – their summer BBQ; we did the Sanderstead Hunt Ball; Sandhurst Military College Ball – did that two or three times. We were a Yuppie band, but it worked.

Chuck Pengilly remembers …

One day I'd gone out shopping. I was keen on gardening at the time and had a lovely strawberry bed full of ripe strawberries. I was looking forward to eating those for my tea. When I came back, there were no strawberries left. I assumed they'd just been scrumped.

A little while later, there's a knock on the door, and it was Alan Hope. I didn't know him from Adam. He asked me if I would like to join his band, Threewheel, as Mike Riley was moving to Germany. He'd obviously heard I was 'unemployed' as it were. I wasn't sure. I didn't know much about Country & Western. He asked that I go to their next rehearsal, in a little pub in Blackwater near where I lived in Vicarage Lane. I eventually agreed. Then I asked if he'd called earlier while I was out. He said he had, and admitted to being the phantom strawberry pincher.

Alan comments …

When we moved to Devon, I gave Chuck my greenhouse. I think that repaid him for the strawberries.

In a Jam …

When we used to play at the Peabody Road Club in North Camp, Aldershot, I used to sing 'In the Early Morning Rain'. Paul Weller told me he liked the song very much. I told him it was written by Gordon Lightfoot, and I'd copied the George Hamilton IV version. Lo and behold, years later, it turned up on one of Paul Weller's solo albums.

The Jam were a local band – from Woking in Surrey. They used to play at the Peabody Road Club in Aldershot, and so did we. It was a Sunday gig, which was a bit unusual, but it meant you could also see a band there. There were always quite a few musicians from other bands in the audience, just for a night out. I got to know The Jam pretty well. They were just a Tamla Motown covers band then. They weren't bad. I was in Threewheel at the time. We were quite popular and we'd done quite a bit of radio work. The club offered us a booking, but we only took it on the basis that if something special came along, we would need to pull out, but we would find them another band. That was accepted. It was a Saturday, and we were booked to play at the Cove Ivy League Club. We got a call to do a radio show or a big ball, something a bit special. So I phoned up Paul Weller and asked if they were free that night. He said they were, and they agreed to do the gig in our place. They went along – and they died a death! Just one of those things – the wrong music for the audience.

And then another time we were booked in at the New Inn Football Club dance at the Hawley Memorial Hall in Blackwater. We had to pull out of that one, and put Jam in there too. We gave them at least two gigs, if not more. At one stage, I was thinking about starting my own Music Agency, and suggesting to The Jam that I act for them. But then I had second thoughts, as I knew by that time we were moving down to Devon. And then, blow me, two years later, there they are on Top of the Pops as big names.

Chuck remembers …

I stayed with Threewheel for quite a few years. We did lots of gigs and tours. I remember doing quite a tour with Jed Ford and others. We were there as ourselves, and also as the backing band for all the other acts. We did some quite big theatres. One I remember in Weymouth, the Winter Gardens, and the Theatre Royal in Norwich. We did lots with people like that – lots of US AF bases. Good fun, having to change our money into the US $ in order to buy drinks and smokes. They were great places. You'd do the gig, and then they'd serve you breakfast at maybe 2am. It was a different world.

And now we're a Country and Western band ...

I'd left Bob Potter by this time. Then the band decided that they quite liked C&W, and they didn't want to play pop anymore. That came out of the blue, at a gig at Southern Instruments Social Club, Frimley. I thought we had the best of both worlds and I was pretty much against it. But that's what we did. I thought we'd lose half our audience, but I was wrong. We made ourselves quite a name on the Country Music circuit. We were travelling all over the country, but the first show we did like that was at Fleet Country Club – Johnny Woodhouse founded it. But I was promoting the shows. When we turned up, the place was all locked-up. I thought, *What are we going to do? I've got the band booked. The audience is coming.* So I came round the corner to the Albert Social Club in Fleet, Hampshire, and they said: "Yeah. We've got nothing on. Come and do it in here." So we just put a big note on the door of the Country Club and everyone came round to the Albert Street Club. It was great. It was wonderful.

From that I made a deal with the club that we would do this once a month every month. First Thursday of the month. I booked the bands, took the money on the door to pay the bands, and they kept all the money taken at the bar. Seemed a fair deal. That went on for a year or so. We had some good people on. People like Tony Goodacre, Brian Maxine. Remember Brian Maxine the wrestler? He had a band called the Ring Rats – Brian Maxine and the Ring Rats.

I remember one Saturday afternoon, Brian 'Goldbelt' Maxine came in the wrestling ring with his acoustic guitar. It was snatched by his opponent, who broke it over his head and back. Obviously it was all a set up, but very dramatic at the time. He was a very likeable chap outside the ring, and there was another guy we used to work with called Jed Ford, although we hadn't met him at this stage. Anyway, the club members realised this was all going pretty well, and they thought they could do it themselves. So the manager made up some cock and bull story about me getting in trouble with the members, so I moved all the gigs to Camberley, first to the Agincourt – once again owned by Johnny Woodhouse – and later, the Civic Hall.

We put on some good people there. Of course, Threewheel were key to every show. We were the house band, and if anyone needed backing then we would back them. That's how we met Jed Ford. We backed him, and a bit like Chuck Berry he said: "When I need a touring band, I'll give you a ring." But this one did materialise. We worked together many, many times and we thoroughly enjoyed it. He was a good act. And through Jed we got to know lots of other Country Music people, like Ron Ryan, Little Ginny, Jon Derek, Tex Withers, the Downtown County Boys, and lots of others.

Jed Ford. (My private collection)

Jed Ford remembers …

Alan Hope and Threewheel were a fine, professional band. A band that I had the great pleasure of having back-me-up on countless stages over a number of years.

Alan led Threewheel for a number of years as a front-man, and a very capable singer and showman. I always appreciated the friendship and professionalism that I was assured of on the multiple occasions that Alan, his band and I shared so many stages, working in happy partnership. But a front-man is only as good as the band behind him providing all that so-necessary music, which Threewheel always delivered.

Chuck remembers …

We were playing nice clubs and getting good money. We played the Ballet School in Camberley, and all the girls were screaming. Alan was a good-looking lad in those days.

For a while he was travelling around with Norma in a camper van. It was quite a nice vehicle. She would pick him up and they would meet us at the gig. We were doing a gig one night and they decided to park up in a multi-storey, but the van was too tall and they took the roof off it. Made it a bit of a wreck. Serves him right for not travelling with the rest of us.

We'd had these really flash stage suits made for us – very fancy. Looked the business.

Of course, Alan's a showman. He knows how to work the cameras. He likes to be the centre of attention. Some of us did go down to the Golden Lion a time or two. He'd put us up for the weekend, and we'd perhaps play a couple of evenings there. Alan would do some guest singing with us. We had some great times there. It was a great place to go. Alan ran a good gig. He and Norma looked after us so well. It would be packed and really rocking.

We did quite a bit of radio for Wally Whyton's BBC programme. We went to the Shepherd's Bush studio a few times. And then we got a chance to make an album for Westwood Recordings based in Montgomery, Wales. I don't recall the reasons, but we ended up making the recording in a house in Huddersfield with Gordon Davies as engineer and producer.

It was an odd deal. The recording session and the subsequent printing of the album were both free. Didn't really cost us a penny. We used to take albums along to our gigs and try to sell them. But for each we sold, we had to give Westwood 50%. I'm sure they would have been selling the album through other channels too. But we never got a share of anything they made.

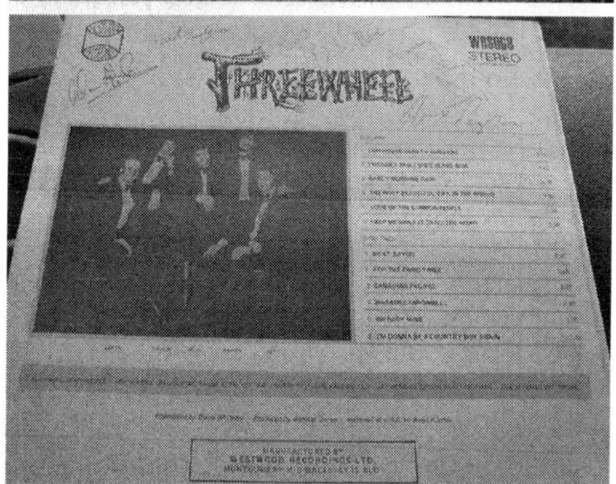

Front and back covers of our album. (My private collection)

And the other day, I was browsing in one of Fleet's charity shops and I found a copy. I had to buy it. It was £1.99 – that's 1p less than the original selling price in 1976. It was a signed copy too. What a bargain!

I'm not sure why I never broke into the big time. With the Blue

Stars and the Soultones, we were managed by Bob Potter. He did his best, but I think he was just too far away from London. We just weren't in the right place at the right time. We stuck with Bob, he was local, and we always had faith in him.

But Threewheel had nothing to do with Bob. We were self-managed. Mainly me and the drummer, although Bob did book us a few times. Threewheel was more of a consortium, we didn't really want a manager – we were doing alright on our own. Most of us had worked for Bob previously. We could get enough gigs, so we were quite content. We were making decent money and having fun.

Of course, I did want to be a big Rock 'n' Roll star in my teens. But I think I more wanted to be an American C&W star if I'm honest. Threewheel was good enough to break into the big-time. Perhaps … if we'd signed with an established manager … who knows???

Happy New Year?

I worked with Threewheel until 1977. My last gig with that band was New Year's Eve 1977. I believe it was in Newbury. Then I signed another contract to do a tour with Jed Ford. The other boys in the band didn't want to do, and that's why I left. Then lo and behold, behind my back, they went off and got another tour without me, which annoyed me a bit. If we hadn't had that bust-up over Jed Ford, we might well have carried on.

I could have been a star and I really did want that. But I guess I was never in the right place at the right time. Perhaps I should have found a London agent. Bob Potter did well for me, but perhaps I was with him for too long.

So now it's 1978 and I'm 36. I've had two failed marriages and I've got four children. I was neither rich nor famous. The only thing that had got bigger was my waistline.

Things were going to have to change.

There was no going back … I'd quit!

ADDENDUM

HOW I BEAT THE BEATLES!

(This section was written as a stand-alone article. It is extremely relevant to my story, so is included here in its entirety. My sincere thanks to Derrill Carr for listening and believing my Beatles in Aldershot story and for undertaking extensive research and conducting in-depth interviews to validate my story.)

What really happened when the Beatles came to Aldershot in December 1961

A true story about the one and only time the Beatles came to Aldershot in December 1961 and ended up playing in a virtually empty venue with a maximum of only 18 people there at any one time. The background and events leading up to this Beatles debacle are fully explained in this story, very little of which has appeared in the public domain before.

"Why tell this story now?" I can hear people ask, to which I would respond that this is due to a recent book publication about The Beatles which has told just part of this story. This book has created a lot of additional interest and raised further questions about what really led to The Beatles' failure in Aldershot. I have decided to reveal everything about what went on in Aldershot during December 1961 as I expect this will be compulsive reading for all the Beatles fans out there with their insatiable appetite for new stories and information about their heroes.

It was recently brought to my attention that a book had been published in 2017 written by David Bedford and Gary Popper titled *Finding the Fourth Beatle* which contained a chapter all about the time when the Beatles came to the Aldershot Palais in December 1961. In Chapter 27 of this book there are extracts from interviews about this Beatles concert in Aldershot with Sam Leach (Beatles agent, promoter and aspiring manager at that time) and Terry McCann (Beatles driver, security/roadie in those days) which specifically mentions conversations they had with me in July 2013. The full extracts from Sam Leach's and Terry McCann's quotes in Chapter 27 of *Finding the Fourth Beatle* are reproduced below. David Bedford, the author of this book, kindly sent me a signed copy in 2018.

'A new twist in the story occurred in 2013. Sam Leach explained: "Alan Hope from Screaming Lord Sutch's band told me that they had a gig the same night near ours in Aldershot and they played regularly at the same venue we were playing in. So he went round tearing my posters down and rang the local paper and said the gig had been cancelled. That's why the other band didn't turn up. He was boasting to my mate Terry McCann, and I saw him recently, and he admitted it to me, in front of my cousin, then of course he tried to backtrack." Terry concurred that there was a deliberate attempt to sabotage the performance and said "Sam went out and found the posters I had put up a few days before had been torn down."'

Front cover of Finding the Fourth Beatle.

An example of the Beatles poster for the event at the Aldershot Palais.

I do remember this conversation with Sam Leach in July 2013 very well and agree with everything Sam Leach and Terry McCann have been quoted as saying about me in Chapter 27 of the *Finding the Fourth Beatle* book.

I feel it is now time, even after 57 years have passed, to put the record straight as part of my involvement in this story has already been published in the *Finding the Fourth Beatle* book. I have decided to share my part in this story which is already part of Beatles folklore, and to fill in the gaps about what really happened when the Beatles came to Aldershot in December 1961 and the reasons they ended up playing to an audience of only 18 people.

I was staying with my good friend Ron Stevenson in Liverpool in July 2013; he asked me out of the blue if I knew, or had heard of Sam Leach. I said, "Yes, of course." Ron then went on to tell me that Sam

Leach was the cousin of his close friend Richard 'Dickie' Leach. I told Ron that I would like to meet up with Sam Leach whilst I was in Liverpool. I also knew Dickie Leach as he often came to Fleet (Hampshire) with Ron Stevenson. I also live In Fleet which is four miles from Aldershot. Dickie Leach had previously told Ron that Sam Leach knew of me; I later found out exactly why Sam knew of me and just how good his memory of the Beatles' Aldershot debacle back in December 1961 still was even after all those years had passed.

So directly through Ron Stevenson and Dickie Leach a meeting was arranged at Sam Leach's house in Liverpool during my stay in July 2013. Sam knew I was coming to see him with his cousin. When we arrived, Dickie stepped forward and knocked on the door; it quickly opened and there was Sam, it was like walking into the Lion's Den as he took one look at me and said, "C'mon in, you bastard, I've always wanted to meet you," with what I think was a smile on his face. We sat down in Sam's lounge and he launched straight into telling me how he still blamed me for the Beatles going off with Brian Epstein in December 1961 and there was no doubt in his mind that he would have been the Beatles' manager if their appearance in Aldershot had been judged to be a success in terms of getting them known in London.

Sam Leach and me. Note the portrait of Rory Storm in the background.

(My private collection)

We drank copious amounts of tea, shared many stories and there was plenty of joking and laughter. I also learnt a lot more about the Liverpool music scene in the 1960s than I ever knew before. I had a photo taken with Sam Leach and there was a picture of Rory Storm in the background and he also gave me a signed copy of his latest book about the Beatles. I left hoping Sam had forgiven me for the role I had played in the Aldershot Palais fiasco in December 1961. We shook hands and parted as friends, hopefully to meet up again one day, but alas, that will never happen now as Sam Leach died in December 2016.

I was born in Mytchett (Surrey) in 1942 and lived in Hawley Estate and went to school in Cove, all of which are only a couple of miles from Aldershot. I was well known in Aldershot having lived in the local area all of my life. Music was in my blood and became a big part of my life from a very early age. I was able to remember all the words of lots of different songs and would often sing to my friends. Musical influences in the early part of my life included Lonnie Donegan, Eddie Cochrane, Chuck Berry and Buddy Holly and the 1960s is still my favourite decade. The late 1950s and early 1960s were a fabulous time to be a teenager involved in the music industry.

It is important to remember that The Beatles in December 1961 were completely unknown outside of Liverpool and they had never appeared in London or the South East before. Very few people, if any, had ever heard of The Beatles when they came to Aldershot. There was no social media, mobile phones or internet in those days so most people in Aldershot were completely unaware of the popularity of The Beatles in Liverpool and their recent successful tour of Hamburg. I myself had also never heard of The Beatles back then and to be honest I never heard of The Beatles again until about a year later.

I was 19 years old when The Beatles came to Aldershot and along with lots of other young people of my age I was able to pursue my dreams, as my age group was one of the first not to be conscripted into the armed forces when National Service ended. I was an aspiring young pop star myself with ambitions to have a successful career as a singer. Like lots of other people of my age I was chasing my big break whilst regularly performing as Kerry Rapid, the lead singer, with my group the Blue Stars every week.

Bob Potter, the agent/promoter of the Aldershot Palais De

Danse, told me he had been contacted by Sam Leach (agent/promoter and aspiring manager of The Beatles) sometime during November 1961 with a request to book the Aldershot Palais for five consecutive Saturday nights from the 9th December. Sam Leach's intention was for The Beatles to appear at the Aldershot Palais at all five of these events and this opportunity was to showcase their talents to the leading agents, press and promoters in London and the South East.

Bob Potter was also the agent/promoter of my group, Kerry Rapid and the Blue Stars. We regularly played at the Aldershot Palais and Bob Potter's other local venues including the Agincourt at Camberley where I played with my band on many occasions. We had built up a very loyal following, particularly amongst local teenagers who would always turn up and ensure our events were complete sell-outs. I was particularly upset when I first saw The Beatles' Aldershot Palais poster that we had not been asked to be one of the advertised two-star supporting groups at any of these five Beatles nights. I was also disappointed that we would not be able to play at the Aldershot Palais, which was our favourite local venue, on the Saturday nights (23rd & 30th December) immediately before Christmas and New Year, which we expected to do every year.

At the time I remember I was angry that this group who I had never heard of from Liverpool were coming onto my patch and throwing all of my plans and bookings up in the air. I knew it was going to be very difficult to find an alternative venue with such little notice but with the help of Rocky Ford (drummer with the Blue Stars) and Mike Burton (agent and promoter for the Central Ballroom in Aldershot) I was able to arrange for Kerry Rapid and the Blue Stars to appear at the Central Ballroom on Short Street in Aldershot on Saturday 9th December 1961 and also on the following Saturday. The Central Ballroom was only a short walk from the Aldershot Palais where The Beatles were appearing and I was well aware we would be in competition for customers that night, but I was determined that Kerry Rapid and the Blue Stars would come out on top and worked hard on promotion in the weeks before with my local fan base and local connections. I even convinced myself that Kerry Rapid and the Blue Stars were a better act than The Beatles back in December 1961.

I then went out of my way and took every opportunity to tell everybody I knew that Kerry Rapid and the Blue Stars would now be appearing at the Central Ballroom in Aldershot on Saturday 9th and 16th December. Promotion was all word of mouth in those days, there was no need for newspaper adverts and posters on the wall were not required. The word soon got around and my event on Saturday 9th December 1961 was a complete sell-out with over 300 people in attendance for the whole night.

I do remember seeing The Beatles' posters on the walls outside the Aldershot Palais and all around Aldershot, advertising and promoting the event on 9th December 1961. I remember thinking, *Who the hell is this Liverpool group, The Beatles?* as I had never heard of them. However, as the Beatles event got closer, I noticed the remaining few posters were badly damaged and unreadable and most of them had been removed. I could imagine my fans would have torn the Beatles posters down and it didn't surprise me at all that the Beatles advert never appeared in the local paper. There was a steady build-up of local resentment regarding this unknown group from Liverpool trying to take over the Aldershot live music scene, especially during the run-up to Christmas and New Year.

I still remember travelling from my home to Aldershot on the bus to my event that Saturday and reminding people on the bus that my group, Kerry Rapid and the Blue Stars, were appearing at the Central Ballroom and would not be appearing at the Aldershot Palais that night. I also went in all the pubs near the Aldershot Palais including the White Hart to remind people that Kerry Rapid and the Blue Stars were appearing at the Central Ballroom in case people went to the Aldershot Palais expecting to see us there. My band did the same and we were all determined to see off The Beatles before Christmas.

During our interval break at the Central Ballroom I decided to get some fresh air and walked the short distance over to the Aldershot Palais to see what was going on. I popped in the White Hart pub on Queens Road for a quick drink and spotted somebody in there with a strong Liverpool accent (I later found out this was Sam Leach) at the bar buying bottles of Watney's Pale Ale to take away and offering free tickets to the customers in the White Hart to come over to see The Beatles at the Aldershot Palais. There was no interest and Sam Leach left the White Hart pub and the customers continued drinking despite

The Beatles appearing live just across the road less than two minutes' walk away. I then looked inside the Aldershot Palais and was very surprised to see there were only about 12 people at this Beatles event. I saw The Beatles (who I later discovered were John, Paul, George and Pete Best) but there were no other groups there and certainly no London agents, press or promoters at this event. The London group advertised on the poster, Ivor Jay and the Jaywalkers, never turned up. I had not heard of them either and unlike The Beatles I have never ever heard of Ivor Jay and The Jaywalkers even to this day. The Beatles were messing about and joking and clowning around on stage with each other; two of The Beatles were not even on the stage when I was there and it all seemed to be a big laugh to them, but certainly not to any of the customers who were there that night.

The Beatles poster referred to The Battle of the Bands at the Aldershot Palais. What the Beatles and Sam Leach didn't realise at the time was that the real battle of the bands contest was with Kerry Rapid and the Blue Stars who were appearing at the Central Ballroom in Aldershot on the same night.

I recognised a few people in the Aldershot Palais who I knew from my concerts and invited them to come back with me to the Central Ballroom for the second half of my show. I sang a few Chuck Berry songs which I was told The Beatles had also sung at the Aldershot Palais that night. After we finished our second slot I was told by two of the people who came back with me to the Central Ballroom from the Aldershot Palais that my versions of Chuck Berry's Johnny B Goode, Memphis Tennessee and Roll Over Beethoven were much better than The Beatles' versions which they had also sung at the Aldershot Palais earlier that night.

Kerry Rapid and the Blue Stars also appeared at the Central Ballroom the following Saturday (16th December) and during our interval break I again went to see what was going on at the Aldershot Palais that same night. Having previously been told The Beatles were going to be appearing at the Aldershot Palais for five consecutive Saturdays, I was very surprised when I first arrived to see that The Beatles were not there this time, and was even more surprised to see another Liverpool group, Rory Storm and the Hurricanes, who I had heard of before, were performing to an audience of about 250 people. There were no publicity posters for this event and I didn't see an advert in the local paper and yet there were lots of people in the Palais that night. However, despite the popularity of Rory Storm and Hurricanes, my event just a short walk away from the Palais at the Central Ballroom was still a sell-out with 300 people there.

I did not see Sam Leach there this time but Terry McCann, who I got to know much later, was there, and everybody seemed to be having a good time. I remember thinking at the time how much better Rory Storm and the Hurricanes were compared to The Beatles. The drummer of the Hurricanes really caught my eye as he was a showman with a big personality and he got everybody up and dancing. I found out later this drummer was Richard Starkey, also known as Ringo Starr, who went on to join The Beatles in August 1962.

Rory Storm and the Hurricanes in 1961. Drummer Ringo Starr is third left.

(Courtesy Dick Matthews)

I then heard through the grapevine during the following week that Sam Leach was not coming back to the Aldershot Palais for the next three Saturdays in December and January he had booked, and these dates became available again. The Beatles were never going to return to Aldershot as by then they were locked into contract negotiations with Brian Epstein following their return to Liverpool on 10th December 1961. It was apparently a nine-hour drive from Liverpool to Aldershot and bad news had travelled very fast in Liverpool with the result that Sam Leach could not get any Liverpool band to fulfil the remaining three Aldershot Palais bookings. These Liverpool acts included Gerry and the Pacemakers, who were lined up to appear at the Aldershot Palais on Saturday 23rd December, but declined the opportunity. There was also no interest at all from any of the main London agents, press and promoters in coming to see any of the Liverpool groups in Aldershot. As soon as the three Saturdays at the Aldershot Palais became available, I arranged for Kerry Rapid and the Blue Stars to step in and fill the void, enabling us to return to our favourite Saturday night venue for two consecutive Saturday nights – 23rd and 30th December. It was a great Christmas present for my group, particularly as both of these Kerry Rapid and the Blue Stars events were sell-outs with around 300 people packed into the Aldershot Palais on each night.

It was about a year afterwards, in late 1962/early 1963, when I first heard of The Beatles and when I realised I had sung on the very same stage, during the very same month and the same year, as The Beatles (John Lennon, Paul McCartney, George Harrison, Pete Best and Ringo Starr who had appeared with Rory Storm and The Hurricanes). During the month of December 1961, Kerry Rapid and the Blue Stars proved to be more popular in Aldershot than The Beatles were. I even thought about booking The Cavern Club in Liverpool in the early part of 1962 and taking on The Beatles at their favourite venue. I still remember my fans being so pleased about our return to Aldershot Palais on Saturday 23rd December 1961 and chanting out, "Kerry, Kerry, Kerry!" when I came on the stage. It was a great welcome and probably was our best ever live performance. We were on fire that night. If only Sam Leach or Brian Epstein had been there to see it.

Sam Leach was intent on becoming the manager of The Beatles. Sam was convinced The Beatles were going to be very famous and even bigger stars than Elvis. The five Saturday night events which Sam had booked and paid for himself at the Aldershot Palais was his final opportunity to impress The Beatles by successfully launching their career in London and the South East by bringing them to the notice of the main London promoters, agents and press. It was also the opportunity to take The Beatles away from Liverpool and from the potential clutches of Brian Epstein. However, the fiasco at the Aldershot Palais on Saturday 9th December 1961 proved to be a real turning point in Sam's relationship with The Beatles. Shortly after The Beatles returned to Liverpool from Aldershot, they informed Sam Leach of their decision to appoint Brian Epstein as their manager. Brian Epstein was delighted with their decision and officially took over as Beatles manager in early January 1962, and The Beatles' career then moved forward quickly.

The original contract between Brian Epstein and The Beatles (John Lennon, Paul McCartney, George Harrison and Pete Best) was signed on 24th January 1962 at Pete Best's house (Casbah Coffee Club). Brian Epstein never signed this contract and explained later that he didn't sign it because he wanted to give The Beatles the opportunity to walk away if the arrangement did not work out for them.

The Beatles, after their appearance in Aldershot on Saturday 9th December 1961 travelled back to London overnight and met up with Brian Epstein in Liverpool the very next day on Sunday 10th December 1961 where they agreed to appoint him as their manager. This just emphasises the importance The Beatles' appearance in Aldershot had on the prospects of Sam Leach becoming their manager.

If the Aldershot appearance had been as big a success as Sam Leach had hoped for and if The Beatles had performed as planned for four consecutive Saturdays at the Aldershot Palais in front of lots of London promoters, agents and record producers, who knows how their career would have progressed.

Brian Epstein produced a new contact in October 1962 after Ringo Starr had replaced Pete Best on drums and this new contract was signed by John Lennon, Paul McCartney, George Harrison and Ringo Starr together with Brain Epstein himself.

The January 1962 contract between Brian Epstein and The Beatles.

The Beatles signed a recording deal with George Martin, a London record producer, and the EMI Parlophone record label in April 1962, and began recording at the Abbey Road Studios in June 1962. Pete Best, The Beatles' drummer who I saw at the Aldershot Palais, was sacked in August 1962 and replaced by Ringo Starr, the drummer with Rory Storm and the Hurricanes. In October 1962 the Beatles had their very first Top 20 UK single hit record (A-side was Love Me Do and the B-side was PS I Love You; both songs were written by Lennon and McCartney) and a month later Love Me Do reached No. 4 in the USA charts. The Beatles went on to become the most influential international music band in history. However, I still cannot believe how the Beatles band of John, Paul, George and Pete Best/Ringo Starr, all of whom I saw perform at the Aldershot Palais in December 1961, were able to achieve such heights less than a year after I had seen The Beatles perform in front of only 12 people.

In hindsight and after further reflection 57 years later, it is perhaps ironic that everything could have turned out so very differently for The Beatles and Sam Leach. For example, if Kerry Rapid and the

Blue Stars had been included on the same Aldershot Palais bill as The Beatles that night, this event would undoubtedly have been a complete sell-out and a big success. There would have been no need for posters or advertising in the local newspaper as I would have done all of the promotion myself. Kerry Rapid and the Blue Stars were a very popular local band with a large loyal following who would have guaranteed The Beatles' event at the Aldershot Palais was a big success. Music lovers would then have seen The Beatles at their very best and they would have happily returned to the Aldershot Palais on the following four Saturdays, providing The Beatles were appearing on the same bill as Kerry Rapid and the Blue Stars. On the back of this success Sam Leach could then have been able to attract some influential London and South East promoters, press and agents to the next four Beatles events at the Aldershot Palais, following the success of this first event. If these five Aldershot Palais Saturday night events had gone on to deliver a huge success for The Beatles then Sam Leach would have become their manager and then who knows what would have happened to them in the future. Either way, The Beatles' appearances in Aldershot played a very big part in their career going forward.

There is no doubt Brian Epstein had a lot more money to invest in The Beatles and being already part of the music business, he had some very good contacts e.g. George Martin, the music producer. Epstein could also open doors and create opportunities with successful record labels in London; these were all contacts which Sam Leach did not have. Brian Epstein also changed The Beatles' image and made them more disciplined and professional which were not qualities I saw them display at the Aldershot Palais.

This example of The Beatles in Aldershot also further highlights how success in the music business in the 1960s could often come from situations when you least expected it. In late 1961, The Beatles only had two options for their manager – Sam Leach or Brian Epstein, there was no genuine interest from anybody else. The shambolic Aldershot event can now perhaps be seen as a the single most important event that gave The Beatles the big break they had been waiting for, because this directly resulted in them appointing Brian Epstein as their manager and as they say, "the rest is history".

In summarising my story, I conclude there now appears to be little doubt, 57 years later, about the impact that the involvement and interventions by Alan Hope/Kerry Rapid had on The Beatles' long-term career. I successfully sabotaged The Beatles' first ever appearance in the South of England and their one and only appearance in Aldershot on 9th December 1961. Alan Hope/Kerry Rapid therefore made a significant contribution to the global success of The Beatles as these actions directly led to the appointment of Brian Epstein as their manager in January 1962, and worldwide success for The Beatles followed soon afterwards. Brian Epstein would have known all about Aldershot as he served the first four months of his National Service in late 1952/early '53 undertaking army training at Aldershot Barracks. He would also have been aware how far Aldershot was away from London as he served part of his National Service in London. Epstein would never have booked the Aldershot Palais to showcase The Beatles' talents in the South of England. Epstein did not enjoy his Aldershot experience, something else he had in common with The Beatles, but it is possible he could have been to an event at the Aldershot Palais and may have visited some of the local pubs whilst he was doing his National Service there.

I was 19 when I saw The Beatles play at Aldershot Palais in December 1961. John Lennon was 21, Pete Best was 20, Paul McCartney was 19, George Harrison was 18 and Ringo Starr who was playing with Rory Storm and The Hurricanes was 21.

Facts about The Beatles connected to the Aldershot gig date and Alan Hope

John Lennon was killed at 4am (UK time) on 9th December 1980, exactly 19 years to the very day (9th December 1961) when The Beatles appeared at Aldershot Palais.

The Beatles praised George Martin's stabilising role in the recording studio. George Harrison said, "I think we just grew through those years together, him as the straight man and us as the loonies, but he was always there for us, to interpret our madness." Alan Hope, after his career as Kerry Rapid, was the joint founder, with Screaming Lord David Sutch, of the Monster Raving Loony Party in June 1982. On the death of Screaming Lord Sutch on 16th June 1999 (Alan Hope's birthday), Alan Hope became the Leader of the Party in 1999 (20 years as Leader in June 2019) so perhaps the

Aldershot experience in December 1961 directly resulted in Alan Hope and The Beatles all becoming loonies.

Alan Hope was born just two days before Paul McCartney. Alan Hope was born on 16th June 1942 and Paul McCartney was born on 18th June 1942.

(Produced by Alan Hope 9th December 2018)

Alan Hope's story has been checked, validated and authenticated through several conversations and interviews with people who were around at the time. Details of these conversations and interviews now follow (all interviews conducted by Derrill Carr):

Interview and conversation with Mike Burton in December 2018

Mike Burton ran a small agency based in Aldershot from 1959 onwards which organised bands/groups to play at local venues. Mike also organised and booked all of the bands/groups for the Central Ballroom in Aldershot.

Mike said the Central Ballroom had an upstairs room which is where the best bands appeared, and then a room downstairs in a club-type cellar where other bands would play. The upstairs room could hold about 300 people and was a very popular local venue.

There was a lot of competition between local venues and promoters to get the best groups. The groups available often included Joe Brown and the Bruvvers and Johnny Kidd and the Pirates. Kerry Rapid and the Blue Stars got most of their gigs through Bob Potter who organised the bands/groups who played at the Aldershot Palais and also at the Agincourt in Camberley.

Mike Burton was very friendly with Rocky Ford (drummer of the Blue Stars) who played with Kerry Rapid. Mike and Rocky saw each other regularly. Sometime during October/November 1961 Mike and Rocky met up at the Wimpey restaurant in Aldershot. Mike told Rocky he had a cancellation in December and Rocky told Mike that Kerry Rapid and the Blue Stars also had cancellation for the same Saturday (9th December 1961) due to Bob Potter taking a booking for the Aldershot Palais from Sam Leach for The Beatles to appear. Mike Burton then asked Rocky if Kerry Rapid and the Blue Stars would like a slot on the bill upstairs in the Central Ballroom on Saturday 9th December 1961. Rocky spoke to Kerry Rapid and the rest of the Blue Stars and they happily agreed to take the booking at the Central Ballroom. Kerry Rapid and the Blue Stars were then in direct competition with The Beatles on Saturday 9th December 1961, as The Beatles were playing a short distance away at the Aldershot Palais.

Mike said Kerry Rapid and the Blue Stars were a very good local group who were extremely popular and had a large loyal following, and they sold out most local venues. Mike was pleased to get them to play at the Central Ballroom for the first ever time, especially as this was just a few weeks after Brian Poole and the Tremeloes had appeared on the very same stage.

Mike said that Kerry Rapid, the lead singer, reminded him a lot of Billy Fury, who at the time was on his way to becoming a very big star.

Mike confirmed that Kerry Rapid and the Blue Stars did their first 45-minute slot upstairs in the Central Ballroom in front of a packed audience and then had a break for at least half an hour before coming back on again. This event was so successful that Mike booked Kerry Rapid and the Blue Stars again for the following Saturday (16th December 1961) when The Beatles were also expected to return to the Aldershot Palais for a second appearance.

Mike said the admission cost to get in the Central Ballroom in December 1961 was 25p (5 shillings) which was the same price as The Beatles' event at Aldershot Palais.

Mike confirmed that he did see The Beatles at Aldershot Palais posters around town but most of them disappeared very quickly. Mike suggested the secret was to follow closely behind the person putting the posters up and then tear the posters down whilst they were still wet and before the paste had time to dry, albeit Mike was then very quick to confirm he had never done this himself. Mike said he had never heard of the other band on the same bill as The Beatles and was not surprised to hear that Ivor Jay and the Jaywalkers didn't turn up. Mike also said he had never heard of The Beatles in December 1961 but he had heard of the other Liverpool group, Rory Storm and the Hurricanes (featuring Ringo Starr on drums), who appeared at the Aldershot Palais a week after The Beatles on Saturday 16th December 1961.

Kerry Rapid and the Blue Stars never appeared at Central Ballroom in Aldershot again after December 1961 because following The Beatles and Rory Storm and the Hurricanes' one-off appearances at the Aldershot Palais in December 1961, Sam Leach decided not to utilise the next three Saturdays he had booked through Bob Potter which enabled Kerry Rapid and the Blue Stars to return to the Aldershot Palais from Saturday 23rd December 1961 onwards.

Interview and conversation with Irene Stoker in December 2018

Irene Stoker was one of the very few people (18) who actually attended the Beatles concert at the Aldershot Palais on 9th December 1961 and she has told her story several times to the Daily Mail and the Aldershot News & Mail. Irene's account also appears in Chapter 27 of the book *Finding the Fourth Beatle* written by David Bedford and Gary Popper, plus also included in many Beatles online blogs, articles and magazines.

Irene Stoker (left) dancing with her friend Pat Hawten at Aldershot Palais on 9th December 1961. George Harrison, John Lennon and Paul McCartney are on stage right behind them. (Courtesy Dick Matthews)

The photo of Irene Stoker on the left dancing with her friend Pat Hawten on the right, was taken at the Aldershot Palais on 9th December 1961, with the Beatles (George, John & Paul) on stage and Pete Best on drums playing in the background.

Irene told me that she always went with her friend Pat to the Aldershot Palais on most Saturday nights. Both Irene and Pat lived on Perowne Street and just a few yards away from the Aldershot Palais. Irene described the Palais as a small venue (held about 250 to 300 people) but it was a very intimate venue and the people were friendly. Irene and Pat went to the Palais early on Saturday 9th December 1961 and paid their 25p (5 shillings) on the door and hung their coats in the cloak room. They walked inside to what was a virtually empty dance floor with less than a handful of people inside; there was no atmosphere. They sat down to weigh up the situation and then got up to dance together but they were not impressed with The Beatles who were messing around and showing off on stage and were not treating the occasion seriously. Irene was not happy when John Lennon criticised the internal decorations and described the Aldershot Palais as a Village Hall. Irene was dancing right next to the stage and told John Lennon he was wrong as the Palais was a great musical venue, and Aldershot had some very good local groups who sold out the Palais every weekend.

Two of The Beatles then came off the stage and started dancing together. Paul McCartney came over and asked Irene for a dance on two occasions but she turned him down both times. Paul McCartney ended up dancing on his own – see photo below, whilst Irene danced a jive with a local boy she knew.

After a few more dances Irene and Pat decided it was time for them to leave the Palais and they then walked the short distance to the Central Ballroom in Aldershot via a short stopover in the Havelock pub. Irene confirmed that Kerry Rapid and the Blue Stars did appear on the Central Ballroom stage that night (Saturday 9th December 1961). Irene also said the Central Ballroom was packed out and both she and Pat ended up having a very good night. Irene said the Central Ballroom was also a very friendly venue where most people knew each other. However, the music was loud and the place was very smoky as most young people smoked cigarettes in those days.

Paul McCartney dancing on his own at the Aldershot Palais on 9th December 1961. (Courtesy Dick Matthews)

Irene said that Aldershot, despite the presence of the Army, was a very safe place for teenage girls to walk around at night in 1961. There were military police on horseback everywhere and Aldershot was a great place for a night out in the 1960s, and she and Pat didn't go anywhere else. There would also be people coming to Aldershot from London on the train at the weekend and at one stage there were so many people coming that Aldershot became known as Little London.

Irene confirmed that she had never heard of The Beatles in December 1961 and it was in the early part of 1963 before she realised from a photo of Paul McCartney that they were the same Beatles she had seen at Aldershot Palais in December 1961, and they were now very famous the world over. Irene and Pat were both convinced back in December 1961 that The Beatles would never make it.

The following weekend (Saturday 16th December 1961) Irene and Pat again went to the Aldershot Palais; this time the Liverpool band on stage was Rory Storm and the Hurricanes featuring Richard Starkey aka Ringo Starr on drums. There were over 200 people already there and lots of people were already dancing. Irene said the music and atmosphere was very good and both she and Pat danced all night and came away very impressed by Rory Storm and the Hurricanes, who they thought at the time were a much better group than The Beatles.

Irene enjoyed the 1960s – she loved the music and fashion but also said it was a carefree period of her life without any pressure and everybody was able to relax and enjoy themselves at weekends. Roy Orbison and Johnny Mathis were her favourite singers at the time but she liked lots of songs by different artists and not just songs from the same artist. Irene went to see Lonnie Donegan (one of Alan Hope's favourites) at the Aldershot Hippodrome in 1957 and afterwards ended up following Lonnie Donegan to Aldershot Station with her friend to get his autograph.

Irene married a Paratrooper who was based in Aldershot. Irene to this day said she has never bought a Beatles record and has never listened to any of their music apart from one song, 'Yesterday', which she still really likes. This song, 'Yesterday', could have been the title of this story from 57 years ago. I can't help thinking Irene's dislike of The Beatles is at least partially due to the very bad Beatles experience she had at the Aldershot Palais on 9th December 1961 which she has never forgotten to this day.

Interview and conversation with Ron Stevenson in December 2018

Ron Stevenson helped to arrange the meeting for Alan Hope with Sam Leach in July 2013 when Alan was staying in Liverpool with him. Ron was also there in Sam Leach's house with Alan Hope that day in July 2013, and confirmed everything Alan and Sam have said in this story is true and accurate. It appeared to Ron at the time that Alan was relieved to get this story off his chest and to put things right with Sam Leach after all these years. Sam Leach understood from this meeting that The Beatles' failure in Aldershot was not purely down to him as there were other forces at work behind the scenes which significantly contributed to this huge failure for The Beatles in Aldershot, when only 18 people turned up to see them perform in December 1961.

Interview and conversation with Bob Potter in 2018

Bob Potter was interviewed for Alan Hope's autobiography. Bob was responsible for booking all of the bands and groups at the Aldershot Palais and Agincourt in Camberley during the early 1960s and was the same person who Sam Leach spoke to when he booked the Aldershot Palais for The Beatles in December 1961. Bob had never heard of The Beatles when he took this booking from Sam Leach. Bob Potter confirmed that Kerry Rapid was top of the bill at the first Rock and Roll tour he ever promoted. He also gave Kerry Rapid lots of gigs at the Aldershot Palais and Agincourt and would often pick him up from home and take him to and from the gigs. Bob described Kerry Rapid as a Jack the Lad character so it should not surprise anybody that knew him what lengths he would go to when The Beatles took over his regular venue when they came to Aldershot in December 1961.

Interview and conversation with Sue Glover in December 2018

Sue Glover is a professional singer and was a member of Brotherhood of Man for three years, and she sang on Joe Cocker's version of 'With a Little Help from my Friends' which was a No. 1 hit record all over the world and coincidentally there is a Beatles connection as this song was written by Lennon & McCartney for Ringo Starr to sing. Sue has appeared on Top of the Pops and at the 1969 Eurovision Song Contest on backing vocals with her sister Sunny when they supported Lulu to win the contest with Boom Bang a Bang. Sue and her sister Sunny were brought up in Camberley and as teenagers they would often go to the Agincourt Club in Camberley which was a Bob Potter venue where Kerry Rapid and the Blue Stars played regularly. Sue and Sunny both wanted to get into the music industry and went along to see Kerry Rapid to listen and learn from the master but Sue admitted they had teenage crushes on him as well as they both thought he was absolutely gorgeous.

Sue said Kerry Rapid's teenage fans would wait for him outside the Agincourt after the concert finished and they would immediately swarm around him when he came out. Sue went on to say that Kerry Rapid had a good heart and was always very patient with his fans and would stand chatting for as long as they wanted.

Sue went on to say that Kerry Rapid was a big draw and would fill the place every time he was on at the Agincourt in Camberley. Sue said Kerry Rapid was such a good-looking guy and he was the local teenage heartthrob. The teenage girls in front of the stage would scream out loud when Kerry Rapid first came on the stage and Sue and her sister could never get near him.

Sue said Kerry Rapid also had the most fantastic rock and roll voice and offered the complete pop star package. She was very surprised Kerry Rapid did not make the big time as he had everything going for him in the early 1960s.

Eventually Sue and Sunny did get to meet Kerry Rapid/Alan Hope and he gave them lots of good professional advice about the music business and they have remained good friends with him ever since. Sue also went out with Brian Allender, who was the drummer for Kerry Rapid's Blue Stars.

Interview and conversation with John Hope in 2017

John Hope was the younger brother of Alan Hope and he was interviewed in 2017 for Alan Hope's autobiography. These extracts below are just about Alan and his music and his pop career as Kerry Rapid.

Alan was always singing around the house and he could sing in lots of different styles and amazingly could remember the words of hundreds of different songs. He kept the family and his friends entertained for many hours. I went to the Aldershot Palais and the Agincourt at Camberley to see my brother Alan appearing as Kerry Rapid with his band the Blue Stars. Alan was a natural entertainer with a great personality who came alive on the stage and the local venues were always packed to capacity whenever Kerry Rapid was in town. Kerry Rapid was very popular with the local teenage girls and they followed and supported him at all of his concerts. John can still remember being at home when Alan was getting ready for a concert at the Aldershot Palais in 1960. Alan looked every inch a pop star and was dressed in a very striking silver lamé jacket which had been specially made for him by his wife.

Another outstanding memory was at the Agincourt in Camberley in February 1967 when Kerry Rapid and the Soultones were the supporting band for Chuck Berry. Kerry Rapid sang a few Chuck Berry songs that night with Chuck Berry stood in the wings listening to every word. Chuck Berry was very impressed with Kerry Rapid's version of Johnny B Goode and after the event asked Alan if Kerry Rapid and the Blue Stars would be interested in being the support band when Chuck Berry the next time he came over to the UK to do another tour. That was all agreed, but nothing ever came of it.

Interview and conversation with Alan Clayson in December 2018

Alan Clayson was a former member of The Savages who were Screaming Lord Sutch's band but for many years he has performed as Alan Clayson and The Argonauts and they still perform live at concerts today.

Alan Clayson lived and went to school in the Aldershot area and followed Kerry Rapid's career from a very young age. He described Kerry Rapid/Alan Hope as his hero and mentor who inspired him to follow his music dreams. Alan Clayson was not surprised to hear that Kerry Rapid was more popular in Aldershot than the Beatles back in December 1961. Alan Clayson confirmed that Kerry Rapid was a huge local attraction and teenage girls mobbed the venues at every one of his events.

Alan Clayson also vividly remembered walking past the Aldershot Palais on a Saturday evening in 1960 when he was aged ten and seeing Kerry Rapid and the Blue Stars unloading all the band's equipment and getting ready to set up for a concert that night.

Alan Clayson forwarded a write up on Kerry Rapid which appeared in the Vintage Rock magazine (April/May 2016 edition), reproduced below:

"KERRY RAPID – in the military borough of Aldershot, local heroes Kerry Rapid and the Blue Stars, were playing at the Central Ballroom on the same December 1961 night when the Beatles undertook a solitary and ill-fated booking at Kerry Rapid's usual Saturday venue."

Interview and conversation with Sylvia McMaster in December 2018

Sylvia McMaster is Bob Potter's PA and she also took the photographs at the concerts at Bob Potter's venues in the 1960s. Sylvia was also the author of *One Man's Dream* which is Bob Potter's autobiography.

Sylvia said, "Kerry Rapid was a blond bombshell and very good looking. He was full of character and great on stage. He could have been famous as a singer; he was just never in the right place at the right time."

The Beatles on stage at the Aldershot Palais. My photo above has a Bobby Darin LP cover pinned to the wall. Note the same LP cover upside down on the back wall near Pete Best. Paul McCartney is standing exactly where I am sitting in the upper photo – could it be that he is following in my footsteps? (Courtesy Dick Matthews)

Sam Leach with George Harrison and John Lennon drinking Watney's Pale Ale that Sam had bought from the White Hart pub (inset) across the road. (Courtesy Dick Matthews)

The Beatles line-up when they appeared at the Aldershot Palais on 9th December 1961. (My private collection)

PART 3

MINE HOST …

In this Part:

Chapter 10: My marriage to Pamela ends, and I marry Norma – the love of my life. But what were we going to do now?

Chapter 11: Buying and running the Golden Lion Hotel in Ashburton, Devon

Chapter 12: Having fun in Ashburton

Chapter 13: The Lion sleeps and I move on

Chapter 14: I'm back in Hampshire and become Landlord of the Dog and Partridge in Yateley.

CHAPTER 10

Reinvention

Oh, Norma …

Yes, I guess it's fair to say that I did fall out with Threewheel over the Jed Ford tour. And that's kind of why I decided to quit as a singer. I just had to sit down and think: *OK. I'm 36 now. What am I going to do for the next 36 years?* I guess I was beginning to realise that I wasn't going to make it big, although I still had it in my mind that I might do one day.

My marriage to Pamela had fallen apart. The same story, I think: Too much time on the road; three daughters at home; not much money. I remember we went to Wales once on a holiday, on the train. I didn't drive then. That's when things started to go wrong. We started having rows and arguing. I'd met Norma by this time. She was quite a fan of Threewheel and she got to know us all pretty well in the band. She was a good friend of Mike Riley and his wife Liz who ran a dance school at Elmhurst in Camberley, but after a while she became quite attached to me. My marriage was just going from bad to worse. Obviously, Pamela was pretty upset and hurt. It was some years later before we could really get along with each other again.

Liz Riley remembers …

At the time, I was teaching ballroom-dance classes in Woking; one of my pupils was Norma Hockley. Some of the members of the class asked if there was any possibility of practicing between lessons. I told them about an up-coming Threewheel gig locally and some of them, including Norma, came along. She met Alan and the rest was history.

They always blamed me, saying it was my fault they got together. Guilty as charged, I suppose.

So it came to the point when I just left, or was thrown out depending on who you want to believe. I moved in with Norma almost straightaway. And we were happy. So very happy, although Norma's mum was a bit put out. I wonder about what she thought of the idea of Norma taking up with a married man and his four children.

But on the day I left and went to Norma's, we filled up Norma's car with all my stuff, and somehow managed to squeeze my son Mark in as well. The next day, I came back to collect my daughters so they could meet Norma properly. But the girls didn't move in with us. It was better that they stayed at home with Pamela.

The daughters reflect …

The break-up wasn't really that upsetting for us as we'd never seen that much of Dad anyway. In some ways it was a relief when all the arguments stopped. Norma didn't have any children, and she was an only child herself, and she did look after us. She treated us as her children really. She would take us shopping for clothes, toys, presents, and we would stay over there whenever we could. We don't think Mum was very happy about it at first – another woman looking after her kids. But that got better. She could see that Norma took care of us, and that was the thing that really mattered to Mum. And she was great with our children too.

Mark Hope remembers …

The first time I met Norma was when she picked us up when Alan and I moved out, and we went to her house in Sandhurst. That must have been 1977. I think I was just about to leave school. I left at the Easter. I hated school. I don't like going back there now with my kids. But I remember having my 18th birthday party in Devon – that would have been 1978. I remember the 'long walk' from Greatfield Road, up Ley Road, to a waiting car in Hawley Lane, the day that Dad moved out. And I just went with him. I think I did have a free choice about that, but it didn't take me long to make up my mind. I was going to stick with Dad. I was a bit bewildered really as it all happened so quickly. We just upped sticks and went. It was very fast. I think Dad had just come home from work and had to go – no notice or anything. I was sitting in her front room, and Dad was shouting up the stairs to Norma – but he kept calling her Pam. That broke the ice. Just me and Dad, the girls didn't come over straight away.

Norma was alright. She never did me any harm. She loved Father. I knew soon after meeting her that she would never have kids. She told me about her mother having MS and it being hereditary. She didn't want to take that chance. I don't know what Dad felt about that. She treated us all as if we were her family. I always called her Norma, not Mum.

It just seemed natural that Norma and I should marry, and we did on April 15th 1978. It was wonderful. We got married in the Methodist Church in Camberley and held the reception in Yateley School hall. It was a big event. Mike Riley from Threewheel was my Best Man, and my three daughters were Bridesmaids. Mark was there of course. We must have had around 250 guests. Many were connected with the music business of course, including some big-wigs from the Country and Western circuit.

Due to the number of guests, the vicar was delighted with the collection taken at the service. He took the plate back to the front of the church, and threw it up in the air: "What the Good Lord wants he'll grab, and we'll use what comes back down." The Emeralds provided the music in the evening, and I joined them on stage for a few songs. It really was a happy day.

In a strange twist of fate, shortly after our wedding the church burned down, and then three months later the place where we had the reception burned down.

So now I had a new life with Norma and Mark. But what were we actually going to do?

Our wedding day. (My private collection)

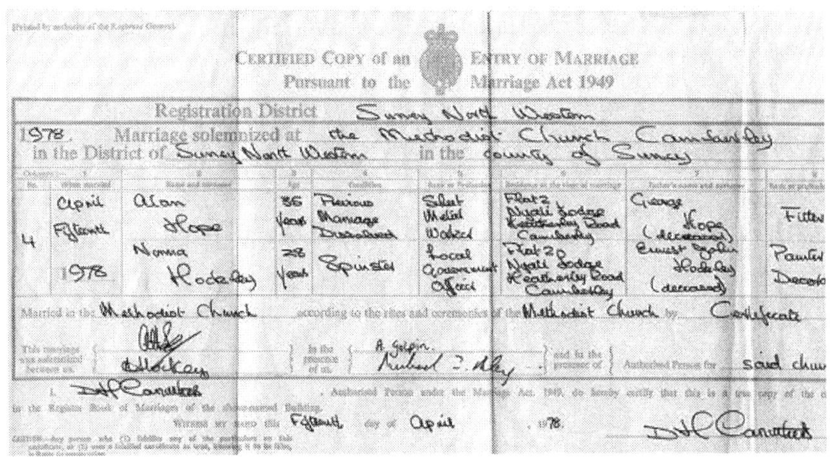

CERTIFIED COPY of an ENTRY OF MARRIAGE
Pursuant to the Marriage Act 1949

Registration District Surrey North Western

1978. Marriage solemnized at the Methodist Church Camberley
in the District of Surrey North Western in the County of Surrey

No.	When married	Name and surname	Age	Condition	Rank or Profession	Residence at the time of marriage	Father's name and surname	Rank or profession
4	April Fifteenth 1978	Alan Hope	35 years	Previous Marriage Dissolved	Sheet Metal Worker	Flat 2 Nyali Lodge Heatherley Road Camberley	George Hope (deceased)	Fitter
		Norma Hodakey	28 years	Spinster	Local Government Officer	Flat 2 Nyali Lodge Heatherley Road Camberley	Ernest John Hodakey (deceased)	Painter Decorator

Married in the Methodist Church according to the rites and ceremonies of the Methodist Church by Certificate

This marriage was solemnized between us, in the presence of us, A. Gilpin, and in the presence of Authorised Person for said church

Witness my hand this Fifteenth day of April 1978.

Our marriage certificate. (My private collection)

In search of a new beginning …

We had to find a new challenge, although we weren't quite sure what that would be. We were living in Norma's house in Sandhurst, and nearby was this place called Rackstraw Farm. I said to Norma one day: "That would make a lovely pub if we could just get permission for it." Around that area, you don't know if farmland is strictly farmland, or whether it belongs to the Church or the Army or whoever. Anyway, I found out it could be licenced, it could be a pub. And I could buy the whole lot for £15,000, the farmhouse and all the land. The deal was £9,000 down and three yearly payments of £2,000.

Rackstraw Farm in 2018. (Courtesy Barry Toms)

We could afford that. I talked with a builder friend of mine called David: "I've got this idea for Rackstraw Farm. It would make a nice pub. If I can get a licence, would you do the building for me?" He thought that was a great idea. This was back in 1977, before I quit Threewheel. I had to go on a six-week tour with them. When I came back, he'd gone behind my back and done it himself. It's still there. Now it's a 'Beefeater' and a hotel and very popular. Clearly, I had the right idea.

The search begins ...

So now we started to look for somewhere else, moving out in ever-increasing circles. We decided it would be too expensive to buy a place to do up, so we'd look for somewhere that was already running. We went to Cambridge, North London, and we ended up in Devon one day. We called in on a local agent. He said: "I think I've got just the place for you. My wife's uncle used to own it." So he took us to see it, and that was the Golden Lion in Ashburton. It was just what we wanted. The hotel had 14 letting rooms in the main building and another 10 out the back. And it had a restaurant, it had a swimming pool, car park, a ballroom – everything we wanted. All built.

Taking a gamble ...

So we had to decide, did we want it? It was very much a gamble, a big risk. But in the end, we set our hearts on this exciting challenge. Ken and Grace Robertson owned it at the time. So we got everything going. But a little later, I got a call back home in Sandhurst from Ken: "Sorry. The sale's fallen through."

"Why's that?"

"Our agent doesn't think we should sell it."

"Well, if you want to sell it, and we want to buy it, what's it got to do with the estate agent?"

In the end he agreed, and we ended up buying it.

The Golden Lion cost us £80,000. That was a lot of money in 1978. We sold the house in Sandhurst for about £30,000 and we were able to secure a mortgage for a further £30,000. That left us £20,000 short. After a bit of bargaining, we were able to convince the owner to take the remaining money over time. That was a gamble, but I did pay him back as promised.

It was time for a change. In a sense, it was still the entertainment business. It had the ballroom, a big public bar with a stage at one end. We could hold ordinary pub events in the bar, and private functions – weddings, birthday parties and so on – in the ballroom upstairs. The bar was my stage, and the customers my audience.

Neither of us had any previous experience of running a hotel or a restaurant, but that didn't worry us. We didn't take any advice from anybody, and we bought the hotel as seen – no survey or anything like that. We felt we could make a success of it. I'd had a little look behind a few bars, but no experience really. Norma worked in local government – for both Guildford and Camberley – and that's what she was doing up until we moved down there. Norma was great with the admin and finance – she was brilliant at that.

Being on stage for many years gave me the confidence, and it just seemed a natural progression where I could still entertain, and sell beer and food, provide accommodation, and make a living.

So yes. It was quite a gamble – an act of blind faith, but we just knew we could make it work. And it did!

Bob Potter comments …

I told Alan not to take on the hotel. I own several and they are very hard work. There's always lots to do and they can eat up your money very quickly.

The deal was that I would make the money and she would look after it. We were a good team. We were there for 22 years. It was October 1978 that we moved down to Ashburton to take over the Golden Lion. On the 1st of November, it actually became ours. We worked there for a week before whilst Ken and Grace were still there. The first person I ever served that day – my first customer – was a local boy called Robbie Boyle, all the way from Scotland. Blow me but many years later I walked into Wetherspoons in Plymouth and there he was.

So we gradually got ourselves sorted out.

About Ashburton and the Golden Lion…

I think I need to give you a little bit of historical context for both Ashburton and the Golden Lion.

Ashburton is an ancient Stannary Town. It claims to be the third oldest town in England after Chester and Totnes. It received its Charter from Edward I in 1285, but it is clear that tin-mining was an important local industry as far back as Roman times. The town was also known for its umber mines.

The Golden Lion c.1900. (Courtesy Pete Webb)

It has somehow managed to retain many of its ancient customs. It still elects a Portreeve, a Bailiff, a Surveyor of Markets, Bread-weighers, Ale-tasters and Constables, annually. These are all dignitaries established in Saxon times.

It lies on the original London to Plymouth road (although now bypassed), and that helped it to become established as a place for coaching inns. Some of these, and many Elizabethan and Georgian residences, can still be found in the town.

The Golden Lion was built in 1768 as a mansion for Nicholas Tripe, a local surgeon. It became an inn in 1795 and became a busy coaching house in the 19th century. The name is said to be based, not on a lion, but on the local name for a breed of Dartmoor sheep that have a distinct bronze hint to their fleece. That is why many pubs are named 'The Golden Fleece' – of which there was one in Ashburton in years gone by.

It was also frequented by sailors and you can still see the entrance to a tunnel in the cellars used to enable them to escape from the press-gangs looking for new recruits.

Norma outside the Golden Lion in 1993. (Courtesy Pete Webb)

The Golden Lion in close-up. (Courtesy Tim Jenkinson)

In 1837, the landlord was called William Barons. He was a strong supporter of the Conservative Party, and the Golden Lion was the 'home' of the local Conservative Party for a while. There was an election that year which caused the Lion's patrons to kidnap the liberal candidate, George Knowling. They spiked his drink and took him up on the moor. Eventually, his supporters rescued him and paraded him up and down the town. It developed into a full-scale riot – sticks with nails in and so on. It got quite vicious.

They say Arthur Conan-Doyle stayed at the Golden Lion when researching for *The Hound of the Baskervilles*. The coachman there used to take him out onto the moors. The coachman was called Thomas Baskerville. Conan-Doyle liked the name so much, he asked for permission to use it. The Baskerville family claim to have a first edition of *The Hound of the Baskervilles*, with a hand-written thank you from Conan-Doyle inside. The fictitious Baskervilles, in the story, were based on the Lord of the manor at Buckfastleigh – the Cavell family.

Prince Rex reflects ...

While researching this book, I stayed at the Golden Lion (now a grand town house). They told me they had put me in the room used by Arthur Conan-Doyle. There were no slobbering hounds to disturb my sleep, but it was a bit eerie. I didn't go barking mad!

During WW2, the hotel was sometimes used to relocate children from St. Faiths in Cambridge, and also by Canadian soldiers as an air-raid shelter. It was surprising how often people turned up out of the blue, just to have another look at where they'd stayed back then.

Much of the 1950 film *"Guilt is My Shadow"* was filmed in the hotel and town. Perhaps not the best-known film in the world, but something of a cult classic and another brownie point for the Golden Lion. Just for completeness, the film starred Elizabeth Sellars, Peter Reynolds and Lana Morris.

And, of course, the Golden Lion was where the Official Monster Raving Loony Party was conceived, and it became the Party Headquarters for some time. We'll get to that in the next section, but it seems the Golden Lion has always been a focal point for political insurrection!

CHAPTER 11

Off we go!

All hands on deck!

The first New Year's Eve, though, was hectic. Everybody wanted to come and see us. They wanted to check out the 'newcomers' and see what we were made of. We didn't realise how busy it could be. There were three of us behind the bar: Norma, me, and another lad called Jersey Joe. He was happy to help behind the bar, but he refused to handle any money. We had to take the money from the customer for him. He was quite an honest bloke in his own way, although he was a bit of a rogue in other ways, mind you. What a character!

So after the first month or two, the Golden Lion was really buzzing. The previous owners did not really run it with any enthusiasm, but that wasn't my approach. Norma and I wanted to make it into the 'go-to' place in Ashburton. We knew we could do it – and we did!

I enjoyed every minute in the hotel. It's hard work, but great fun too. If you're doing the business, you've got the customers, you've got staff so you don't have to do it all yourself, it's alright. OK, so it's 24 hours a day, 7 days a week. But if you've got good staff, you can get time off. We went to America twice, and Canada, and other places. You have to have staff you can trust.

"Dukes of Hazzard?" Me as Boss Hogg and Norma as Daisy Duke.
(My private collection)

Driving in America ...

Perhaps now is the time for a quick aside about our holidays in America. I had a provisional UK licence, but had never taken a driving test. That didn't seem to matter. I don't think the US car hire companies realised that it wasn't a full licence. It never occurred to me that I might not be insured, and I tended to do quite a bit of driving over there. I got stopped for speeding twice.

The first time, I noticed a squad car behind me with his lights on, but I just assumed he was after someone else, so kept on driving. Eventually he pulls alongside and made it pretty clear he wanted me to stop. I showed him my licence, but he'd never seen a UK one before. He made us follow him to Bullock County Jailhouse. Having seen all the films, read all the stories, to say I'm feeling worried is an understatement. I'm taken to the main desk, and the officer explained to the desk sergeant that I'd been speeding and handed me over. She said: "You've been fined $90."

All I had was a $200-dollar traveller's check. "We can't accept or change them. Where are you going?"

I replied: "We're on our way to Atlanta to fly home." (Although that was a lie.)

She said, "When you get home, if you want, you can send the money on to us."

I replied: "You said, if I want. What if I don't want?" I was only teasing.

She said: "Go on. Get out of here." That was the end of it.

On a second holiday I was pulled over again. The policeman comes over and tells me I've been stopped for speeding. "Sorry, Officer. What happens now?"

He said: "You have three choices: pay a cash fine now; come to court and try to plead you weren't speeding; or take a four-hour instruction course." I chose the course but told him we were going home next day (we weren't … I was lying … again). He'd already written out the citation. He leaned on the window as only an American cop can do. He said: "Don't tell anyone I just did this." and tore up the citation in front of me.

Perhaps I wouldn't do it now, and I'm sorry to say I lied shamelessly to the cops. But blow me! It worked both times. If I'd have been rumbled, I'd probably be seeing out my days wearing an orange jumpsuit in a penitentiary somewhere in the mid-west!

Meanwhile, back in Devon …

Lots of the family helped out: Norma; my mother; my sister Mary; my daughter Angela came down; Mark came down and worked for us in the kitchen for a little while; and my other daughter Gina came down. She met her future husband, Phillip, down there, got married, and then moved back up to Hampshire. Mary also met her husband, Paul, down there.

Mary remembers …

My mother, Paddy (a friend of Alan's mum) and I went down to live with Alan (at the hotel) in 1980. And we helped out there. Paddy was a kind of odd-job man, Mum and I worked in the kitchen cooking bulk food for the freezer to cater for the fast-food side of the business. I lived in the hotel until I met my husband down there. Life in the hotel was hard work. I worked in the kitchen and also did some housekeeping. I didn't do bar work. I felt there was some jealousy amongst the staff. Because I was family, they thought I was getting favourable treatment, which I wasn't. I was on the same pay as them. There was nothing to be jealous of.

My sister Mary on her wedding day. I gave her away.

(My private collection)

The other staff were mainly casual labour. They didn't seem to mind having family working in the hotel. My mum was the cook – she was the best. I don't think you should ever employ a chef – you need a good cook. Chefs want too much money for too little work. They won't do this, and they won't do that. Employ a local lady who's a good cook. That's all you need in a restaurant, and that works. Chefs have attitude.

A couple of sisters, Angela and Pat Brooks, worked for me for years. Various bar-staff over the years. Henry Scarrett, a bit of a character as I remember. John Raffles, Denis Waterman (not the actor!) and I was well-known for employing the prettiest barmaids in town.

Even before they were old enough to work in the hotel, my daughters would come down in the holidays. I'd try to spend as much time as I could with them, but that wasn't easy. Norma was great though. She'd take the kids out, take them shopping, and she became very much a mother to them.

My daughters' children always called Pamela 'Nanny', and Norma 'Nanny-Pub'. I guess they had to invent a way of differentiating between them.

From the daughters …

The holidays at the Golden Lion were wonderful. We were just so young everyone seemed to mother us when we were there. Nan always cooked great food, and we could help ourselves to bars of chocolate and drinks from behind the bar when Dad went to bed in the afternoon for a siesta. And the pool table was free. It was fun. There were seven or eight beds up in the attic. We would bring our friends and we'd all stay up there in the attic.

Although Dad didn't have much free time, Norma looked after us so well that it was always great fun. But Dad always did make time to have a proper slap-up family meal with us on our last night. The food was always so good there.

Coach trips would come to Ashburton, just to see the HQ of the Loony Party. It was a trip out from Torquay: up onto Dartmoor; have a cream-tea somewhere; and call in and see me at the Golden Lion – just part of their itinerary. I was a local celebrity … or perhaps a curiosity!

My mother was there from about 1984, until she died from cancer in 1996. I think she must have worked there for seven or eight years before she got ill. She died in Ashburton. And we moved my wife's mother down to Ashburton too, as she was left up in Hampshire on her own. She died in a hospice in Torquay. So we still have a lot of connections down there, I suppose. One of my grandsons is an Ashburtonian. His father is from Ashburton, my daughter married him in Ashburton, and he was born in the hospital at Torquay.

My son Mark married an Ashburton girl … although she's passed on now as well. So Mark's children are half Ashburtonian as well.

On top of all that, I also had two sheep that lived in the 'orchard' at the back of the hotel, and a boxer dog called Bomber. He was a real character and I'll tell you more about him later. And in addition to the rooms in the hotel, we also had three cottages in the grounds.

They were mainly used by staff and visiting family. You can see there was lots to look after.

Mark remembers …

I moved down to Devon with Dad and Norma – in a little MG. That was cramped with the three of us and whatever we could take. That was an eye-opener really. I worked in a factory, worked on a building site. Next thing I know, I'm behind the bar. Big hotel with thirteen rooms and an attic. There were three flats at the bottom of the car park. I rented one of those. At first, they were still owned by the previous owner. Dad only bought those after I got married.

Norma looked after me well. I was 17 when I went down there. I married a local girl there when I was 21. My honeymoon was spent back at 3 Ley Road in Hawley Estate in Alan's mother's house.

It was long hours working at the hotel – and very little pay. I worked behind the bar, went to catering school for a year or so, and generally helped out where and when I could. In a busy hotel, you just do it. You don't worry about the Job Description.

I was sacked by my dad. I forgot to read the roster one day. I was supposed to open up that night, but I hadn't realised. I got sacked over the phone, so I went and found a job next day.

But, of course. I was still in love with music.

And the bands play on …

I wanted to make the Golden Lion THE place in Ashburton, so as well as running the bar, the restaurant and the hotel, I just had to provide more.

I was my own DJ, as I had a great record collection. I reckon that, perhaps not in quantity but in content, I had one of the finest record collections outside of the BBC archives. There was a time, in those days, wouldn't happen now because everything's on CD and DVD, when if the local radio stations didn't have a record they needed, they'd ring me up to see if I had it. That was quite an accolade. I focused mainly on some quite obscure Country and Western music. Whenever I went to America, I would bring lots of vinyl 45s back with me.

Entertaining at the Golden Lion.
(My private collection)

I always used to close my disco nights with 'Every Time We Say Goodbye' by Ella Fitzgerald. It was written by Cole Porter, and perfect to close off an evening.

Norma with Dave Berry in the Golden Lion.
(My private collection)

We had a lot of bands come down: Screaming Lord Sutch and the Savages of course; Captain Sensible – who had a post-punk hit with a remake of 'Happy, Happy, Happy, Happy Talk'; Kenny Ball and his Jazzmen; Dave Berry – 'The Crying Game'; the Jets; the Searchers – rivals to The Beatles in the 1960s; Jon Derrick. All the C&W bands would stay at the hotel if they were touring the area – maybe a week, maybe ten days, and in return they'd do me a free gig.

So some of the bands I put on were going down to Carlyon Bay, which was a big venue in Cornwall, and perhaps they would be getting £3,000 to £4,000 per night down there. You could see them at the Golden Lion for nothing. Amazing. It doesn't matter really. No matter how much money you earn; how much money you don't earn; at the end of it, you are only a human being. No matter how many millions you've got, you'll still eat a cheese sandwich, won't you? Or a bacon sandwich, depending on your faith! So the Golden Lion got to be known as the best local venue.

Poster for Golden Lion gig.
(My private collection)

I didn't charge customers coming to see the bands that visited and played for free. Might have cost you £25 to see them anywhere else. They were playing in the bar, and it was a public house, so charging would not have worked. Of course, the bar would be packed so our takings went up which was enough. If we'd put them on in the ballroom upstairs, a cover charge would have made sense. But then we would have had to hire in extra staff and our costs would go up.

One band that used to come down was called 'In the Red'. They were a 12-piece orchestra. They were brilliant. Absolutely wonderful. And they all come from around Hampshire and Surrey. They were originally called the Brian Allen Band, but they all wore red jackets. They came down one time and they were playing fantastic. I heard one of the locals asking: "'Ere, Al. When's they in the red coming back again?" They liked that, so they changed their name. I still think they are still around in some form or another.

From the daughters …

David Sutch (Screaming Lord Sutch – but David to us) came down a few times. Dad didn't drive at the time. Angela had to go to Newton Abbot station to pick him up. She had quite a new car then – a D-Reg Ford Escort Ghia with electric windows. That seemed to be a new thing for David because he kept playing with the windows. David Sutch was a very quiet man. Completely different from what you saw on stage. He was tee-total. And he did suffer from depression, but I don't think we realised that at the time.

He came down to the hotel fairly often especially for the Party Conferences. He would bring his band with him and they'd put on a show. The hotel was definitely the place to go to on a Saturday night. The hotel was definitely the place to be for quite a long time, it was always a focus on carnival days and the like.

I had two people appearing at the Golden Lion who had had No. 1 hits. One was Captain Sensible with 'Happy, Happy, Happy, Happy Talk'; and Kenny Ball of course – 'Midnight in Moscow'. And Dave Berry stayed here a few times, although he didn't perform there. He had a good few hits as well.

Liz Riley remembers …

The next time we saw Alan and Norma was in October 1989 when they hosted a 'Threewheel Reunion' at the Golden Lion. We did not realise it at the time, but this marked the 20th anniversary of Alan joining Threewheel (and coincidentally celebrated Alan's daughter Helen's 21st birthday.) Further reunions were held in 1990, 1991 and 1992. Then, in 1993, a special one marked the 15th anniversary of Alan and Norma being at the Golden Lion.

Sadly, Mike had died in January 1993 but I was at the reunion with our two daughters, as we had been for the previous four – an indication of the importance of Threewheel in all our lives.

There was another No. 1 artist too. All the way from America – Marvin Rainwater with 'Whole Lotta Woman'. That was a great song. He played the Golden Lion twice.

I said to him once: "Hey Marvin. Wouldn't it be great if you had another No. 1 hit sometime?"

He said, "Boy. No it would NOT! I just couldn't afford to drink all that Bourbon again."

He came down with the Jon Derrick Band. Jon was pretty well-known on the country music scene. He had a band called 'Country Fever'. That had Chas and Dave in it, and Albert Lee at one time.

In March 1982, I saw an advert for Screaming Lord Sutch in Plymouth. I think it was in a place called 'The Crypt' underneath an old church. Very appropriate. So I phoned up the venue and asked to speak to him. They went and fetched him.

"Hi. I'm Kerry Rapid. Do you remember me?"

"Yes. Of course I remember you."

I explained that I now owned this hotel in Ashburton, 20 miles away, and that he would have to come past on his way home.

The gig was on the Saturday night, and on the Sunday, he called in – much to the surprise of my wife. When I told her he might be coming, she said: "No. We don't want the likes of him in here!" but she'd never met him, so that was just based on reputation. But he was just a likable bloke. Everybody fell in love with him. He didn't swear, he didn't smoke, he didn't drink. If you swore in front of him, he'd tell you off. He was everything that people thought he wasn't really.

Well we got to talking, and he decided to stay the night. He had a drummer with him called Bob Burgos – he stayed as well. I asked Sutch what he was doing in June. I was going to be 40. "OK," he said, "I'll come down for that. That'll be good." I will continue that story in Part 4 …

David Sutch would ring up from time to time: "I fancy a weekend out of London. Can I come down?" Well of course he could, and he did. He loved coming down and just walking around the town. He loved junk shops – second-hand shops. He'd always buy you a present. He bought loads of junk. His house in London was full of it. If the stairway was five feet wide, there would maybe one foot in the middle that wasn't full of junk. He was a hoarder. Once when he was down in Ashburton, he bought me a darts trophy. Somebody else's name on it. He said: "You can soon get that taken off, and put your name on instead."

He was always buying stuff like that … and he'd buy me shirts. He loved my mother's steak and kidney pie. I don't know how much real home-cooking he got in his life.

Relaxing in the Golden Lion with Tony Dangerfield, Angelo, me, David Sutch, Bob Burgos and David Dix. (Courtesy Bob Burgos)

Bob Burgos recalls …

I first met Alan when I was touring the west country with Screaming Lord Sutch and the Savages. Alan and David Sutch had been friends for many years, and at the end of our tour Alan invited David to stay at his hotel for a short break before he went back to London. Being old friends, it was inevitable that David would be returning to Devon, and so he did many times in the early 80s that also included us all in the Savages too. I got to know Alan very well and it was wonderful to hear some of the great memories and stories that David and Alan both shared together from those days when they first met in 1959.

They were wonderful and priceless times that we all had back then because we all had so much fun, and this I believe was the key that unlocked everything that was to follow. It's never been easy to explain to people who have asked me time and time again what it was like in those days, and did it really happen? Well you really had to be there to believe it. But believe me, it did happen. And I wouldn't change it for the world!!

Pure madness …

I became great friends with Cynthia Payne. 'Madame Cyn', as she was known, was a notorious woman who kept one of the most exclusive brothels in London. She allegedly had clients drawn from the rich, famous, and influential, but she was always totally discreet and never confirmed nor denied specific questions about the identity of her clientele.

Cynthia knew Screaming Lord Sutch and she came to a number of Party Conferences at the Golden Lion. She was great fun and we got on really well.

One time when Cynthia Payne was staying for a few days, I put up a sign behind the bar that read: 'The House of Fun'. Coincidentally, the bar was also known as the Lion's Den. It was shortly after that when Madness had one of their biggest hits: 'House of Fun', which has the tag-line "Welcome to the lion's den."

The story goes that originally the song had the working title of 'Chemist Façade'. When they tested out the song on their record company, the Head of Stiff Records was unimpressed. He felt it needed a catchy chorus/hook and that was missing. It seems that Mike Barson – the keyboard player for Madness – almost immediately came up with the now-famous chorus that made the song into a No. 1 hit.

Now, I cannot prove a connection, but the timing is spot-on. The signs were up in the bar at exactly the same time as Madness were touring the West Country, and before the song was recorded. They must have passed by Ashburton on those tours, and could easily have popped in to check out the Golden Lion. It had an established reputation with musicians as a great place to take a break and check out whatever was going on. It could be coincidence, but to my mind, there has to be a link. How else could 'Welcome to the House of Fun' and 'Welcome to the Lion's Den' get linked in one chorus unless they had seen it?

CHAPTER 12

Cricket, Rugby and Football

Roll out the barrels ...

"Let's have a barrel of fun." And we did. Lots of them.

We had our own darts team and pool team, and we had lots of visiting cricket teams. The first team that came down, and booked in, were from Datchett – near Slough. I thoroughly enjoyed their company. I started advertising in cricket magazines, offering a base for any team touring the West Country. That really took off. We were turning teams down in the end, we couldn't put them all up. Did very, very well out of that. We had lots of teams come down. One I remember was from St. Thomas' Hospital in Tooting. Every member seemed to be from the Caribbean, and they really were great fun, and quite prepared to take the mickey out of themselves as well. I was doing the disco one night, and played 'Brown Girl in the Ring'. They got this white boy (my barman, Henry Scarret) and surrounded him, singing, "White Boy in the Ring." Great fun.

And on another occasion, I had a team staying here, things got even more lively. It was past hours, but they were residents so I carried on serving. It happened that there were two police in the bar in plain clothes – a policeman and a policewoman. I just assumed they were with the team.

A couple of the lads had got a bit merry, and at one stage they were running round the bar minus their trousers – showing their genitalia. I got taken to court for that, and I had to say that I didn't even know it had happened. But when I told the court how much the police had had to drink, they were reprimanded by the judge. I told the judge that the policewoman had drunk a whole bottle of cherry brandy, and he believed me. I kept my licence – just a £30 fine.

Surprise, Surprise ...

In Ashburton, I helped start up a thing called 'Young Sports' with a friend of mine called Tom Arnold. We used to take the kids down to the playing fields on Sunday morning and get them playing football. That gave them something to do, and I really enjoyed it.

Around the same time, Ashburton decided that they would have a rugby team. A couple of the lads in the bar – Ron Southcombe and Laurence Frediani – were talking about getting a rugby team together. So they got this group of lads together and started doing some training. A local farmer – called Roger Parker – let them use one of his fields for a pitch. They got it all marked out and everything. And the Golden Lion bar was the Ashburton Rugby Club's HQ. That was an obvious choice, as the guys who thought up the idea were regulars. All the lads knew me, and most of them drank there.

This Ashburton rugby team never, ever won a game. So me and Ron, we conjured up this idea that we would put an ad in the local newspapers – the Mid-Devon Advertiser and the Herald Express: "Ashburton Rugby Club has never won a game. We challenge any other sports team to play their game, as long as THEY have never won a game." I think we were expecting (or hoping) that a girls' hockey or netball team to phone up. It didn't matter who it was. Lo and behold, my phone rings, and a voice on the other end says: "Hello Chuck." It was Cilla Black. Our advert had got into a national newspaper somehow. Surprise, Surprise. "We've got a team that wants to play you." But I have to admit that it wasn't Cilla herself, it was her PA. But Cilla did say "Hello Chuck" to me when I did meet her.

Well, we got it all arranged. We didn't know who we were playing or what we were playing, just a team called 'The All Stars'. A coach came down from London to pick us up. We knew we were going to Highbury (Arsenal), so we thought it would be football. So we're on our way, but just the other side of Exeter, the coach breaks down. So we had to wait for another coach to come and pick us up. But we were on a tight deadline. We thought we were going to miss out, but we did get there eventually.

The Ashburton Rugby Team with their esteemed leader!
(My private collection)

When we got to Highbury I was met by Billy Wright, the Manager of the All Stars team. I started supporting Wolves in the 1950s so Billy Wright who played for Wolves and England was a hero of mine. Billy took me into the 'Away team' dressing room and introduced me to members of the All Stars team which included George Cohen (Fulham and England) who played in the 1966 World Cup final, Nat Lofthouse (Bolton and England), Tom Finney (Preston and England), Danny Blanchflower (Spurs and Northern Ireland), Geoff Hurst (West Ham And England) who scored a hat trick in the 1966 World Cup final, Gerry Francis (QPR and England), George Best (Manchester Utd and Northern Ireland), Peter Osgood (Chelsea and England), Emlyn Hughes (Liverpool and England), Peter Bonetti (Chelsea and England) plus John Hollins (Chelsea), Steve Perryman (Spurs), Paul Walsh (Liverpool) and Jimmy Case (Liverpool). Of course, as a team, these heroes had never played a match together, so the requirement that they had never won a match held true.

I left the away team dressing room and made my way back to our dressing room. I was thinking about how I was going to tell my lads about the opposition. When I walked in I was immediately asked who are we playing against and I told my team: "Nobody special. I have heard of a few of their players but they are well past it now." The look on my players' faces as they went on the Highbury pitch and saw who they were playing against was priceless.

Team photo of Ashburton Rugby Club and the TV All Stars. I'm in the middle shaking hands with Billy Wright. The All Stars pictured are:

Back row left to right — 3rd from left George Cohen (Fulham and England); 4th Nat Lofthouse (Bolton Wanders and England); 5th Tom Finney (Preston North End and England); 6th Danny Blanchflower (Tottenham Hotspur and Northern Ireland); 8th Geoff Hurst (West Ham United and England); 9th Gerry Francis (Tottenham Hotspur and England); 10th George Best (Manchester United and Northern Ireland); 11th Peter Osgood (Chelsea, Southampton and England); 14th Emlyn Hughes (Liverpool and England).

Front row left to right — 4th John Hollins (Chelsea and England); 5th Steve Perryman (Tottenham Hotspur and England; 6th Paul Walsh (Liverpool and England); 7th Peter Bonetti (Chelsea and England); 11th Jimmy Case (Liverpool and Southampton). (My private collection)

And the referee was 'Diddy' David Hamilton, the DJ.

We lost 2-1, but we were lucky to score. We had Emlyn Hughes playing on our side. Towards the end, George Best tripped him in the penalty area. We got a penalty, and Emyln scored. That gave us our goal. It was all a set up though … George and Emlyn laughed all the way back to the centre-spot. But that came from that advert … "We'll play anybody." And we got on that big show. Great fun. That was in 1984. I've got a lovely photograph at home somewhere, of George Best swanning around, and I'm stood on the side-line in my white suit. I've got a signed football somewhere, but I can't find it. I'll come across it one day, I'm sure I will. It wouldn't be blown up anymore.

27th April, 1984

Mr. Alan Hope.
The Golden Lion Hotel.
Ashburton,
Devon.

Dear Alan,

May I on behalf of London Weekend Television and Cilla's 'Surprise, Surprise' team, thank you and the Ashburton Rams for all your help in making such a successful film. We hope that you are as pleased as we are with the results.

Best wishes,

Yours sincerely,

Michael Longmire

Michael Longmire.
Researcher - SURPRISE, SURPRISE

Nice letter from LWT. (My private collection)

A lot of these boys in the rugby team were also in the Ashburton tug-of-war team. I had a meadow – perhaps more an orchard – at the back of the Golden Lion. Well, there was only one tree left – the others had gone. It was my dog's paddock really. At one corner of this orchard, they fixed up a big oil drum full of concrete and a hoist, so they could pull against it. In the early 90s, Ashburton became one of the centres for tug-of-war contests in the country. All through a chappie called Nicky Major who was one of my customers. And as the rugby team and the tug-of-war team were linked, they both used the Golden Lion as HQ. It was all good business.

Sinbad (friend in Ashburton) remembers …

Everyone in Ashburton – if they've been here a while – knows Alan. He was always up to something. Every Friday and Saturday at the Golden Lion was a riot. He put this cheese on the bar once. I tried a piece. It was horrible. I nearly spewed up. It was joke-shop cheese. Late on, Alan would always make fried bread and cheese – Sunday morning special that was.

Oh Bomber!

And of course, Bomber the boxer dog. A customer came in one day and asked if I knew anywhere he could pitch his tent. I said he could put his tent up in the back garden in the paddock. I didn't charge for that, I thought I might be able to sell him a meal or some drinks. The next thing we know, the dog is in the man's tent, and being very 'amorous' with his ruck-sack. We were in fits. The poor guy didn't know what to do. We had to get in there and drag Bomber away. He was very 'excited'.

Sinbad remembers …

At the top of the stairs, there used to be a suit of armour. That used to disappear from time to time. It might end up on the porch over the door next to the lion statue. Or we'd put it against someone's bedroom door, so next morning when they opened their door, it would fall on them.

There was a girl called Julie who worked behind the bar. She came to me once and said: "Quick. Come here." I followed her upstairs and there was this guy who had got his hand stuck in the sash window. "This might hurt a bit, mate. When I lift the window, pull your hands out." He did, and he fell back on the bed with Julie and the bed collapsed. We gave him a few brandies, and he seemed to recover. He was playing the piano later so there couldn't have been much wrong with him.

Ashburton Chamber of Commerce meetings were held at the Golden Lion. They normally ended up with just me, Pete Webb and Roger Parker. Roger was one of the town's eccentrics. He had a farm and put out some corrugated iron sheets on a hill-side that spelled out 'camping'. The National Park people got upset and asked him to move them. He said it wasn't his fault – the wind must have blown them there. When he did remove them, he'd killed the grass underneath so the word 'camping' was still clearly visible. Eventually, the boundaries were re-drawn taking his farm outside of the Park. A pragmatic solution!

Pete Webb remembers …

You gave coach companies permission to park in your yard. That brought people into the town. Modern coaches couldn't get into the main car park because of the hump bridge. That was a great idea.

Visiting coaches were always good for trade, but sometimes it got a bit out of hand …

Dave Brooks remembers …

There was this guy, John Raffles and me, thought it might be fun to dress up as Arabs. We thought that would be a laugh, so we got some head gear and robes and blacked up our faces with brown shoe polish. We're walking down the road and this coach went by. We waved, and they all waved back, and then it turned into the Golden Lion. We walked in to work behind the bar which really surprised all the old dears from the coach – nobody recognised us – we pretended we couldn't speak English so people were pointing at the beer-pumps to get a pint. A friend of mine, Johnny Worthington, was standing near to me, and he moved along a couple of feet, so I moved along, then him, then me etc. He was looking a bit uncomfortable till I told him who I was in a whisper.

The coach party had gone upstairs to the function room, so we decided that it would be fun if we started serving them behind the bar dressed as Arabs. When we went in, it all went dead quiet. It was all old ladies and John said: "I'm looking for some new girls for my Harem." One of them came back from the ladies': "You'll do for me." They were all a bit shocked. But they saw the joke, and went away happy and smiling.

I always held great Christmas Parties for the kids on Boxing Day. They loved it. I'd play all the Christmas songs, and there would be bags of little sweets everywhere. I played Father Christmas and I made sure I had a little present for all of them. They had to sit on my knee and give me a kiss to get their present. That's why there are so many in Ashburton in their late 30s and early 40s who remember me and those days. They get a bit embarrassed sometimes when I mention it in front of their friends!

Mobile pub …

On top of all of this, I would run the bar for local shows and events.

One stands out in my mind. It was Buckfastleigh show and it was a terrible day for rain and wind.

The marquee was pitched in the field and it was raining so hard it was coming in one side and flowing out at the other. We were serving behind the bar. At the end of the show, it was so bad, that we didn't take the marquee down. I decided we should leave it there until the weather improved.

Sinbad remembers …

We piled everything in the back of the Transit and Alan sat in the front with Denis Waterman his driver, and Raffles and myself rolled in the back. We got into that transit stone-cold sober, and fell out at the Golden Lion completely pissed. It was so uncomfortable we just sat in the back with the stock and drank all Alan's profits.

We went up two or three days later and picked up what was left of the marquee. Happy days!

C'mon you 'Shots!

Aldershot were playing Torquay one weekend. The team called into the Golden Lion for breakfast. Three of us – Charlie Dennis, Maurice Worth and me – went to the match in the team coach. The match was rained off!! We ended up in this pub and we started playing Euchre – a traditional regional card game – and we beat all the local lads. We had to get a taxi home to Ashburton. It was about five in the morning when we got back, and I invited the lads in for a 'night-cap'. Then I discovered that I didn't have a key so I had to go round the back and break into my own pub!

I've always been a supporter of Aldershot Football Club. So I thought it was a good idea to make up a story that the Golden Lion was now the headquarters of the Aldershot Supporters' club in the South-West. Just publicity. The paper picked up on it, and a guy from Bovey Tracy came in one day. He said he'd read the story, and wanted to become a member. I asked why. He said because he was from Odiham, a small town in Hampshire, and only about ten miles from where I was born. There were only ever the two of us as members, but Aldershot does have quite a following in Ashburton now as a result of that. Eventually, the story got picked up by the club and they put it in one of their magazines – it pulled in a few visitors from time to time.

Whenever the 'Shots were playing away at a South-West team, they would call in to my hotel and stay over. I remember it always had to be eggs for breakfast, don't know why. After the match the team would go home, but the non-playing staff would often come back here and stay another night. That all had something to do with Colin Hancock – he was a dentist in Frimley (and 'Shots Chairman). Last I heard, he had moved up to Newark and he was trying to buy Mansfield Town. Don't know if he succeeded. The manager of 'Shots at the time was Len Walker.

Charlie Dennis remembers …

It was about two in the morning; I had an earring at the time. There were quite a few staying as guests and one of them started teasing me about my earring. Alan joined in. He said, "The only guys who wear earrings where I come from are gypsies and sailors."

I took exception to that. I'd been working in the bar all day. I leaned over the bar and grabbed hold of Alan by his shirt. All the buttons started to pop so I kept pulling at it. I pulled the whole shirt off him. I threw it back at him and said: "Stick your bloody job, I've had enough of it." Norma rang up and sacked me the following day. I told her I wasn't going to go in anyway.

Sam Howis was in the finals of the area singles darts for the Golden Lion. We went to Newton Abbot for the final and he won. We had some drinks. It was a Friday night and when we got back here there was a band on and the place was busy. When Sam's had a few drinks, he gets a bit loud. Nothing really wrong with him, and if you know him, you can control him, obviously. This particular time, there was a policeman in the bar. He said to me that I was breaking the law. "You're serving a man who is clearly drunk, and that's against the law." And he pointed out Sam. He told me I had to chuck him out. I wanted to just have a quiet word with Sam, but the policeman wouldn't have it. "You've got to get rid of him."

So I took Sam over to the door and said, in front of the policeman: "Look, Sam. This has nothing to do with me. But this man's a policeman, and he says I've got to throw you out or I'll lose my licence." Sam looked at the policeman, stuck up two fingers, said two choice words, and walked away with his tail between his legs. We had a great darts team.

CHAPTER 13

OMG Norma …

We ran the hotel for 22 years – until 2000. The last ten years or so, my wife was slowly getting ill with Multiple Sclerosis (MS). It comes on slowly. The first time I noticed something might be wrong was maybe 1990 or thereabouts. We'd gone to Swindon, and we were walking through a shopping arcade. We heard someone singing, and we thought that's a nice voice. It was Don Estelle. He was selling his latest album out of a wheelbarrow. I'd met Don Estelle before, so I started walking towards him to give him a surprise. All of a sudden, my wife seemed to trip, or stumble. I was holding her hand at the time, so she couldn't fall. But there was nothing to trip over. And then I began to notice this happening a bit more, just a trip.

So I began to realise that something might be wrong. Then one day, in the bedroom, she just burst out crying. She was just standing there, crying.

I said: "What's wrong? What's the matter?"

She said: "Look at my body." It was all twisted. I asked her if she could stand up straight, but she said she just couldn't. It scared the life out of her (and me).

First of all, we thought it was just a spinal problem, and someone suggested we try a chiropractor. But it did no good and just cost us quite a bit of money – all wasted. But in due course, it was confirmed that it was Multiple Sclerosis (MS) – and that was a real problem. We'd had a great time in Ashburton up to that time, and now it was going to get difficult. For a start, I had to learn to drive – a challenge in itself, although I did pass on my second attempt.

It was 1994 when Norma really got too ill to help. I had to have some carers coming in for a while before she went into the first home. I couldn't manage her any more – not and run the hotel. If she fell out of bed, which she often did, she was too heavy for me to lift her.

She was getting worse, and quite quickly. She spent the last five years of her life in a hospice. She never saw the hotel at all in that time. And I think I lost interest in it too, because she wasn't there. And we were running into a little bit of debt as well. It just wasn't being run as well as it had been while Norma was well.

The daughters reflect ...

It was hard for Dad. He had to step up to the mark, and take on more work. He'd really just done the social side of things while Norma looked after the business. And he had to learn to drive. I think it all got a bit too much for him. Things did start to go downhill. Not sure if he started getting into debt, but they did sell off some land – what they called the orchard. They were struggling financially. Things started to need repair. The ceilings in the toilets began to look like they might come down on you.

Last orders ...

Barney Bettesworth was the estate agent who sold the hotel for me. He came by one day and said he had a chappie who wanted to buy it. He'd pay off any debts and give me a lump sum. Simple as that. I thought about it but quickly agreed. Then I had to think about moving my stuff out.

It's just a rumour that it was converted to apartments. I sold it to a builder called Carl Frogmore, and he turned it into two townhouses. It's most certainly not apartments. The townhouses are big three/four storeys. Old Georgian in style. And with a cellar. I'd wanted to convert the cellar into a nightclub, but I couldn't get another door out as an emergency route.

One of my barmaids, Jayne Hatfield who I always referred to as Jane Mansfield, has carried on as a kind of housekeeper for the new owners. The upshot of that was that they invited me down one week when the carnival was on. It was great fun and I thoroughly enjoyed it.

The hotel needed an awful lot doing to it. I couldn't really sell it as a going concern. People comment on the ACROs in the bar, but there's nothing safer than an ACRO, and anyway they were already there when I bought it. I didn't put them there. People used to think that the ballroom floor upstairs was sprung. But it wasn't. It was the main beam that was bending.

So we had 22 years at the Golden Lion. Thoroughly enjoyed it. Had a lot of fun. Met some nice people. And now if I go back down there, people will say to me: "For Christ's sake, Al. Get yer arse back down 'ere. The place ain't the same without you." When I moved away, they re-wrote the history book of the town. It hadn't been changed for many years. It has a page listing the 'worthies' of Ashburton – people like Lord Ashburton himself, who was connected with Barings Bank; Thomas Carlyle; a lot of well-known royals. They updated the book and re-published it to include me in the worthies. I was very humbled by that. It says Alan Hope: … blah … blah … did this … did that .. he was great for the town … he was the town's publicity officer.

So the hotel was sold, and Norma was now in a nursing home in Farnborough. My life had hit another brick wall. What was I to do?

CHAPTER 14

Coming home

The Dog and Partridge …

I could have stayed in Ashburton after I sold the Golden Lion. But I wanted to move Norma back to where her family and friends were – and that's why we came back to the Fleet area. That was where we had planned to retire. It was quite easy to get Norma into the second care home. The fact that she was technically the Mayoress of Ashburton helped – we'll cover that in Part 5. She was known as the Mayoress to everyone in the home. I made a sign, and put it on her door. Both homes were funded by Social Services; I could never have afforded to pay for her care.

I moved Norma back up to Farnborough on January 1st 2000. In March 2000, I came up to see her, and that's when I saw the lease for the Dog and Partridge in Yateley up for sale. So I made some tentative enquiries and I was asked to put in my CV. I hand-wrote the CV and submitted it to Scottish and Newcastle, that would be March 2000. Come May, I got a phone call telling me the pub was mine if I wanted it.

I was pleased to leave the Golden Lion in the end. When I came back from Ashburton for the last time, I stopped the car by the 'Welcome to Hampshire' sign on the A303, got out and cheered: "I'm home!" I think I got a fair price for the Golden Lion. I had to sell, so I was happy with what I got.

What spare cash I had went into the lease of the Dog and Partridge, after all I didn't have anywhere to live – or to work. Again, I opened up straightaway, although that first week I went down with 'flu. It was a full repair and insuring lease, so I was responsible for any work on the pub, but I never had any major problems. The brewery makes sure you carry all the risk – not them.

The Dog and Partridge in Yateley. (My private collection)

It was just amazing that the Dog and Partridge came up just as I was selling the hotel and had to get out. When I moved Norma to the nursing home that January, I made a promise to her that I would be sold up and back up here within a year, and on June the 1st I moved in – I'd kept my promise. In time to celebrate my next birthday on the 16th. My birthdays lasted a week in those days. I'd have a band on every night for a week.

Norma was now too ill to take any part in it. The home brought her to the Dog and Partridge once, but it was too much for her, and she had to leave after about ten minutes. Too many people, too noisy. She just got very confused.

The pub did have some rooms that I could let out – really for guys working in the area. But I didn't do breakfast or anything – there was a café over the road. There was no point in me getting up at 6.30 to cook breakfast when the café was just there. I didn't charge them much to stay anyway.

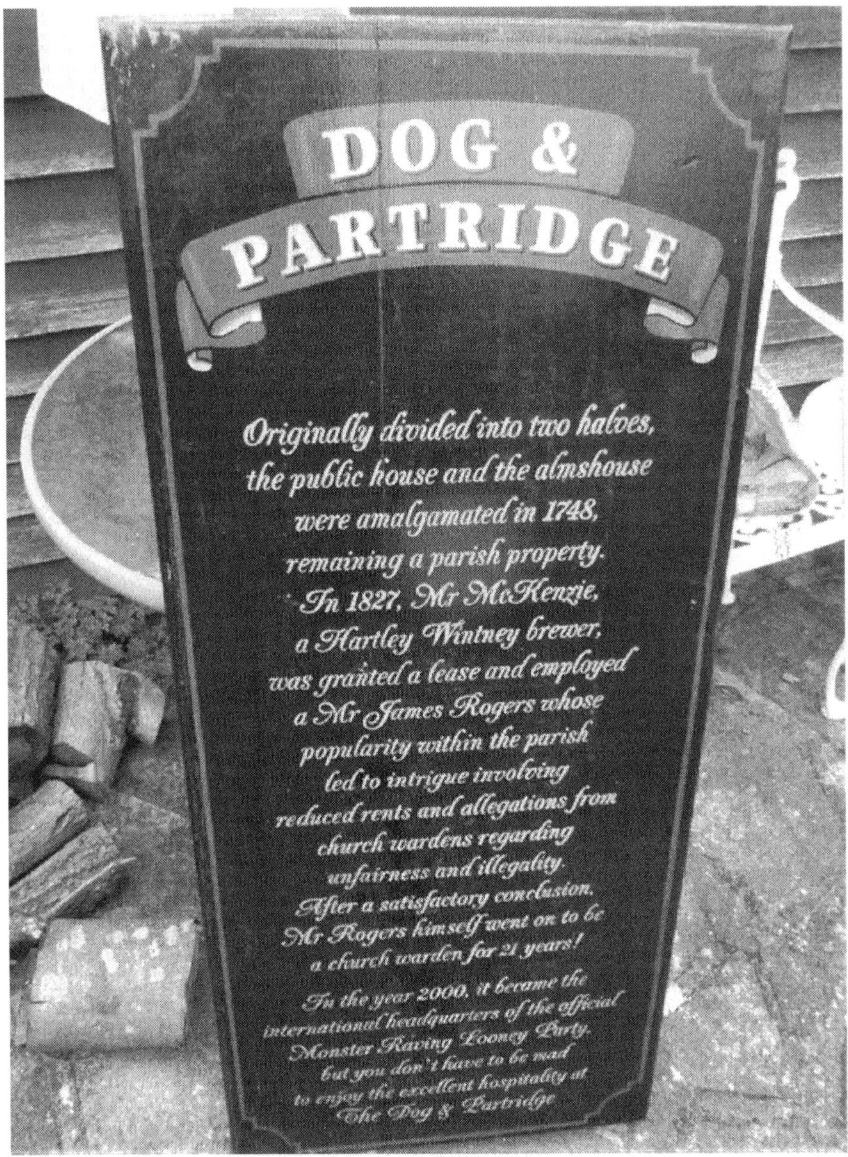

I had this sign made for the Dog and Partridge.

(My private collection)

I remember winding up a truck driver who asked what I charged. I said £20. He thought that was great and handed over the money. "What time is breakfast?" I told it was served whenever he wanted to cross the road to the café. He was a bit put out, but he stayed anyway.

The letting rooms were not much more than dormitories with camp beds and fairly basic facilities. But it was cheap and cheerful, and the pub downstairs seemed to more than compensate!

Mike Carlin remembers …

I was living in County Durham but working in Camberley (Surrey) in 2002 and stayed at the Dog and Partridge in Yateley for six weeks (Sunday evening to Friday morning and some weekends). A great place to stay but the highlight was every evening when Alan entertained the customers, telling stories and singing songs in the bar, I didn't want to leave, every night was party time.

Chris Bryant remembers …

A group of us were sat in 'Codger's Corner' of the Dog and Partridge one afternoon, and the conversation turned to old cowboy movies. I posed a question: "What was the name of Roy Roger's dog?" I cannot recall Alan's answer but he was adamant that he was right. We ended up agreeing on a £20 bet.

After getting home I had to find some convincing proof and managed to locate a picture showing Roy along with his dog and a caption.

I won. The dog's name was 'Bullet'. Begrudgingly, Alan handed over a tatty £20 note – I was as amazed as those around us. Magnanimously, I offered to buy him a drink. "I'll have a large G+T, but make sure they pour it from the Gordon's bottle – not the rubbish in the optic."

That's Alan, bless him. I recall that my £20 winnings were soon back safely in his pub till.

The guy who gazumped me on Rackstraw Farm was a Freemason, as well as a number of friends at the time, and they asked me to join. I didn't because we were about to go to Devon. They told me to get in touch with the Lodge in Devon and they would vouch for me. Dan Thompson was the local head man in Ashburton – he was the landlord of another pub – he hated me.

It wasn't till I came back to Yateley that I became a Freemason. But I'm not a paid-up member anymore. Although I enjoyed it and you make some good friends and have fun, in a sense it's the older man's Boy Scouts. It's not really the self-supporting clique that most people think. It wasn't for influence. I've kept all the regalia though.

Chis Bryant remembers …

There was an occasion when Alan attended a Masonic Ladies Weekend in Bournemouth. Lucky old me. He was on my table for the banquet dinner, and was seated next to my mother-in-law, Dolly.

He simply could not resist a potato on Dolly's plate, and (with his fork poised for action) asked if she was going to eat it or not. A slight hesitation on her part was a good enough sign, and the potato had gone!

I was landlord of the Dog and Partridge from 2000 to 2005 – five years. And it was going ever so well. I built it up from nothing. It wasn't doing anything at all when I got there. If you ask around, you'll find people who will tell you how I built it up over that time. But we did have some fun there too. Lots of bands came along. All the local musicians I knew before we moved to Devon would come to the Dog and Partridge and play for next to nothing. They were friends.

The 'Old Codgers' (Dog and Partridge regulars) remember …

The Dog and Partridge got much better when Alan was here. It went through bad times after he left – lots of changes of managers. No stability.

At one of the Loony Party Conferences we brought along a fellow Mason – Douglas – he was only a little chap – about 5ft 4. Alan persuaded him to join up on the spot, and then decided he should be in the Loony Cabinet as the Minster for Smaller Affairs. I'd been in the Army for quite a long time, so I became the Minister for War.

He'll deny this, but I know he used to take his shirts to a charity shop. When they'd washed and cleaned them, he'd go in and buy them back – much cheaper than dry-cleaning them himself.

Alan: How clever of me to think of that!

He put on a lot of live music here. The best band he ever had was the Savages – brilliant. They came here a few times. But Alan made the pub what it was – he was a real character and put Yateley on the map.

Alan helped out my daughter when she was doing a school project on politics. She got top marks for that simply because of Alan's help – the other parties wouldn't talk to her.

Eric Bristow came in here a time or two. He always won at darts.

Alan comments: One time Eric Bristow announced he had to play the pub landlord. I'd won a championship the year before so I was pretty good. He said he would play down from 901, against my 301. He still won.

Years later when Alan got on Fleet Town Council, I thought he meant he'd got a job as a mobile roundabout.

We think the book should be called 'Beyond all Hope'.

We used to do karaoke as well. I used to get up there and sing a few songs and encourage everyone else to get up as well. It's much easier to persuade them if you are taking the lead. You need to inveigle them into doing it.

Mark remembers …

When he first ran the Dog and Partridge it was amazing. It was buzzing. There were bands on every weekend. He knew a lot of musicians – especially David Sutch – so there were always different bands turning up. I think they played for free and he put them up. But he left after five years because they wouldn't renew his lease. The brewery wanted to redevelop it. The rent would have gone sky-high, and Dad wouldn't have been able to afford it.

From 2003 on, I'd begun to ask the agent for Scottish and Newcastle about renewing the franchise. I was really interested in carrying on and I was making a decent living. He kept assuring me there was no problem. Same in 2004. Then in 2005 with just six months to go, I was still reminding the agent about renewal. He was still telling me, "No problem … it's all in hand … it's all in order … I've got it worked out for you." But he kept very quiet about whether or how much they would put up my payments to them.

Now three months to go. Colin McDonald was the agent's name.

"What about this franchise, Colin?"

"Yeah … yeah … yeah. It's fine. Don't worry about it."

Two months to go, still no further on, but he promised to have it all ready for his next visit. On the day, no visit. I rang him and he told me: "There's been a bit of a glitch. I'll come and see you next Monday."

I was getting suspicious. What had happened, unknown to me, was that a customer of mine had later taken on another pub. That franchise was up too, and he let the brewery know that he wanted to run the Dog and Partridge, and for whatever reason – I guess money – they got the franchise. I was out on my ear. I'm convinced that I'd made such a success of the Dog and Partridge, that the brewery just wanted to take back control … put a manager in … and keep more of the money themselves. But between 2005 and now, the Dog and Partridge has had about nine or ten landlords. The one who is there now has been there three years or so, so there was pretty quick turnover of people at the beginning.

I was annoyed about that at the time. And I'm still annoyed about it. If that hadn't happened, there's every chance that I would still be there now. It was quite a shock.

This was June 2005. There I was for the first time in my life: out of work; evicted from my home; nowhere to live; and Norma, my wife, terminally ill in the hospice. When I closed the front door of the Dog and Partridge for the very last time, I was really low. I sat on one of the benches on the green outside and, for once, I actually cried. It just seemed like everything was coming to an end.

Goodnight Norma …

Norma's MS developed over ten years. It was awful to watch it happening. As time went on she just got worse and worse, and there was little or nothing I could do to help. She gave up the fight in April 2007. I had been preparing myself for Norma's death. We both knew it was going to happen one day, so you just have to accept it and get on as best you can.

But I can't describe what it's like to watch someone you love slowly die. There are no words…

The daughters remember …

When Norma died, Dad got a phone call from the home saying she hadn't got long, and they wanted us to go up. When we went into the room and she was still breathing. Dad asked if they could get her to hospital. They said that if they tried to move her she would probably pass away. Dad said: "I want her to know that I've done everything I could for her, and I really would like you to get her to hospital now." They asked us to leave the room while they got her ready. After about two minutes, the nurse came out crying.

The doctor called us in: "She's gone."

"Do you mean she's passed away?"

"Yes," replied the doctor. We just sat there with her, and we could just see the colour wash from her face.

We stayed there a little while. Dad talked to the doctors. Then the ambulance came and took her away. We decided we should go to the Oat Sheaf pub in Fleet, and just talked about her. Dad made a couple of phone calls to tell people, and really that was it. He definitely loved her.

Norma's funeral was an event. Dad organised it all at the Masons' club. Considering she didn't know that many people up here anymore, it was an incredible turnout. Norma didn't often drink, but when she did it was brandy and a banana milkshake – or brandy and milk. We had a lot to drink that day and Angela fell over.

Norma would have been proud of us.

So I was with Norma for longer than my other wives. I loved them all at the time. I wouldn't want to hurt any of them. But the difference is that Norma was taken from me. I'm glad I've stayed friends with Pamela, and it was lovely that she felt able to come down to Ashburton with the daughters. Gina married in Ashburton – to a guy called Phillip Teague – and the reception was held in the ballroom at the Golden Lion – that was nice. As for my first wife … I have some good memories and some bad memories.

And so another chapter closes in my life. I'm now 63, my wife has just died, I've lost my livelihood, and I have nowhere to live.

Perhaps it was just time to retire … but then I had my alter-ego to look after …

PART 4

MY POLITICAL LIFE …

BEING A LOONY

In this Part:

Chapter 15: The birth of the Official Monster Raving Loony Party with Screaming Lord Sutch as Leader

Chapter 16: The serious side of running a Party, and matters of policy

Chapter 17: My leadership of the Party, and my personal beliefs

Chapter 18: Our famous Conferences and our re-shuffles

Chapter 19: Keeping this show on the road.

CHAPTER 15

The Official Monster Raving Loony Party is born …

After the first visit that David Sutch made to the Golden Lion in Ashburton, he went home the next day, having promised to come back for my 40th birthday.

I never really gave it another thought. Then, come June 16th 1982, the door opened and in walked David. He had a couple of musicians with him, and they did a bit of an impromptu show for my birthday that night. I think he stayed for perhaps a week. We got talking, and this is where we formulated the OMRLP. It had been talked about before, although nothing ever really got done about it. So we decided that from that day – 16th June 1982 – the Golden Lion Hotel would become the 'Loony-versal' Headquarters. He would be Leader. I would be Chairman and Deputy Leader, and Norma, my wife, would be the Membership Secretary. Technically there already was a Secretary, Janice Healey, but she was really David's Private Secretary.

Bob Burgos reflects …

We sat around that night in the Golden Lion with Screaming Lord Sutch drinking his customary cup of tea, and it just all seemed to come together – the Party was born.

Sutch was a great guy. He was like a father to many of us in the band – including Alan. We learned so much from him.

And so The Loony Party was formed with Alan 'Howling Laud' Hope being the Co-Founder, Chairman and Deputy Leader alongside his dear friend and Leader of the Party, Lord David Sutch. The news was out and many bookings and tours followed for us all in the Savages, together with David and Alan at the helm with their Party's huge following of supporters. Not only around Britain, but all over Europe too.

Appearances on television and radio, national press coverage, and at elections became a regular occurrence and a part of everyday life in those unforgettable, glorious, crazy years we all had back then.

It really was a true partnership when Alan and David got together because they were so closely connected to what they both wanted to do. It was a kind of marriage if you like. They were inseparable and a perfect team.

When the launch of the Party went public, Devon Life got in touch with me. They realised there were two Party Chairmen living in the same constituency: me and Norman Tebbit. They wanted to take a photograph of us standing back to back. But he wouldn't do it.

David Sutch already had the idea of a political party in the back of his mind, but it hadn't really got underway. I think it was originally called 'The Mad Maniacs Monster Raving Loony Party', or something like that. But then we found out that the Electoral Commission would only allow a maximum of six words in the party title, so it became 'The Official Monster Raving Loony Party'. This was to avoid confusion with the 'unofficial' Loony Parties – Conservative, Labour and Liberal – or any other pretender to our throne.

Commemorative plaque.
(My private collection)

I find it quite heart-warming that the OMRLP and me share the same birthday – even if the Party is a tad younger.

In the bar of the Royal Standard, Aldershot with The Jersey Flyer, Prof. Stanton and 'Elvis Presley'. (Courtesy of the Jersey Flyer)

Sutch good times …

David Sutch had already stood for election under a number of different names: The National Teenage Party was the first incarnation back in 1964. That was in Stratford-upon-Avon – the seat that Profumo had to vacate because of the involvement with Christine Keeler. David always blamed prostitution for getting him into politics. But he would say that, wouldn't he?

The second time he stood was in Huyton against Harold Wilson in 1966. That was quite famous. He offered his hand to Harold Wilson, but he was having none of it. Then I think he stood once again in 1970 for 'The Go To Blazes Party'. Things went a bit quiet for a while after that although he was still getting some national newspaper coverage with his band the Savages. I think he stood in Brecon under that party name. I sent him a telegram. I was in Wales at the time with Norma, so we sent a Good Luck telegram to Brecon

Town Hall. Whether he actually got it or not, I don't know. On his Wikipedia page, it says he stood 39 times – I'm only up to 28 as of 2019. He's in the Guinness Book of records for standing the most times.

So the OMRLP got under way, and the first time that Sutch stood under that name was in February 1983, in Bermondsey, London, against Simon Hughes – the Liberal. Wikipedia states that the Party started in 1983 – because that was the first election where the name was used – but it actually started on June 16th 1982 – around 10 in the evening … or was it 4am?? So that's how it all started.

David and me at No. 10. (My private collection)

We never really thought the Party would get as big as it is. We get messages from all over the world: congratulations; good luck; all this kind of thing. It's absolutely amazing. I always tell people that we are the Party that everybody loves. Nobody hates us. We are on everybody's side. No matter what your political persuasion may be, we are on your side. But they don't vote for us – maybe this time!

I don't think people realise or remember just how active David Sutch was in politics. Here are a few facts:

- In total he stood in 33 by-elections and got 7,522 votes;
- He stood in two national elections (but in four different constituencies gaining 1848 votes;
- He first stood for the OMRLP in Bermondsey in 1983. He got 97 votes and came 6th out of 16 candidates. The seat was won by Simon Hughes with a massive swing from Labour. It is notable for the 'dirty tricks' and smears made by some candidates against Peter Tatchell who was standing for Labour and was a prominent gay rights campaigner;
- In May 1990, David stood in Bootle, Liverpool, against Jack Holmes of the SDLP and polled more votes – 418 for David and 155 for the SDLP. That signalled the death-knell of the SDP and they joined with the Liberal Party. The Labour candidate was elected, but died 57 days later, so the by-election was re-run that November. David beat the Liberal candidate by 311 to 291;
- He last stood in Winchester in November 1997, gaining 316 votes. This was a re-run of an earlier election in May where, after investigation, the result had been declared void.

Playing for laughs …

People say we're just a joke, but politics is all a joke. We are the Official Loony Party, as opposed to all the others. So you might call it a joke, but we do get votes, and we rarely come last in any count. I do wonder what these others think. They stand with what they think is a good cause in their mind, and they get beaten by the OMRLP. I don't know what they think, but I'd love to know. If I asked them I don't think I'd get an answer. They'd tell me to bog off, I would think.

R U Seerius comments ...

I have met so many interesting and fascinating people who are members of the Party, and many are now long-time friends. Most are cynical of politics and dare I say it slightly eccentric. But all fight to keep the OMRLP going as a tradition. Some people think the OMRLP is just wearing silly clothes and acting daft. It is not. We do it because we can. It is living satire.

In Alan's words "We are Loonies ... not nutters."

The Party developed through music. Most people who have ever stood for the OMRLP are involved in music one way or another. Freddie Zapp down in Cornwall, won two council seats. He won Redruth and Camborne on the same day. He was a DJ. Stuart Hughes in Sidmouth. He's now a county councillor, although not on a Loony ticket. He jumped ship and went Conservative. He's a 'trait-Tory'. We're still the best of friends. He was a disc-jockey. Nigel Knapp who stands in North London. He's a singer with a band called the Big Fibbers. R U Seerius who stands up in Derbyshire; he plays banjo in a morris-dance team. Nick Delves aka The Flying Brick also in Derbyshire; he plays bass in a punk rock band. And so it goes on and on. It's all built around musicians. That's our heritage as a Party.

I think Sutch saw the Party as mainly a way of getting publicity. He got loads of that. But it has got more serious. I was in the pub business for 30 years. The publicity we got for the hotel and the pub was phenomenal. In Ashburton we had a Japanese TV crew come over, and Danish and Argentinian TV crews too. Argentina came because in Patagonia there are a lot of Welsh people. It the biggest welsh-speaking community in the world – bizarre really. They love us there. German TV, French TV, Swedish TV and so on. When I sold up and we moved the HQ to the Dog and Partridge in Yateley, we had a crew come over from North Korea. They brought a Korean comedian over with them. The idea was that he would challenge me for the right to run the Party. They promised and promised that they would give me a copy of that, but I never did get one. I'm not really annoyed about that, but I am disappointed with them. I did get in touch with them, but they just denied all knowledge of it. The locals in Yateley were amazed that a crew from North Korea turned up. It made the local papers. It generated business because everyone came along to see what was going on. That's how it works.

I love the cartoon below from the Daily Mirror in March 1988. It focuses on Eric Heffer and Tony Benn during one of the many Labour Party crises. But who's that in the back? Why! It's David and me.

Courtesy of Charles Griffin.

Sutch did a series of ads for Heineken. There he is in the Prime Minister's seat in the House of Commons: "Only Heineken can do this." He made a series of six. I don't know if they were ever shown because Sutch died. They had to pay the fee into his estate. I wanted his fee to go to the Party, but they said they couldn't do that. But I no longer have a copy of those ads. It would be good to get hold of a copy.

Whipping up the crowds …

There have been other well-known people who have joined in with us over the years. We were very friendly with Cynthia Payne – the woman who ran the brothel – Madame Cyn. She started her own political party called 'The Rainbow Alliance Pain and Pleasure Party'. The first time that she and David Sutch met was at the Kensington By-Election in 1988. Cynthia finished 6th out of 15, and David Sutch came in 7th. They became the best of friends. She used to turn up at our Conferences. We used to say that she was our Chief Whip. She kind of went along with it but would always deny it in a proper interview.

Me and Cynthia Payne – Our Chief Whip. (My private collection)

The daughters remember …

We do remember meeting Cynthia Payne. Both at the Dog and Partridge and the Golden Lion. When we were all introduced to her she said: "Oh. I'm thinking about recruiting." We thought, *Noooo*. She was their Chief Whip. Sometimes we felt a bit embarrassed about the OMRLP. People would ask us if we were Loonies, but we would always say that we were the sane ones. We were not really embarrassed; people can think what they like. We'll go to any of his local events, or Conferences. We had a Conference once at the Links Hotel in Fleet. That was when Adam Ant turned up. That was a good Conference. We don't tend to go to the Conferences now. They are usually in Blackpool and it's just too far away. The way we look at it is that he enjoys it; it gets him out the house; he meets a lot of people – so why not?

Alan comments: That same day there was a birthday reception for Gina, the landlady of the Links. Adam Ant's girlfriend went to the buffet and took a sandwich. No-one knew who she was and she was told off by another guest, even though the landlady had said that it would be OK.

Cynthia was good fun. She used to come down to the Golden Lion. She could keep all the girls spell-bound with all the stories she could tell. I think David Sutch stayed with her for a little while. She was always happy to join in the fun. We had a campaign to move the Houses of Parliament to the Scilly Isles (which we thought made sense) and she was all for that.

Alas, she's not around anymore. The last time I saw her was at our Conference in the Dog and Partridge in 2004. Her funeral in December 2015 was a grand occasion: horse-drawn gold coach, a great jazz band and so on. So many friends and well-wishers from across every walk of life.

David Sutch was a very quiet man. He didn't smoke; didn't drink; didn't swear. He drank tea, and only tea. A true Tea-Totaller. He was everything people thought he wasn't. He liked to come down to Devon and just walk around town. People knew him by then. Ashburton is only a small town. He was just an ordinary guy. But once he put on his leopard-skin jacket and jumped on stage, he was a different person. He was a very thoughtful man, not too sure if I would say he was clever. He used to have a lot of jokes. Many people thought they were his, but he'd 'borrowed' most of them. There was one that Terry Wogan always liked: "Why is there only one Monopolies Commission?" But it was Charlie Denis who I first heard use that, and I think he told it to Sutch.

But it had to end …

I really don't know why David committed suicide. He was very depressed towards the end. One day I found him just pacing up and down in the cellar of my hotel.

I said: "David, what's the matter?"

"Oh just stress, stress."

"Come and talk to me."

But he wouldn't say anything. His mother had died a little while before. He was a dog lover, and a cat lover. Hence the passports for pets policy. He had a little dog called Rosie (his mother's dog). It went everywhere with him. It never left his side. Some people say that when the dog died, he decided to end it. But I don't think that is really true.

Part of his legacy was the Radio Sutch pirate radio station. This was set up on a shoe-string in the 60s on an old fort in the Thames Estuary. I don't think it ever made any money – it probably ran at a loss – and eventually David sold the station to Reg Calvert – who used to run the Agincourt in Camberley – and his business partner, a retired major – Oliver Smedley. It was perhaps just as well, because some time later Reg Calvert was shot and killed in an argument over the station. The Major was put on trial, but amazingly, he was acquitted.

So he did have some money troubles. His mother lived in Harrow, and one of our Party members – Lord Tiverton – lived down in Brighton. He had spotted a house down there for sale. David always wanted to move his mother down there for her last days to be near the sea. He went and looked at it. If he could sell his mother's house, then he could afford to buy the house in Brighton outright – no problem. He had a buyer, but it fell through after he had signed contracts to buy the Brighton house. He took out a bridging loan. The worst thing he ever did. He did owe a lot of money. But then

NatWest Bank bailed him out. They got some advertising from that: "Only NatWest can do this" or something like that. I've got a lovely photo of Sutch with a NatWest bank behind him. The photo's about 4ft by 4ft.

David had lots to look forward to. He'd been booked for a series of shows in Las Vegas and was planning to get married while he was there – to Yvonne Elwood. Carlo Little and me were to be the Best Men at Sutch's wedding in Las Vegas. Carlo was one of David's original drummers. He was there to represent his music life, and I was there to represent his political life.

Poster for Sutch in Las Vegas. (My private collection)

Then came that fateful Wednesday night down in Devon – it was on my birthday. In Devon there's a card game called Euchre. I was in the Euchre team. It's a North American card game very popular in the West Country for two to four players, played with the 32 highest playing cards.

We had an away match, and we got back and we were having a late drink in the bar, and all of a sudden, the phone rang. It must have been about 12.30/1am. I glibly picked up the phone:

"You're a bit late to be ringing the OMRLP HQ aren't you?"

And the voice the other end said: "So you haven't heard then?"

As soon as I heard that, I knew what had happened – David had died. It was a reporter from the Times. I thought, *What a silly bugger.* If only he'd spoken to me that day in the cellar, things might have been different. Who knows? Took us all by surprise. But in the book that Graham Sharp wrote, *The Man who was Screaming Lord Sutch*, the opening words are my words. "I knew it would happen one day." Or I had an idea it would happen one day. That was very sad. But all in all, he was a well-liked man. Everyone who met him loved him.

It was Yvonne who found David. It must have been terrible for her.

Mark Hope remembers …

Not sure how I would describe David Sutch – perhaps 'Lost'. He was a loner, he was always on his own. He seemed really troubled and lost, especially towards the end. Like my dad, very quiet and private … but put him in a crowd and he blossomed. That was David, with all his stage props and stuff. He had to cut back on some of that at the hotel – it wasn't a big enough stage.

Alan comments: It wasn't just that. He used to perform 'Great Balls of Fire' wearing a hat soaked in lighter fuel. He frequently set his hair on fire, and I thought he might burn the place down. Arthur Brown used that idea some years later.

But we had some great times in Devon and elsewhere during the 17 years or so that David was the Party Leader. One time we were invited to entertain on a Thames river-cruise. There was some fuss at the time with the EU and our sausages. Mungo Jerry were there with us, so we re-wrote their famous song and it became 'In the sausage time'. There was a video of it, but it wasn't that great and was largely ignored in terms of publicity.

Bob Burgos reflects …

When David sadly passed away it ripped the heart out of so many of us who knew him, and I shall always salute Alan for all that he did for David, being the true friend that he most certainly was. I also salute Alan for all that he's achieved throughout the years as the new Party Leader because I know it couldn't have been easy for him running the Party on his own. But being the Alan we all know, he came through for us all like the champion that he is, and I will always admire him for that. His dedication, loyalty and belief in all that he does, especially in this throwaway society that we all live in today. He has kept the Loony flag flying for all of us to enjoy. If it wasn't for Alan, the Loony Party would never have happened, because our dear friend 'Lord David Edward Sutch' could never have achieved so much without him.

We just seemed to have lots of 'daft' ideas – like holding a Summit Meeting on the top of the Hay Tor, or going to the Scilly Isles with a plan to walk round them backwards. These little stunts generate loads of publicity though. And then we had the idea for a famous cabinet reshuffles. An annual Conference tradition that continues to this day.

OMRLP Summit Meeting. (My private collection)

In the same area we held the Summit Meeting, there are three notable landmarks on the coast: Thatchers Rock; Corbyn Head; and Hope's Nose! Isn't that odd?

Hopeful signs (Courtesy 'Lord Charles').

CHAPTER 16

The serious stuff

Matters of policy ...

But it wasn't all fun and games. There was some more serious stuff too. We've always had good policies and a fair few of them have been 'stolen' by our political rivals.

Back in the 'Teenage Party' years, David Sutch had campaigned to lower the voting age to 18. That did become law, and it was David who started that.

Over the years, we have promoted Passports for Pets; all-day pub opening, and having St. George's Day made a public holiday. The first two have happened, and the third was adopted by the Labour Party in their manifesto for 2017. That was a headline-writer's dream: "Corbyn's 'Loony' Policy" and the like. But it's good publicity for us.

One of our current policies that is getting some attention is the idea that if you pay your taxes on time, you get Nectar points. That's a good idea. And many years back we suggested that £5 and £10 notes should be made of plastic. They are now, but we don't get the credit!

We know we won't get elected. We do it for the hell of it – just because we can. People say that this is one reason they love Britain. We wouldn't get away with this in any other country. This is the democracy of our politics. It costs us some money. But if I hadn't done this, there would have been no point in this book. It wasn't my aim, but I always hoped a book might happen someday. I didn't expect I'd ever be on the Daily Politics show either, but I have been four times now. Andrew Neil introduced me and said I had every right to be on the programme. We are registered officially as a political party. A lot of the odd-bods aren't.

Daily Politics – Jo Coburn, me, Steve Lawson and Andrew Neil. I presented Jo and Andrew with bottles of our Co-ALE-ition Monster Mash ale which I had sneaked through BBC Security.

Chinners comments …

I've always been hopeful that one day we will have one elected MP, but I don't know if we will. But we will continue to get more local councillors. We work well with local communities and they vote for us. That's the way we will need to do it. It's right to say there's a big gap in the centre of politics at present. Alan's a big bloke, so I reckon he could fill it. He's got the guts for it.

We need to get more younger members. Most of us are getting on now, and the young vote was our original strength. I'm campaigning to give five-year-olds the vote. After all, our politicians act like little kids, so they might as well have the vote. We do support getting the age down to 16. You are a legal adult so why can't you vote? We need to get back to that. Youth involvement is key to the future. I came up with that slogan: "The only wasted vote, is one that isn't used." Everyone should vote – even if they spoil their ballot paper. I've made a replica polling booth, which we're going to put up in the pub. "Come in and practice voting." It'll generate some interest and publicity. But it's a serious message really.

> Alan may not have a coherent political philosophy in national terms, but he does take local issues very seriously, and he's well respected as a result. He's had a road named after him in Fleet where he lives.

But sometimes I just can't help winding up journalists. I was being interviewed by Sky News one time, and they asked to see our manifesto. I simply showed them a blank sheet of paper!

And on the BBC Politics show, I won a coveted BBC Politics show mug for the best one-liner for the picture of David Cameron, Angela Merkel, the Dutch Prime Minister Mark Rutte and Swedish Prime Minster Fredrik Reinfeldt in a rowing boat. It was a phone-in. I said I had a very good one-liner, and Jo Coburn insisted that I got my chance: "Is this the Coxless Four?" I asked!

> ***Bob Hickson comments …***
>
> People seem genuinely interested in what we have to say, but of course, we keep it quite light. We don't generally get a negative reaction from people.

We're always open to new policies. You can just go to the OMRLP website and submit your ideas – you don't have to be a Party Member. We take these along to our next Conference, and if we like them, they get adopted. I think some our policies are quite serious. The idea of a 99p coin has got to be good, hasn't it? It would make shopping much easier and save money; a 1p coin costs more than 1p to make. Richard Branson liked that. Maybe he would sponsor us – but he's a staunch Conservative.

It is showbiz. I've always thought the best publicity a band, or a landlord of a pub, can get is to spend £500 on a general election, or even just a by-election. The publicity you get for that £500, you wouldn't be able to buy. And that goes for anybody who's in a band, or a DJ. In the June 2017 Election, our candidate in Gorton in Manchester was Johnny Disco – a DJ, again. There was a by-election planned for Gorton, but then the general election was called, and the by-election cancelled. We'd already paid our deposit for the by-election, so that had to be refunded to us. That's the only time we've got our deposit back – so far! It is the music connection that holds us together. The people who stand have got friends, and they in turn have friends. Just yesterday we got 350 new clicks on Twitter. That's because of the election. Everyone wants to have a look to see what we're doing.

We like Theresa May's leopard-skin shoes, because it shows she's sympathetic to the Loony Party. Our Party Animal is the leopard – there's always some leopard-skin image in our publicity. I always wear a leopard-skin bow tie. We adopted the leopard as the Party Animal because we are the Party that won't change our spots.

We do get some success as a Party. We fielded a number of candidates in the 1994 European Elections and got 7,798 votes. We also did well when we stood for the Welsh Assembly in 2016. We fielded 30 candidates across the five Welsh regions. We came in 8th out of 16 with 5,743 votes. We were very proud of that.

Our base for the Radnor By-Election in 2019 was the Neaudd Arms in Llanwrtyd Wells, which claims to be the smallest town in the country with just 850 inhabitants. Coincidentally this was the place where Screaming Lord Sutch played his last gig. There's a plaque on the wall, and it is the Welsh Headquarters for the Party.

They play some silly games – like the man vs horse marathon. No prize for the horse, but if the man wins a prize, it has always been £1,000. If it isn't won, it rolls over to the next year, thereby increasing the prize. After 25 years, the prize of £25,000 was won by Huw Lobb, William Hill were the sponsor and paid up the £25,000, but I think they withdrew their sponsorship after that. Hundreds take part – lots of running clubs fielding around 600 runners, and about 60 horses. They run the World Alternative Games that take place every two years. It's a kind of alternative Olympics full of Loony games. I've been invited to open the games next year. That will be fun.

And in the 2019 General Election, we fielded 24 candidates and got a total of 9,739 votes. The table details this achievement:

1.	The Iconic Arty Pole	Louth & Horncastle	1044
2.	Earl Elvis of Outwell	South West Norfolk	836
3.	Barmy Lord Brockman	Mid Worcestershire	638
4.	Citizen Mark Lawrence	Chelmsford	580
5.	Howling 'Laud' Hope	North East Hampshire	576
6.	Baron Von Thunderclap	Mid Sussex	550
7.	The Mid Bed Minx	Mid Bedfordshire	536
8.	Reverend Martin Hogbin	East Surrey	521
9.	Nick Blunderbuss Green	Kenilworth & Southam	457
10.	Rambling George Ridgeon	Cheltenham	445
11.	Mad Mike Young	Sittingbourne & Sheppey	404
12.	Lily The Pink	Brecon and Radnorshire	345
13.	Sir Mark Beech	Aldridge & Brownhills	336
14.	Badger	Esher and Walton	326
15.	Farming Lord F'tang Dave	Denton and Reddish	324
16.	Citizen Squiff	Brighton Pavilion	301
17.	Sir Archibald Stanton	Dewsbury	252
18.	The Flying Brick	Islington North	236
19.	Just John	Clacton-on-Sea	224
20.	Dame Dixon	Hove and Portslade	195
21.	Chinners	Kingston and Surbiton	193
22.	Lord Sandys of Bunhill	Islington South	182
23.	Lord Buckethead	Uxbridge and South Ruislip	125
24.	The Raving Mr P.	Peterborough	113

But it's not cheap. Many candidates fund their own deposit. But if you add it all up, over the 36 years, OMRLP candidates have paid £85,800 to the Treasury in lost deposits at general elections and at least £27,100 to the Treasury in lost deposits at by-elections. This comes to more than £100,000 paid to the Treasury on behalf of the Official Monster Raving Loony Party. How crazy is that? Which brings me to …

Sponsorship …

Graham Sharp, who used to work for the local paper in Harrow where David Sutch lived, would write endorsements of him, and those would make the national papers. Then Graham Sharp got himself a job with William Hill. He became their PR man, and they decided they would sponsor David – just him. He used to wear a rosette that said: "I bet I can beat William Hill". Not a lot of people realised that. Then it came about that he sponsored me, and two or three others as well. But there were strings attached. You had to get 100 votes to get your money back. The idea was always to try and get yourself photographed outside a William Hill shop. If the newspaper would let you get away with giving them free advertising.

OMRLP/William Hill Rosette.

(My private collection)

Then in the 2010 General Election, William Hill told me they would sponsor all our candidates. I think that only cost them £12,500 for 25 candidates and lots of publicity. They sponsored the next election too. But then the Board changed, the Directors changed, and they decided to do something else. I think they sponsor Scottish Football now. I did contact Graham again before the 2017 general election, and told him I was standing in Maidenhead against Theresa May, and asked if would help. He emailed back with the sad news that he couldn't help, and that he was parting company with William Hill. But he did give me the email address for their political PR man there. But we have no sponsorship as of now. We are in contact with Paddy Power, but I don't know if that will come to anything.

I sent an email to Arron Banks as well. I know him very well. UKIP seems to be failing, so I asked if he would sponsor me. I am waiting his reply. But he did sponsor me in one general election, so you never know. And Wetherspoons might help out. They have before. It's just a matter of finding a businessman with the right sense of fun and frivolity.

Sometimes we get offered money we can't accept. We received a substantial donation one time from our sympathisers in the Isle of Man. We were gutted when we found out the Electoral Commission would not allow us to accept it. We had to send it back.

And I must mention my appearance on Top Gear. That just came out of the blue. I got a phone call one day asking if I would do it. They wanted to find out who was the fastest political party on the track. Of course, I was up for that. It was on Dunsfold Airfield near Chiddingfold in Surrey. They told me they didn't expect me to win, they just wanted me to make them laugh. There's a video on our Party website. Jeremy Clarkson was very approachable; we shared the same changing room in one of the trailers. It rained all day though which wasn't so good. I wanted to go round backwards, but they wouldn't let me. I should have just done that anyway as I got to the finishing line. I actually stopped just short of the line. They made me go back and do another circuit. Still, I hold the record for the slowest lap!

The chappie who won, John Ault, he was in the LibDem Party then. The other guests on that 2003 show were Jamie Oliver (the TV chef), Bernard Jenkin (Senior Conservative) and Perry McCarthy (the Stig).

We've got quite a few local councillors, and that brings a sense of achievement. I remember being on a TV chat show in the West Country. The Conservatives were ruling there. They had 7/8 minutes; Labour had 5/6 minutes; Liberals had 3/4 minutes; Greens had a couple of minutes; and I was last. The question that was being put to everybody was: "What ceiling would you put on the European Monetary Unit?" All of them blabbered on without really saying anything – or anything anyone understood. Now it's my turn. I've got the shortest slot.

"What ceiling would you put on?"

"Artex," was my reply. Done. Brought the house down.

Over the years, all the things we needed to set up – websites – registration – and so on – have been done. Not many by me, but by people who knew how to do it. I don't know about IT – I can use the computer and the phone – but we have people who are into IT and can set things up for us.

But there are things we have to do. For example, every party has to have a Nominations Officer. You can't just go to the electoral office and say you want to stand for the OMRLP. You need a piece of paper whichever party it is, that says that you can. That applies in the same way to all parties. The bigger parties might have several Nominating Officers around the country, but I'm the Nominating Officer for us. We are well organised. We've got a Membership Secretary. We've got a merchandising man. I'm the Leader and the Nominating Officer, so I am the king-pin. Lots of delegation.

Baron von Thunderclap remarks …

I am Membership Secretary. We have about 150/200 active members, and quite a few abroad. I probably get two or three membership requests every week, but close to a general election it goes haywire – it can be several hundred in a month. We must have had 1000s of members world-wide. A lot of memberships are given as presents for birthdays etc. At the core there's probably about 20/30 active members. If you don't renew, you cease to be a member, regardless of what Alan says.

Alan comments: Once a Member, always a Member. Although we do now have a renewals system.

CHAPTER 17

Now I'm in charge …

So to recap. The Party was born at the Golden Lion in June 1982, and I served as Deputy Leader up to June 1999 when David Sutch died. Then it just followed that I would step into David's shoes, as it were.

In a sense, under David's leadership, the Party was rather more the Screaming Lord Sutch fan-club. But it's not like that now. It has its own identity.

So we had to formally elect a new Leader, but my cat, Catmando, wanted to stand too. I had to settle for Joint Party Leader for a while. We both got the same number of votes in the Leadership election. Very strange! But it was OK. I was Party Chairman too, so I had a casting vote! We also voted for David Sutch to be our spiritual leader for eternity.

Because of that I announced that we were the only party in the world ever to be led by Man and Beast. But I was heckled. "No you're not, what about John Major and Margaret Thatcher?"

Catmando was a lovely cat with a great nose for publicity. If there were cameras around, he would strut around and pose for them. He was a natural showman, just like me. He was originally called 'Catman'. But one day, I was asked some question about when some song was recorded, and I couldn't remember the answer, and one of my customers said: "I bet Catman do." And the name just stuck. I only became sole Leader a few years later when Catmando got run over and was killed. The locals of the Dog and Partridge accused me of assassinating him, but he was MY cat. I couldn't have done that!

Catmando and me. (My private collection)

I wouldn't have said that I was worried about taking over after Sutch died. I was a bit apprehensive, but the Party Members wanted me to carry on. So I did, and I'm still here 20 years later. I've had a couple of challenges since, but they've never come to anything. Nothing got far enough to force a vote. But we have a rule that the Leader is the Leader till death, unless they choose to resign. We haven't had a Deputy Leader for some years. It would be good to find one. They could learn the ropes and then take over. I would settle for President.

Sutch showed me how to use the media. You need to feed stories one at a time to one newspaper at a time – they need to feel they have an exclusive – even if they haven't. I enjoy working with the media – it comes easily to me.

Lady Muck comments ...

Alan is a kind and gentle man. A rough diamond. He always tries to do the right thing and he does not like confrontation. But when he has had to make hard decisions (e.g. rebellious factions) he has done so. He ran the Conferences at the Golden Lion very well, and dealt quickly with any issues or trouble-makers/gate-crashers. He takes his politics seriously.

So I'm Leader, and there is a serious side. So what do I really believe in? I'll try to explain.

I'm a Town Councillor – we'll get to that in the next section – so people are entitled to know what I think. I'm an ordinary-living kind of bloke. Yes, I serve under the OMRLP, but I don't think politics should come into it on Town Councils. Underneath it all when you meet these other politicians, whoever they are, they are just ordinary people. From the Prime Minister down. I'm no different to them, and they're no different to me. Do I believe in politics? I suppose it has to be there. But I don't think I really do believe in politics. The country shouldn't be run by politicians. It should be run by the '12 Just Men'. The 12 people who are the best for it. You can see each party refusing to accept a good idea from another party because they didn't think of it first – and that's what it seems to be about all the time. If that's not loony, I don't know what is.

I didn't mind Maggie Thatcher. I thought she did quite a good job, but I also thought she let a lot of people down. I didn't like it when she died, and some people had 'Good riddance. We hate the witch' parties. Not right.

But my real hero was Winston Churchill. He was the man who saved us all in my lifetime.

The white suit that I always wear on election nights was inspired by a statue of Winston Churchill in a white suit. Mine is not really a suit, more of a three-piece. A white jacket from BHS; white trousers from a cricket shop; a white waistcoat one of my customers made for me – all separates. In the early 80s the Dukes of Hazzard was a very popular TV programme. One of the characters, Boss Hogg, always wore a white suit. So I immediately got called Boss Hogg. But it was Churchill who I was copying. I first wore it in Ashburton carnival way before I stood in any elections. I certainly wore it at my first election in 1983. And we've always dressed up to get noticed – unusual clothes and lots of badges. We were the first party to have t-shirts and badges made for us. The yellow and black came from the leopard – we are the Party that never changes its spots.

Churchill in white. (My private collection)

'Howling Laud' was just a variation on Screaming Lord Sutch. 'Laud' came from William Laud, Archbishop of Canterbury from 1633 to 1640. He had quite a reputation but fell foul of Cromwell. He was imprisoned in the Tower of London and was eventually executed for treason in 1645.

So these are my 'politics' in no particular order:

Our National Health Service should be preserved, invested in and publicly owned. I'm generally against privatisation of public assets. But that was Maggie Thatcher's way of smashing the Unions, which was a good thing. Coal mining was a dying industry anyway – so it would have gone in any event. But national assets should be owned by us all. We should take them back into public ownership.

We should invest in our country. We should stop all Overseas Aid, we should invest it here – for us. We spend too little, but I don't support higher taxation – we should use the Aid money. Money we give to the EU I regard as Overseas Aid.

Our MPs have been very ineffective since the EU Referendum in 2016. We voted out. No good saying that we didn't know what we were voting for. Any MP saying that, doesn't deserve to be an MP and I hope they get voted out at the next election. I am a Parliamentarian at heart, but it needs the right people. I don't understand why we have a House of Lords – they are unelected, just like the Commission in Brussels.

The police service has been allowed to go astray. Too few police on the street. Closing police stations is a bad idea. The police need to be visible, and a station helps. Now Fleet's police station is in the council offices, it just looks like an admin office. We need more police powers to deal with knife crime, gangs and drugs on the street.

I don't object to immigration. But it needs to be controlled, and immigrants need a good reason to come here – like essential skills and so on. Of course we need to provide asylum, but asylum seekers should stay in the first safe country they get to. They shouldn't be moved on. Our off-shore patrols need to be more vigilant to stop those boats coming over. Once they're here they are a problem to find and deport. But we supply them with too much in benefits over and above our own people.

Initially, I did not support the ban on smoking in pubs and other places. But now I think it's a good thing. The air is cleaner. Lots of smokers don't smoke inside their houses now.

I think we did try to do the right thing in Iran/Iraq/Afghanistan and so on. Some people say that Tony Blair is a murderer and should be up in the European Courts. I don't know if that's right or not. But you can see that a lot of young boys went out there for no very good reason, and didn't come back. Their mothers and fathers are bound to feel really aggrieved. I think I would have voted against the Iraq War. What's been the outcome? We get rid of all these despots. And we replace that with chaos. We didn't have to get involved.

In general, I support investment in new infrastructure. For example: the third runway at Heathrow, smart motorways, HS2 and so on. But projects need to be carefully costed against the benefits. What is a few minutes shorter journey from London to Manchester really worth? I'm not sure.

Anyone who wants to go to university, and has the ability to better themselves that way, should be allowed to go. Remember it was an early Loony Party policy to abolish the 11+. We always felt that was too early to push schoolkids down one route or the other. Children need to be given every opportunity that they can build on.

I did not and still do not agree with the sale of council houses. They fill a social need. They should not be privatised and then fall into the hands of private landlords. The old council estates, were strong close-knit communities – and we've lost that.

I don't believe the voting age should be lowered any further. 18 seems right to me.

I am a staunch Royalist. Charles should take the throne when he gets the opportunity – that's his right.

I thought Tony Blair would be good. I was wrong. Gordon Brown gave away all our gold. Nick Clegg was destroyed by the Coalition. Cameron just walked away, and I don't think May did a good job at all. We should never have had a Remainer in charge of Brexit. It was never going to work. Corbyn doesn't seem to be very patriotic – he does seem to support Hamas, the IRA and so on.

I do like Donald Trump and I believe Nigel Farage has done great things for this country. He made the Referendum happen, and he's trying to make sure the people are listened to.

If I were Prime Minister I would: fill in the pot-holes; stop giving away money overseas; encourage Commonwealth countries to work more closely with us. We can work with Canada, Australia and New Zealand and so on.

And now … BREXIT!!!

This has been, and still is, a complete shambles. It should have been led by Boris Johnson from the start, and we would have been out the next day at 12 noon. Instead, it's been completely messed up by a bunch of real loonies. We wouldn't let them into the OMRLP – they are far too mad for us.

If you listen to people now, they've stopped saying whether they are Tory or Labour – it's Brexiteer or Remainer. A lot of the smaller parties will profit from all of this, including ourselves. I don't know how many factions there are in the Tory Party – lots it seems. But the

Labour Party has at least three factions: Momentum; the Blairites; and the traditional Labour people.

The Referendum was won for Brexit, but a majority of MPs want to remain – and that's the problem.

Yvonne Elwood reflects …

I think the end result will be a big rise in right-wing parties. That's a real danger. When we have the Euro Elections in June 2019, I think Nigel Farage's new Brexit Party will end up with more MEPs than UKIP have today. They will win more seats. And where there are Loony candidates, I think they will do very well. People will vote for them, rather than spoil their paper.

Over the last few months we have had a real surge in membership enquiries – perhaps up to 1,000. And that's mainly down to Brexit.

I do think that I can think logically. I'm not really a Loony, I just pretend to be, and I'm happy living my life the way I want. I deliberately chose to fail my 11+. Mr Bannister, the sports master, had bet Mr Griggs the head master 2/6d that I would pass. I bumped into him some time later – he told me off for making him lose the bet. Year 1 – 1st, Year 2 – 3rd; Year 3 – 7th, at the end I was bottom of the class (32nd). I took no exams and left at 15.

My only weakness is that I don't think I have any. My other strengths are knowledge and leadership especially for the Party and local politics. I can lead, but I like to be a team player – but they have to agree with me. I make decisions very quickly and get things moving forward.

Blue plaque fame. (My private collection)

Yvonne Elwood remembers …

After David's death, many people said that the OMRLP was finished, but some of us thought it should continue and that Alan should take over as Leader. Had Alan not stepped up, the Party probably would have gone. It wasn't on the up at that time. No-one else could have brought the Party back. It's an institution now.

I'm 77 now and I've been Leader for over 20 years. That means that I've been Leader of the Party for longer than David Sutch, and I'm the one of the longest serving Party Leaders ever. Clement Attlee, who oddly played junior football at Fleet in his youth, managed 20 years and two months – I've just got past that milestone. Next target is Edward Smith-Stanley. He was Tory Leader from 1846 to 1868. So just two more years!!

I've seen off 17 Party Leaders of major parties, and four Prime Ministers – Blair, Brown, Cameron and May – since I became OMRLP Leader in 1999. And then there have been many leadership changes in the minor parties. Nigel Farage was UKIP Leader three times, and UKIP has had many other leaders too. Not to mention the SNP, Plaid Cymru, the Greens and so on.

The table shows the leaders of the three main political parties in the UK that I have seen off. It's quite some list!

1999	Paddy Ashdown	Lib-Dem
2001	William Hague	Conservative
2003	Iain Duncan-Smith	Conservative
2005	Michael Howard	Conservative
2006	Charles Kennedy	Lib-Dem
2007	Menzies Campbell	Lib-Dem
2007	Tony Blair	Labour
2007	Vince Cable	Lib-Dem
2010	Gordon Brown	Labour
2015	Nick Clegg	Lib-Dem
2016	David Cameron	Conservative
2017	Ed Miliband	Labour
2017	Tim Farron	Lib-Dem
2019	Theresa May	Conservative
2019	Vince Cable	Lib-Dem
2019	Jo Swinson	Lib-Dem
2020	Jeremy Corbyn	Labour

CHAPTER 18

Conferences and re-shuffles

Time for a re-shuffle …

From the beginning, the Party Conference was always held at the Golden Lion in Ashburton. The very first was in 1984. And when I took over the Dog and Partridge in Yateley, the Conference venue moved with me.

Commemorative plaques. (My private collection)

We've had 36 Conferences now, and I've been to them all. Here's a summary:

Years	Location
1984 to 1999	Golden Lion Hotel, Ashburton, Devon
2000 to 2004	Dog & Partridge, Yateley, Hampshire
2005	Tudor's Bar, Aldershot, Hampshire
2006	Newmarket Arms, Torrington, Devon
2007	Hotel Ommaroo, St Helier, Jersey
2008 & 2009	Raven Hotel, Hook, Hampshire
2010 & 2011	Links Hotel, Fleet, Hampshire
2012	White Hart Hotel, Uttoxeter, Staffordshire
2013	Pavilion, Matlock Bath, Derbyshire
2014	Ridgebourne Inn, Llandrindod Wells, Wales
2015 & 2016	Uncle Tom's Cabin, Blackpool, Lancashire
2017	Molloys Bar, Blackpool, Lancashire
2018 & 2019	George & Dragon, Belper, Derbyshire

Then we had the idea for our 'Famous Cabinet Re-Shuffle'. We got an old wardrobe, took it out into the garden and laid it on its back. We climbed in and literally shuffled around the garden in it. Randomly, someone might announce they are, perhaps, "The Minister for Dog Poo!" and jump out. Someone else might jump in proclaiming themselves "The Minister for Chocolate", or whatever. Again, great fun, and the TV crews loved it because it was so spontaneous and visual.

Fathers for Justice were getting active, and there were a number of incidents involving public figures and flour bombs. We thought we could use that, so my dog Bomber, became our 'sniffer dog'. We'd dress him up and take him round the hotel looking for any flour bombs.

Sinbad (friend from Ashburton) remembers …

I have a video with Sutch singing at the Golden Lion. I think Cynthia Payne is on there too. She was a great laugh. Those days are long gone. Sutch came to Ashburton loads of times. Alan really revived him. He'd been forgotten, but started singing again down here. Once Alan launched the Loony Party, 'Screaming Lord Sutch' started getting invited to go sing places again.

Wild Willie Becket, David Sutch, me, Lionel Digby and Sir John Rowe at the Golden Lion in 1966. (Courtesy The Jersey Flyer)

A montage of Loony Conferences. (My private collection)

After I sold the Golden Lion, the Conferences moved to the Dog and Partridge in Yateley. Having moved on from there, we now hold the Conferences up and down the country to even out the travelling for our members. But a few years back, we did hold one at the Links Hotel in Fleet in 2010. That was a memorable night as Adam Ant showed up and played a great set for us, including many of his best-known hits.

Terry Twinn remembers …

Alan kept inviting me and lots of others to the Monster Raving Loony Party Conference at the Links Hotel in Fleet; he told us that Adam Ant would definitely be appearing but nobody believed him. Imagine my surprise when I turned up with a small group and Adam Ant was on stage getting ready to sing.

Yvonne Elwood remembers …

I've been to quite a few Conferences and some by-elections. It's all good fun and I've met some interesting people – Boris Johnson and his sister, Nigel Farage, David Davies, Nick Clegg, Zac Goldsmith. The Conferences have changed a bit over the years, especially after the ones at the Golden Lion. I think I'm nostalgic about those. At the Golden Lion, Alan was in charge of everything. It's not the same when it's someone else's venue – but they are still successful. Lots of publicity and people. Always lots of fun.

People think our Party Conferences are just three days of getting drunk, but it's not like that at all. We arrive and meet up, all a bit cheeky-grinned, wondering what's going to happen over the weekend. There is some drinking. The first night, we put some music on. We held three in Blackpool, where we had access to an open-topped Blackpool sight-seeing bus. One of our members drives buses up there. So we toured the town in the open-top, with me and my loud-hailer. Shouting out our slogans: "Vote for Insanity – You know it makes sense!" Telling people where we'll be that night, and asking people to come along and meet us. It's not a big piss-up. Honestly!!!!!!!!!

Ron Stephenson remembers …

I've been a drinking buddy with Alan for many years now and I did go to one of the Conferences in Blackpool. Great fun! I really enjoyed the open-top bus ride through Blackpool and admire the way Alan can just perform to the crowd. The great thing is, he puts a smile on people's faces. And that's a good thing, eh?

On the bus in Blackpool. (My private collection)

And every year we do our Cabinet re-shuffle, where we all change our 'jobs' in an instant. We're just taking the micky out of the big parties really. How can the Minister of Transport become the Minister for Education overnight? That's what they do. What do they know about it? But the newspapers love it. We'll have our Conference in a proper hall. The Chairman will introduce me, and I might speak for, say, about 25 minutes. Our Chairman lives in Jersey. We've nicknamed him 'The Jersey Flyer'. Obviously because he's always flying over. His name is Anthony Blyth. He's a big man in Jersey. He has a lot to do with the British Legion over there. He's an ex-Army man. He was stationed in Aldershot once. He organises the gun salutes in Jersey every year.

The Jersey Flyer remembers …

It was David Sutch's idea that I should start a branch of the Party in Jersey. That's how that came about. Then one time, Alan and Norma came to stay with me in Jersey. We were sitting here one night, when we decided to start the Isles of Deliberation Party, but I've been a member of the Loony Party almost since it started. I always try to get over for the Conferences.

At the Dog and Partridge, Alan would let most of us stay there in the upstairs rooms. He was very generous to us all. He didn't charge us. There were a couple of rooms up there that had a number of beds in each. The pub was very popular. Everyone was so kind and very generous. We had a wonderful time.

One Saturday when the Conference was on, we had guy dressed as a Bishop. There was a wedding taking place at the church next door to the Dog and Partridge, so we all went over there and formed a guard of honour for the Bride and Groom (or a Guard of Lunacy).

We held one Conference here in Jersey. One of our members – Baron Apple Jack – had a friend in France who makes wine, so we had cases of red and white wine made – I've still got some bottles. We made up our own labels for this Loony Wine and put the next year's date on just to confuse everyone. We had a Rock 'n' Roll night in one of the hotels, and everyone who came over was given a bottle of red and a bottle of white. I had some fake money made, and a 99p coin – to save on change.

Alan is a very well-meaning man, and Norma was a sweet, loving, gentle lady, and her death must have affected him a lot. He's quite private, and I think sometimes, he keeps too much to himself.

Norma and Alan made a great team. She could keep Alan under control, especially in Ashburton. It was bit of a wild-west town. I remember down at the London Inn, the landlord – Mike Delaney – had a juke box with all the old Rock 'n' Roll records. It was very popular, but Alan upstaged him once he got the Golden Lion up and running.

Alan came up with the name The Isles of Deliberation Party. The Channel Islands were called the States of Deliberation historically due to them having their own legislature. You'll have to ask Alan how he came up with that title.

I only see Alan from time to time now, but I try to see him whenever I come over. We had a pub crawl in Fleet once – that was a good afternoon!

The Party went into a state of limbo when Sutch died, and it was Alan that really held it all together. I hope the Party has a future. Some people got upset when we had sponsorship of William Hill – some people left over that association.

I think the OMRLP must be the only party in Britain that has held a Party Conference in a land where nobody can vote for us. We held a Conference in Jersey once, and nobody can vote for us there at all. Now that was good fun … and a piss-up. The local winery man out there made us 'Raving Loony' bottles of wine – red and white. And the local cider man made us cider as well. We have a lot of ex-pat members. Quite a few in Jersey, and all over the world: Australia, New Zealand, Canada, India, Africa. I have a cousin in Zimbabwe – well, not my cousin, my cousin's husband. My cousin Julie Archibald, who was there, is no longer with us. But he seems to be holding his own out there. He owns a donkey sanctuary. I'm pretty sure if he could stand out there for us, he probably would. But that might be a dangerous thing to do against Mugabe and his successors.

At our Conference in Jersey (Courtesy the Jersey Flyer).

R U Seerius remembers …

Most Conferences have memorable parts, and one that stands out was in 2001. The previous year (I think) the IRA had attacked the MI5 headquarters in London.

I had decided to bring my caravan to Yateley for the Conference and advised Alan that it was to be designated a temporary HQ for MI5 if required. I asked Alan if security would be a problem and he replied, "Probably not but I will ask the police if they would provide security."

Nearer the date of the Conference I enquired what if anything had happened, and Alan said he had phoned the Chief Superintendent of Hampshire Police and asked them for protection of my caravan.

"What did they say?" I asked, to which he replied that he was told to 'bugger off'.

The 2019 Loony Cabinet: Knigel Knapp, Baron von Thunderclap, Chinners, The Flying Brick, R U Seerius and me at the back. (My private collection)

Our 2019 Conference was held in Belper in Derbyshire. As always, it was great fun. We also achieved a world record, which has been accepted by the Guinness Book of Records. We had 119 people all playing *Eye of the Tiger* on kazoos. Then they played the Laurel and Hardy theme. That was in honour of Bob Hickson who is Chairman of the UK Laurel and Hardy Appreciation Society. And of course, *Land of Hope and Glory* in my honour.

Two photos (above and below) of Me, Freddy Zapp and 'Basil Fawlty'.

(My private collection)

Plain Scilly…

Down in Exmouth, we had a Party Member, Stuart Hughes, who was a lookalike for Basil Fawlty – and he ran a B&B called Fawlty Towers. He became our Minister for Funny Walks. He was just like Basil – very funny.

Stuart got in trouble with the Council. He stood for the OMRLP for the Town Council and Stuart, Freddie and me painted his house as a big Union Jack. Later he absconded and joined the Conservatives. There was John Rowe from Torquay. He had a Jack Russell with bladder problems. It pissed everywhere. You'd hear him ask: "Do you know where my pissing dog is?" If he was challenged about taking his dog into a pub perched on his shoulder, he would say: "That's not a dog, that's a parrot."

The newspapers had picked up on our plan to walk backwards round the Scilly Isles, and they wanted a story, so on our way down we stopped off in Redruth to meet the press.

We were collecting for charity along the way, and for some reason or another (the details escape me now), 'Basil' got all bitter and upset about this and accused us of keeping the money for ourselves. Nothing could have been further from the truth, the trip actually cost us money, and what we collected went to good causes as we had promised.

David Sutch, Lord Tiverton and me called in on him on the way home to try to set things right. But he wouldn't have it. He told us in no uncertain terms to get off his property. It was a good while before he would talk to us again.

We never did walk round the Scilly Isles backwards, but we visited the pubs and Harold Wilson's house, but he wasn't in. The woman who owned the B&B we were staying at decided she wanted to have a romp with me. She sent her husband to bed, and produced a bottle of brandy. They do say that the only virgin in the Scilly Isles, is the one who can run faster than her father.

George remembers …

When we were going to the Scilly Isles we stopped over at Lands' End. During the night, Alan kept telling me to shut up. I was snoring so much he couldn't get to sleep. That went on all night. That was how I became known as the 'back-bench snorer'. When we did get to the Scilly

Isles, no-one would share a room with me. I was put in a tiny room halfway down the stairs, but they all complained they could still hear me. It got into the papers, and I got stuck with that name for a while. We went in one pub with our rosettes on, just the two of us. It went dead quiet and then we heard: "Look. It's the Loony Party, and one of them's the back-bench snorer."

Me, Lord Tiverton, Cynthia Payne and David Sutch outside Harold Wilson's house on the Isles of Scilly. (My private collection)

And whatever we did, it just seemed to be for fun and a laugh. Once, in Sidmouth (although David was not with us that day), we saw the vicar walking up the hill with his bike. I stopped him and asked: "Excuse me, Vicar. Can I ask you a question?"

"Of course you can, my son."

"Would you like some more tea?"

He told me to '*bleep*' off. He said it with a smile on his face though.

We were there because it was Sidmouth carnival, so we were all dressed up. When the procession came along we jumped out in front of it and led it along the street.

We decided we'd have a Loony trip to the Munich Beer Fest. Someone we knew from the Bath Ball said they had friends in Holland, who owned a bar, and could probably put us up. There were four of us on the trip: George, Alan who was Minister for Vinyl and Shellac, Shaver Paul who was Minister for Nothing in Particular, and me.

There had been quite a lot of car bombs at the time, and we thought we might be a target, as I'd told the press about our trip and we were getting some coverage. I walked up the road a way, and refused to get in the car till the rest of them had got in and driven up to me. After all, you have to protect your leader!

George remembers …

I didn't enjoy the ferry crossing. It was a bit rough out of the harbour and I didn't like it. I was quite ill. It was too rough to go outside, so I sat in the stairway down to the car decks and just wedged myself in till we got across. We stopped overnight in some place in Dunkerque. Shaver and Alan had gone ahead. When we got there, we could see them inside through a crack in the curtains, but the door was locked. We knocked and this woman all dressed in black, opened up and invited us in. Shaver was at the bar surrounded by young women. We began to realise that we were in a brothel. Shaver spent loads on drinks, we had to drag him out in the end. And then we made our way to the bar in Holland. The husband of the couple who owned it went to work, and Shaver decided to make a play for his wife. She went to bed, and we noticed Shaver trying to crawl quietly up the stairs. We thought there was going to be trouble, but there wasn't and after just a minute or two he came back down. About ten minutes later, I heard the stairs creaking. I looked out, and the wife was standing on the stairs calling for Shaver, but she was stark naked. Shaver had gone back to sleep. I didn't wake him. He was annoyed in the morning when I told him.

We eventually got to Kitzbuhel in Austria and stayed at a place called the Club Continental. It was owned by Aussies, and all the clientele were Aussie too. We were in the bar that afternoon when all of a sudden two coaches pulled up outside and the place was flooded with young Aussies and Kiwis. They sold a liquor called 'Eauck'. Of course, the label had been altered to 'Fuck'. And that's all you could hear people shouting. It was a bit like Tia Maria. It was quite strong, but it was a bit different. If you managed 12 shots you were presented with a certificate. We had a good time with them.

The next day we drove up to Munich for the beer festival. We made our way back but not too directly. We got up to the top of the French Alps at one point. On the way back down the brake warning light came on. We were a bit worried about that all the way down. We found a garage and tried to explain, but it was just overheating.

I don't like these terms left, right, centre … the best right-winger I ever saw was Stanley Matthews. I like to think of ourselves as the goal-keepers. We're trying to save you. We want to save the world, if not the LoonyVerse. My father, being a Northerner, always told me to vote Labour, so I did. I remember voting LibDem once as well. But since 1982, I've been able to vote for myself in local elections. There might have been a couple of times pre-1983, when I didn't vote at all, but since then it's always been the OMRLP, where there has been a candidate.

CHAPTER 19

The show must go on …

The real buzz for me now, is that I'm 77 years old and I'm still able to do it. I was singing a song a while back at my party at Lakeside in Frimley Green (23rd April 2017). I was singing a song called 'Amanda'. It comes to the part: "I got my first guitar when I was 14. Now I'm proud and I'm 30, and I'm still wearing jeans." But I changed the second part: "Now I'm proud, and I'm 74, and I'm still on the scene." That is the buzz. It is an ego-trip. Of course it is. I was in the newspaper again, having done a show with Chuck Berry 50 years ago. Great stuff. I like the idea that my old schoolfriends of 60/70 years ago, know I'm still alive and what I'm doing. There's quite a lot of 'professional bull-shit'.

Long Tall Sally remembers …

In 2001 I told Alan I would be standing for Devizes as a candidate for OMRLP. He asked me to attend the Mountbatten School in Hampshire as a student wanted to have an OMRLP person at a debate they were holding. So off I went, unaware that I would be making my speech in a large school auditorium to 200-300 6th formers against many other more political candidates including Michael Anchram and Ludovic Kennedy. THANK YOU, ALAN. Out of them all, Mr Anchram befriended me, and I WON the majority vote, which appeared on BBC Newsround. A WIN!! Having watched how Alan can catch and work a crowd. I went onto get 471 votes in the election, much to many people's surprise. Quite how he managed to encourage me to offer myself as a sacrifice, I still wonder, but he did, along with sending me to a large parish church in Devizes and surviving the hecklers, winning over many, even though I was asked by the vicar to please ensure that I was suitably clothed for the church. Alan's advice was to KNOCK THEM DEAD, but I did comply with the request, the vicar's that is.

With Bob Burgos and Chris Fender Black of The Savages (Courtesy Bob Burgos).

I've had invitations to speak at Oxford, Eton, and Trinity College Dublin. It was the Shelley Supper Club at Eton. I was the guest speaker, and Prince William was there – he was still a kid. Next day, the Sun had the headline: "Prince William's a Loony". They wanted to know how the Party had started. So I talked about David Sutch standing in Stratford following Profumo's resignation. I didn't know it, but Profumo's grandson was in the audience, and Spencer – Churchill's grandson. I went down well. I was doing the Chelsea and Kensington By-Election at the time, against Michael Portillo, and that generated the Eton invite. I wasn't apprehensive. They were just another audience after all. Oxford was rather similar.

With Michael Portillo at Kensington. (My private collection)

A bit odd going to Dublin. We have no presence there of course. But it was just an after-dinner speech. I never rehearse these speeches; they are always ad-lib. I've done quite a few of those type of events, and I'd like to do more.

But I've missed out one person. My real all-time football hero, Jimmy Greaves. I never, ever thought I'd get to meet him … but I did! The photo below was taken in Central TV's Birmingham studios when I was guest of honour on his chat show. The invitation came out the blue, like so many others that I get. He said I was the most interesting guest he'd ever had on his show. That was in the early 90s. I asked him out for a drink afterwards, but he was tee-total by this time.

Jimmy Greaves – Tottenham Hotspur, Chelsea and England – and me!
(My private collection)

PART 5

VOTE FOR HOPE!

In this Part:

Chapter 20: My involvement with local politics in Ashburton; being the Millennium Mayor; and being a Fleet Town Councillor

Chapter 21: My 'victories' in general elections and by-elections

Chapter 22: My 'victories' against David Cameron and Theresa May

CHAPTER 20

Big fish in a little pond …

We'll get on to national politics later, but first I want to cover my career in local politics. In 1987 there were elections in Ashburton for the Town Council, and I'd threatened to stand on an Official Monster Raving Loony Party (OMRLP) ticket. Ron Southcombe, one of my customers was a Town Councillor. One Sunday afternoon, Ron asked me if I'd put my papers in to stand. I hadn't. He said: "They've got to be in tomorrow." I hadn't realised that either. He marched me out of the hotel and down the road to another house belonging to Major John Joiner, the Town Clerk. He knocked on the door. Ron suggested that the Major got the papers for me to stand. So all three of us walked over to the Clerk's office in the Town Hall. He got the papers out. Ron Southcombe proposed me, and the John Joiner seconded me. That was all I needed. In the event, I was elected unopposed. There were only 8 candidates for 12 seats, so no election was needed. So I was the first person in the world to hold elected office for the OMRLP, even though no-one had actually voted for me. I'd told the papers and there was a lot of press interest. I was told at the time that I would be front-page news in every newspaper, but, lo and behold, and much to my dismay (and everyone else's) the Herald of Free Enterprise flipped over that night. Kept me off the front page – perhaps a little bit on page three, next to the lady showing her boobs. What a shame that was. But we've made up for it since. We've had lots of headlines all over the country.

Dave Brooks remembers …

I was in the Golden Lion one day, and Alan passed this form over, and asked me to sign it. I just thought it was sponsorship for some charity and gave it no more thought, I didn't realise I'd just nominated him! The following day, Alan comes round with a reporter, and says: "Stick these in your window." Posters to vote OMRLP. I told him where to go. Think I called him some rude words. I'd been duped. I'm a true-blue Tory. I was on the Conservative Club Committee and they called me in to explain. I just had to say I'd been stupid. I got a smacked wrist.

Alan comments: I was a Conservative Club Member too – mainly for the bar and the locals. I was hauled in front of the Committee as well. I had stood against Patrick Nichols and we'd chased Geoffrey Howe out of town. Gordon Dumball, the Chairman, said to me: "When you joined the Loony Party, did you think you'd got yourself into deep water?"

"No. Not at all. In fact, the deeper the water became the better swimmer I was."

They kicked me out though.

After the election, the very first person who came through the hotel door to congratulate me was Paddy Ashdown. He was in the area and he called in with his wife. "I love it," he said. "What a great breath of fresh air for politics having a Monster Raving Loony Party councillor." My phone never stopped ringing. David Frost loved it. He called me three or four times for different quotes.

I told you about Stuart Hughes from Sidmouth – the Basil Fawlty lookalike. He got on the council as a Loony Party member. I have to be honest, although I was the first to hold office, he was the first to hold office with enough votes to win. Freddie Zapp got on the council in Redruth at about the same time, but he was elected unopposed, like me. But then Stuart deserted us in favour of the Conservatives!

John Hope remembers …

The local conservative organisation said he was going to be kicked out for standing against the Conservative candidate. And Alan said: "Excuse me. I put my deposit in first. So you are standing against me." But his membership of the Conservative Club was cancelled. He was banned for life!

I served on the Town Council in Ashburton for 13 years. I was on the Planning Committee, and Chairman of the Emergency Relief team. My hotel was on high ground, so I was expected to put everyone up if there was a flood. That sort of thing. I worked hard to set up a proper Tourist Information Centre in the town. That's still operating and has been a great success.

It was good publicity for the Party, and also for the town. It brought people in, and once here they spent money. It certainly helped the takings at the Golden Lion.

Dave Berry remembers …

I stayed at the Golden Lion a couple of times when the Party Conferences were held there. It certainly made the town buzz.

I remember one time when Alan and David Sutch decided to run round the rugby pitch backwards. Just for some publicity. It was an awful day, pouring with rain and there was hardly anyone there. But they insisted on going through with it.

Alan comments: Dave turned up a week early one year, but he enjoyed being here so much, he just stayed on.

Prince Rex comments: Dave Berry has been a long-time friend of Alan. He had two major hits in the 1960s, most notably with the "Cryin' Game".

We won!

But the first OMRLP candidate to be elected through a popular vote was Stuart Hughes in Sidmouth, even though he did get into trouble for painting his house like a Union Jack – but then he went and defected to the Conservatives.

Pete Webb remembers …

Well, the town did have a bit of a weird opinion of you and the OMRLP, I must admit. But it's part of the town's history now. It pulled in visitors from all over the world – Russia, China etc. TV crews from all over would come to the Party Conferences.

The town felt the OMRLP was a bit disparaging for the town. It wasn't.

It was something a little bit different. But it brought publicity to the town. And it wasn't bad publicity. In a sense, Alan put the town on the map.

I remember when I was Portreeve. Alan put on a charity fundraising event, and nobody would go to it. That would be about 1993. I was disgusted with that. And Alan got drummed out of the Conservative Club (barred for life!). I could see the point though as Alan was involved with a different Party. They did get a bit funny, and they still are. I don't go there myself.

I'm in the Guinness Book of Records for returning the least (election) expenses. There was an expense record that had stood from sometime in the 1700s, for £3 13s and 3 3/4d, I think. I thought, I could beat that. So in 1987, I put in an expense sheet of Nil. About two years later I got a phone call from the Guinness Book of Records, saying they'd put me in there. I asked what for. They said they'd checked with Teignbridge District Council, and were satisfied that I'd broken the record. I was certainly in the 1999 version. I don't think that record is now in the current editions. One of my greater claims to fame, that was.

I was on the Ashburton Carnival Committee for some years. We used to move our meetings around each of the town pubs, just to keep them all happy. The first meeting after I'd become a councillor, was in the London Inn. I walked down there with John German who lived across the road from my hotel – he was on the Committee too. We walked in, and I went over to Dan Thompson who was the landlord to order some drinks.

"Before I serve you," he said, "I've got something to say."

"What's that?"

"Well, now you've proved yourself to be the Official Town Idiot, I don't want you in my pub anymore. You are a disgrace to my profession. Go on. Get out. Sling your hook."

I thought he was joking, and waited for him to laugh. But he meant it. I went out, but I was seething. His son Melvin Thompson came round the corner. He was also on the Carnival Committee. I told him what had happened and I thought he would sort it out. But he just shrugged his shoulders and said: "Well, I can't go against my father, can I?" I was very annoyed by that!

About three or four years ago I was invited by the Carnival Committee to open the Town Carnival. I was quite proud to be asked. In previous years, it had been opened by Little and Large, Colleen Nolan (one of the Nolan Sisters), and Sid James. It was an honour for a lad from Farnborough. I suppose I was the closest thing they had to a home-grown celebrity.

His Worship ... the Mayor ...

I was Deputy Mayor for one year, and then the following year, 1998, I became Mayor. The normal term of office is just one year unless you put yourself forward again, which the previous Mayor did not. It wasn't universally welcomed. I remember one councillor proclaiming: "If you ever become Mayor, this town will be dragged through the mud." But once I was officially the Mayor, the Conservative Club lifted the ban!

The Good Burghers of Ashburton – I'm standing right behind the Mayor. (My private collection)

I stood for the following in year, 1999. It was a close-run thing. When we took the vote, the council was split 50:50. Then one councillor who was opposed to me (previously a Mayor) turned up late and demanded that we re-run the vote. Council Clerk John German put him in his place though, and told him that the vote was valid and could not be dismissed. I was Chairman of the Council at that time, so I got to use my casting vote. That was a lucky break wasn't it? Guess who I voted for.

John Belmont, a local journalist, wrote up those proceedings as a kind of Brian Rix farce. I guess it was in a way.

Ashburton, Buckfastleigh & Mid-Devon Advertiser

Loony? Not Mr Mayor

Monster Raver uses casting vote to re-elect himself

Lottery winner

Proof of my election. (My private collection)

Rosemary Christophers remembers ...

I was on the council at the same time as Alan. When Alan got elected it was quite amusing. He only got in by one vote, but one councillor had got the time wrong, turned up late and demanded a re-count. I strongly agreed that was not possible, and inappropriate. Alan actually had two votes. It was a tie, so Alan had to use his casting vote for himself.

In 1999 I became Town Mayor, Chairman of the Council, and Lord of the Borough, with Norma as my Mayoress. I was the Millennium Mayor. I was very instrumental in getting the Tourist Information Office up and running. It started up in a caravan, and later moved into the Town Hall. I generated lots of world-wide publicity for the town. I used to have to lead various parades – Veterans' Day for example. We were twinned with a town in France called Cleder. I made an official visit there one time and stayed with their Town Mayor. We had a good time and I met his friends and the local dignitaries. I don't speak a word of French though, and he couldn't speak a word of English. The mosquitoes there really took a liking to me – I was almost stung to death by them. But I did make Ashburton a better place – made it much more popular as a place to visit.

While I was Town Mayor I was invited on the Richard and Judy show. They were having a party on the roof-top garden and they asked me to open it. They thought it quite novel that the OMRLP should now have a Mayor in Ashburton in Devon.

They invited me up there and asked if I could bring my regalia with me. I told them I couldn't take the chain because we are not allowed to wear it outside of the area, and we didn't have a cloak or a cap.

So they fitted me out from the BBC wardrobe with robes and a mock chain. It looked OK. So we did the interview with me in these fake robes and chain, and when the Ashburton Town Council saw it, they got so upset. They questioned me at a council meeting. They wanted to know where the robes had come from. I told them from the Wardrobe Department of course, but the newspapers picked up on this and made a bit of a 'thing' about it.

I don't think I did anything wrong. I think it was just jealousy as I was getting more publicity than they were. But you can see that the BBC would want me to look the part. I was forgiven in the end, although a previous Town Mayor who was still on the council remained pretty upset.

Sinbad remarks …

Alan did a good job on the Town Council. He took it seriously and did it properly.

Now you can see the value of me being on the Town Council. I can shout about whatever I like. I'm a Loony. A member of the OMRLP which is recognised by the Electoral Commission.

Freddy Zapp remembers …

Alan has spent years on local councils. He knows how they work and he takes it seriously. He will try to do the right thing.

He was a great singer and frontman – you never forget how to do that. He was an entertainer – not just a singer – he could fill a stage by himself. If you've got the energy behind you, you can really reach out to the crowd. Alan was good at doing that.

Alan can lift a town as a councillor using those frontman skills. "If you haven't done it, you can't see it", but Alan has, and he can. It's a tradition that goes back to the Wandering Minstrels.

Fleet Town Council …

I stood for Fleet Town Council (FTC) just because I could, and I enjoy being there on a Loony ticket. There was nobody more surprised than me when I put in my nomination, and I got in unopposed. I expected there would be an election and I wouldn't win. But there we are. Not enough candidates stood, so we all got in unopposed. And I'm still there now. I know FTC doesn't have a lot of power. But bearing in mind I was on the Town Council in Devon for 13 years, I was always interested in the planning side of it, so I'm Vice-Chairman of the Planning Committee here. And I'm Chairman of the Highways and Transport Committee too. That's alright. I can keep an eye on the pot-holes. I don't think I'd want to be in finance, or anything like that. Each Town Councillor is expected to be on at least two committees, and those are my two.

I'm very focused on FTC. Meeting are a lot shorter if I'm in the chair. I won't put up with rambling pointless discussion. It has to be focused on the matter in hand. You have to get decisions made. But I have to accept that these committees are only advisory. Hart District Council is the planning authority; and Hampshire County looks after highways and transport.

Cllr. Steve Forster (Hampshire County Councillor for Fleet) remembers …

I've worked with Alan on FTC for a number of years. His image is one that means many don't take him seriously, but my experience of working with him is that he is one of the best councillors I've met. Great understanding of rules, process and procedures – and he appreciates the need to run the council efficiently and fairly, and to listen to residents and ensure they are never ignored or forced to accept something which isn't right for the community.

He spends much time engaging with locals – sometimes over a pint or three in the Prince Arthur, but just as often on the street, in a shop, or anywhere residents gather or happen to pigeon hole him. His attention to detail is exemplary, and he always raises and follows through on residents' issues to ensure they are addressed. I know as I often get calls asking for action!

As an example of his approach, a few years ago there was concern about the state of disrepair of the Fleet Town pavements. This was raised at a council meeting and none of the other councillors stepped forward to take any action. Nonetheless Alan offered to write a report and I volunteered to help him, with detail of what needed doing and that required evidence.

We arranged to meet – and he ensured it happened within a few days. Rather than a fast (15 minute) walk up and down the street, we spent some hours – actually around five hours – together walking the length of the high street in both directions – where we carefully noted each and every fault we found. Broken paving, temporary asphalt repairs, dirty bus stops, graffiti, weeds, overgrown trees. The list was comprehensive and complete. It took so long as we both found much to comment upon, as well as being stopped by many to enquire of us, 'What are you doing?' And many more who just wanted to engage with Alan as a friend and councillor.

It was a pleasurable and informative day, and we subsequently presented this evidence to colleagues so that the issues were addressed. That involved County Council and highways staff, Hart and Fleet council officers, and as a result most defects were resolved. There was even a volunteer day where Fleet Council volunteers washed the bus shelters and lampposts and painted the benches. This was real community spirit in action and much was a result of Alan's focus. It was a Town Council Action Day initiative – which has carried on each year.

I spent much time that day with Alan and had good opportunity to talk with him. His political views on the whole are pragmatic and frequently sensible, but with a good bit of hilarity and humour thrown in. However, they're underpinned by a sound approach to supporting residents and making the community better for all. I enjoyed that day, and the few pints we drank, then and subsequently. It's a pleasure to have Alan as one of our local councillors.

Dan Proctor (former manager of the Prince Arthur in Fleet) remembers …

Alan was the local Fleet Town Councillor when the pub's planning application for an expanded garden area with floodlights was refused. Alan was on holiday at the time but promised me he would sort it out when he got back and true to his word he got the planning permission agreed the day he got back from holiday.

I've generated quite a bit of publicity for Fleet too – lots of articles in the local paper and so on. I've just started my third term of four years so I must be doing something right. We really should have built the bypass round the town, it would have improved the town centre. The night-time economy is thriving now, and there is not a lot of trouble at night. A bit of vandalism sometimes and that's about it. But we do need to find a way of making the town more attractive to shoppers. We pay to park here. Why would you when you can park in the local supermarkets for free?

And that brings us to Hope Walk, some new houses close to the station. Hart District Council wanted to call it Village Way. Fleet Town Council didn't like that name because Fleet's not a village. So we wrote back objecting, and they asked for our suggestions. Well. It's quite close to Fleet Pond, so one of the councillors, with a glint in his eye, suggested Hope Springs. That was agreed and we put that forward. But the County Council felt that Hope Walk would be better. We agreed with that. So it's named after me … Hope Walk. If you go past now, you'll see that the road name is missing on one side. The Town will swear blind that I nicked that, and it's on my toilet wall.

It's not. I wish it was. I wish I'd thought of it first.

NEWS & MAIL
6TH JUNE 2013

Loony idea ended up as a nice Walk

Fame at last! (Courtesy Fleet News and Mail)

CHAPTER 21

Little fish in a big pond …

I've stood 27 times for general elections and by-elections over a period of 36 years. They are usually great fun and I love doing it. I have some good memories of those various campaigns.

General elections

I've stood in all general elections since 1983, except for 1997 when Norma was very ill. Sutch was also having a bad time after his mother's death so he didn't stand either. That year, the Party polled over 8,000 votes. A total only surpassed in the 2019 General Election. Here's a list of my results:

Year	Constituency	Votes	% votes	Position
1983	Teignbridge	241	0.46	4 of 4
1987	Teignbridge	312	0.45	4 of 4
1992	Teignbridge	437	0.70	4 of 5
2001	Aldershot	390	0.90	4 of 6
2005	Aldershot	553	1.00	6 of 6
2010	Witney	234	0.40	6 of 11
2015	Uxbridge and South Ruislip	72	0.20	8 of 13
2017	Maidenhead	119	0.20	9 of 13
2019	North-East Hampshire	576	1.00	6 of 6

In all of these elections, the Conservative candidate has won. I must be their lucky mascot!

Teignbridge (Devon) – 1983, 1987, 1992

I first stood against Patrick Nichols – my local MP in Devon – in 1983.

I put it in the local paper that Screaming Lord Sutch was to come into town to support his candidate in the general election. Patrick Nicholls saw this and decided to do a similar thing on the same day and bring in Geoffrey Howe. What a mistake that was! The town loved it. It was a Wednesday – Market Day. The town was packed – all the farmers were there; all the traders were there.

Geoffrey Howe was standing on the steps of a pub called 'The Silent Whistle' making a speech … "Blah blah blah." I was standing down there in my white suit, waving bits of paper at him. His entourage kept snatching the paper out of my hand, but I just produced another one, and another one. We didn't heckle him, and we were still waiting for Sutch to turn up – he was always late. Anyway, I heard this shout through a megaphone. I turned round and there were about 20 of them getting out of this coach, walking down the road towards Geoffrey Howe. You couldn't have timed it any better. Perfect timing. Geoffrey Howe was supposed to be on a 45-minute walkabout around the town. But he went after ten minutes. He couldn't put up with us. I remember following him around. All the time Patrick Nicholls kept trying to trip me up. You know, the schoolboy trip-up. That was a day that Ashburton will never forget – the day Geoffrey Howe came to town. And the headlines in the paper: "The Chancellor didn't budget for 'The Great White Hope'" What a fantastic headline. Geoffrey Howe's debating skills were once described as "like being savaged by a dead sheep". That day, he was a lamb to the slaughter.

Rosemary Christophers remembers …

That was quite an event when Geoffrey Howe was chased by Alan and David Sutch. He cut short his speech and ran across the road to take refuge in my care home. Great fun!

In 1987 and 1992 I stood again against Patrick Nichols. I remember being at the 1992 Candidates and Agents meeting and Patrick Nichols saying: "Hello, Alan. You're standing again. Lots of publicity for the Golden Lion again, isn't it?" And indeed, it was.

In 1997 I didn't stand due to Norma's MS. But I do remember standing twice in Aldershot in 2001 and 2005.

Aldershot (Hampshire) – 2001 and 2005

In 2001 King Arthur Pendragon was standing. He was a local man, but now lives down by Stonehenge. I know him very well. I was next to him on the stage. I said: "You know what? I've never come last yet in an election."

When they read the results out he nudged me and said: "You have now." He beat me by just a few votes. What a Loony Disaster!

Conference at the Dog and Partridge. (My private collection)

Then in 2005 I got more votes in a general election than ever before – 553. The Sunday Express picked up on that. They billed it as one of the most amazing things to happen in politics. "Look out, politicians. They're behind you!" It was quite a big story. It's odd. I got 553 in Aldershot, and I got 553 votes in the Leicester South By-Election. What odds would I have got on that? But that's the most votes I ever got until 2019; 553, but in two different places. Once again, the papers have picked up on that as unusual. It's all good fun. It's not an ego-trip. It's good fun.

Sir Gerald Howarth remembers …

I did have the temerity to stand against Alan twice in Aldershot, and narrowly managed to defeat him by several thousand votes on both occasions.

The key thing about Alan is that he is always very good-natured. There is no nastiness about him. Actually, he secured his best ever result against me when he won 553 votes, but not enough to retain his deposit.

I have a wonderful story about one of their Annual Conferences held at his pub – the Dog and Partridge at Yateley. Watching them do the Cabinet Reshuffle with a wardrobe on the green outside the pub. It was absolutely hilarious, wonderful. Amusing, fun, and a real mickey-take of the political system. That just encapsulates the essence of the OMRLP and demonstrates their complete lack of malice.

At the count at one General Election in the Prince's Hall in Aldershot, I started getting some pretty nasty grief from some Labour supporters, none of whom I knew. They were not Labour councillors (all of whom I knew well), certainly not mainstream party people. They were accusing me of being a warmonger and a murderer, and it was getting quite nasty. Quite a bit of alcohol was flowing and it was looking like it could get physical. Then all of a sudden about three OMRLP people with Alan, just stepped in and came to my defence. That episode left an indelible mark on me, and it demonstrated that these guys were serious, intelligent guys. They are all a bit quirky, but they are not stupid, and they add to the spice of electioneering.

For me, the real purpose of the party is to add that sense of fun and lightening things up a bit. Elections are important. They do determine the future direction and the destiny of the nation for the next five years. And ergo they are absolutely critical. Those of us who are active with the main political parties are really fighting for the soul of the nations, and for the destiny of the nation.

The OMRLP acts as a kind of foil to all that earnestness which you find in the major political parties, particularly the Tory Party and the Labour Party. So it's an amusing diversion. Adds to the gaiety of life. And that's the thing, these guys invest a lot of money and time in standing at elections. It's not so expensive, but it's not cheap either, especially if you lose your deposit.

It's true there is no coherent political philosophy to the OMRLP. But if the day ever comes when one emerges, the party will become irrelevant, or perhaps redundant would be a better term.

Although there are some of their policies that have found their way onto the Statute Book: Passports for Pets, for one. And perhaps Pets for Passports may become a post-Brexit Loony policy – as long as we spray all the poodles blue.

Uxbridge – 2015

Then I stood in Uxbridge against Boris Johnson in 2015. I got on well with his sister Sarah, and Rod Liddle, the journalist.

Thinks: "You are a real Loony, Boris!" (Courtesy Steve Lawson)

The photo of me gazing at Boris was taken as he was proclaiming that he would lie down in front of the bulldozers to prevent the 3rd runway being built at Heathrow. I thought that was a Loony idea!

I only got 72 votes. Boris sent me a present to remember the night – a copy of his book *72 Virgins*.

Steve Lawson remarks …

Both myself and Joy, my wife, have supported Alan at seven major elections including three general elections at Uxbridge, Maidenhead and North-East Hampshire where I was his agent. We usually stay in the count location for a few days and get involved in campaigning. Personal highlight was taking that photograph of Alan looking into Boris Johnson's eyes as he did his acceptance speech.

I don't do door-knocking, but I do try to get round the public houses. That's where you meet the real people. I'm not loony enough to knock on doors.

The Flying Brick comments …

With national elections, you have to get nominated by ten local electors. That can be hard. Alan's approach was always to try and get people in the pub.

I prefer to go door-knocking, and that's much easier. I'm 6ft 5in and in full regalia, and a top-hat that adds another 2½ ft, I make quite an impression! When I explain who I am, they are normally relieved. People under 40, often haven't heard of us, but older voters have, and they are normally happy to nominate.

So we have different approaches. I don't think I'd focus on Wetherspoons so much, but Alan loves them, and it works for him.

The media always love us 'cause we're interesting and different – we relieve their boredom. But you do get some people who want to have a go at you – you're a disgrace to this country and so on. But it's quite rare, most people are friendly and nearly always say they will vote for us. But of course, we never know if they do. But if a smile was a vote, we'd win by a landslide.

North-East Hampshire – 2019

In this most recent election, I decided to stand on my home ground in Hampshire. Lord Buckethead has decided to join the Loony Party and he was taking on Boris Johnson in Uxbridge. It was an interesting campaign. I took part in a debate at Balliol College, Oxford, a podcast for The Times, and I was interviewed at length for Japanese TV. It was all good fun and it seemed to work. I polled 576 votes, 1% of the vote. My best ever.

Making my 'acceptance speech' in NE Hampshire. (My private collection)

But of course, the sitting MP Ranil Jayawardena won with 60% of the vote and a massive majority!

With Ranil Jayawardena at the count. (My private collection)

You might have noticed that the general elections in 2010 and 2017 are missing here. I'll come back to those two in a bit.

R U Seerius remembers …

I remained in contact with Alan and he asked that I attend an election in 1999 at Kensington and Chelsea (Michael Portillo was standing).

We spent most of the time in a local pub, surrounded by reporters, and I felt totally out of place, but Alan kept me near and reassured me that he would get me into the count. (I didn't have a pass)

There were several other Loony Party stalwarts there and I didn't think I stood a chance, but somehow Alan and his agent Peter Stockton sorted it for me to attend. It was surreal, the security was very tight and I ended up on the balcony.

By-elections

Quite an impressive list of by-election 'victories', don't you think!

Year	*Constituency*	*Votes*	*% Votes*	*Position*
1999	Eddisbury	238	0.70	4 of 6
1999	Kensington and Chelsea	20	0.10	17 of 18
2003	Brent East	59	0.28	13 of 16
2004	Hartlepool	80	0.30	12 of 14
2006	Blaenau Gwent	318	1.20	6 of 6
2007	Sedgefield	129	0.50	10 of 11
2009	Norwich North	144	0.40	9 of 12
2011	Leicester South	553	1.60	5 of 5
2011	Barnsley Central	198	0.80	8 of 9
2012	Bradford West	111	0.30	8 of 8
2012	Manchester Central	78	0.40	10 of 12
2013	Eastleigh	136	0.30	9 of 14
2013	South Shields	197	0.80	8 of 9
2014	Clacton-on-Sea	127	0.40	7 of 8
2016	Tooting	54	0.20	7 of 14
2016	Richmond Park	184	0.80	4 of 8
2018	Lewisham East	93	0.40	9 of 14
2019	Peterborough	112	0.33	10 of 15

Celebrating another Victory: The Iconic Arty Pole, The Incredible Flying Brick, Lady Hell 'n' Back, and me. (My private collection)

Eddisbury – 1999

This was the first one I stood in after David Sutch died. Tony Blair was there one day. Never got close to him. He was PM at the time and well protected.

Kensington and Chelsea – 1999

My worse ever result. Just 20 votes. But I didn't come last.

Brent-East – 2003

I don't remember much of this one, although I got on with Sarah Tether (LibDem) really well. We were both in the same Indian restaurant one night, and it was a good chat.

She was at another by-election, I think Leicester South in 2004. R U Seerius stood for us, but Sarah was there too. She introduced me to her candidate, saying: "I quite like Alan, 'cos whenever he comes along, we win."

Hartlepool – 2004

Ronnie Carroll, the singer who had a hit with the song 'Roses are Red', stood for the Rainbow Alliance Party, linked to Cynthia Payne. But I got more votes than he did. At the end when all the results had been read out, he and I sang 'Danny Boy'. It went down really well. Fathers for Justice were causing a fuss at that time. There was a young female candidate standing for the Liberal Democrats and they threw loads of purple flour over her at the count. They got arrested. She cried her eyes out. It was not a nice thing to do. She came a close second though.

Blaenau Gwent – 2006

Blaenau Gwent. That was a very depressing place to be. Just a big empty space where the steel works used to be. Everyone seemed to be out of work as a result. It's almost enough to make you vote Labour! Although the election was won by an independent.

Sedgefield – 2007

Tony Blair's old seat. Not much happened there really. I didn't stand against him in the 2005 general election, but our 'Mad Cow Girl' did and came a very credible 9th out of 15.

Norwich North – 2009

I got a gross of votes there – 144. I came 9th out of 12 so that was pretty good.

Leicester South – 2011

This was where my votes equalled the 553 I got in Aldershot. Keith Vaz MP was there. He asked us to do a speech to his supporters. I guess there were about 20 of us there. We had to introduce ourselves and explain who we were and what we stood for. It went down well. We had a lot of people saying to us afterwards that they'd followed us for years, but never actually met us before. It was a good turnout.

Barnsley Central – 2011

Dan Jarvis, an ex-soldier, was standing there for Labour and he won easily with the UKIP candidate a distant second. This is where I met Nigel Farage (then UKIP Leader) for the first time and we have been close friends ever since.

> ***Nigel Farage remembers …***
>
> The first by-election in which we (UKIP) came second was Barnsley in 2011. When the result was announced there were a load of UKIP people there holding up placards, and there is a wonderful photograph of Alan holding up a UKIP placard – terrific.

Two great photos from Barnsley. (My private collection)

Bradford West – 2012

Bradford West was good fun against George Galloway. He refused to have his photograph taken with us. He's as irascible as he seems on TV. Our boys in Manchester had written a song about him, which they sang to him. It was quite a funny song, but I don't think he liked it. Really he won because of the Asian vote.

On the platform with George Galloway. (My private collection)

Nigel Farage comments …

Well Alan is a regular at by-elections and I've been at the same counts with him many times over the years. I've always had a very good relationship with him. He has a terrific sense of humour. He's great fun, but how he's still alive is completely beyond me.

I have watched him everywhere from Eastleigh to Bradford. I watched him arrive in a constituency, find a friendly pub, and that's base-camp. Then he sits there from midday till closing time – he loves a beer – and he waits for people to come to him. Over the years, I've always made an effort to pop in and see him.

Manchester Central – 2012

Manchester Central. That was pretty dull. There was no vibe. The count was in a massive hall, so cold. The by-election was triggered when the sitting MP – Tony Lloyd (Labour) – resigned in order to stand for Police and Crime Commissioner. Lucy Powell retained the seat for Labour. She got ten times the votes of the second-place candidate.

Eastleigh – 2013

Eastleigh in 2013 was good fun, and I enjoyed myself when the result was announced – over to Derrill …

Derrill Carr remembers …

I attended the count at Eastleigh and witnessed for myself the complete transformation of Alan Hope into the 'Howling Laud' – the charismatic Leader of the Monster Raving Loony Party. He didn't even get close to winning, but everybody wanted to interview and take photos of him and towards the end of the night around 3am he stepped forward to give his closing speech and surprised everybody when he burst into song and treated us all to his version of 'Mack The Knife'.

Nigel Farage was at Eastleigh supporting Diane James (future UKIP Leader). She came second, less than 1,800 votes behind the winner. Chris Huhne Lib Dem MP and senior member of the Conservative/Lib Dems Coalition Government (2010 to 2012) had resigned, so it was a very high-profile election. There were cameras and reporters from all around the world.

'Mack the Knife' live at Eastleigh. (My private collection)

South Shields – 2013

I remember haranguing Harriet Harman in the street – outside Greggs – there are loads of them in South Shields. She didn't want to engage at first, but eventually I got a smile and a handshake out of her. Nigel Farage spent some time there too. The UKIP office was just across from the hotel we were staying in. We had some good fun with them. I've always liked Nigel. He's really friendly, and always telling people how great we are. He's always saying that we have had more policies adopted than they have.

Harriet Harman caught in the street. (My private collection)

R U Seerius remembers …

When we were in South Shields, we couldn't find Alan. So I asked some locals to direct me to the nearest Wetherspoons. Sure enough, there was Alan holding fort at the bar!

I was invited along to the UKIP post-election party, and Nigel was very welcoming. He made a great fuss of me and announced that I had come along to defect to UKIP. I had to correct him: "No, Nigel. Not to defect. I've come to INFECT you with Loonyism."

Clacton – 2014

Clacton was interesting as this was when Douglas Carswell defected from the Tories, forced a by-election, and stood for UKIP … and won. He didn't look very happy when the result was announced. When I congratulated him on his win, he replied: "I'm not too sure I've done the right thing you know." History has been the judge of that!

Tooting – 2016

Tooting was not the place I expected it to be, but we ran a fun campaign. We met up with Rainbow George from the Rainbow Alliance Party. We made a record outside Tooting Bec station. George Weiss was his real name. Big friend of Ronnie Carroll and Peter Cook, and Ian Drury. Because of that we put it about that Ian Drury and Peter Cook where Loony Party members. I'm pretty sure Peter Cook would have liked to join us.

That by-election was triggered by Sadiq Khan resigning. It was won by Rosena Allin-Khan. I didn't get many votes – only 54. But there were seven candidates who got less that I did. I finished in the top half of the table. So that was really a good result.

Richmond – 2016

Richmond was good because I came in 4th behind Labour. I came in halfway. I remember standing next to Zac Goldsmith in Richmond. Everyone expected him to win, but he came a very close second. He was very dejected. I said: "Zac. You know how I feel now, don't you?" He just had a little wry smile.

Consoling Zac Goldsmith. (My private collection)

His father James started the Referendum Party, later to be led by Kilroy-Silk. Goldsmith liked us and suggested that one day he might sponsor us himself, but then he died so it never happened. I did email Zac after the by-election to ask him if he would carry out his father's wishes and sponsor us. He never replied!

I've got one of those in-flight airline magazines at home somewhere. It has James Goldsmith on the front cover, and a report about our Party Conference further on inside. It has a lovely photograph of us all in the ballroom at the Golden Lion.

R U Seerius remembers ...

I have attended many other elections as an agent with Alan and the thing one notices is the way he is always able (despite the chagrin of the Returning Officers) to stand next to the winning candidate, and invariably be the first to shake the winner's hand, in full view of the world's press.

I think the one time he did not next get to the winner, he still managed to sit on the stage in the front directly beneath the winning candidate. He's a Class Act. So he managed to be shown again with the winner, to the point where most photos of the winner are now head shots.

Making plans for Nigel! (My private collection)

Lewisham East – 2018

This was triggered by the resignation of Heidi Alexander to take up a role in the London Assembly. It was handsomely retained by Janet Daby for Labour, although her majority was reduced. Pretty uneventful.

Peterborough – 2019

This was an interesting by-election in that the incumbent MP had been de-selected by the constituency after she was convicted of Perverting the Course of Justice. It was also the first outing for the new BREXIT Party that Nigel Farage had created. BREXIT came second, only 600 votes away from victory. They were both delighted and disappointed. Maybe next time, Nigel!

With Katie Hopkins in Peterborough. (My private collection)

I had set up my HQ in a local pub. One day, Katie Hopkins was in town interviewing all the candidates in the market square. I refused to go. She had to come to me. We had a great time together, and she later Tweeted that she had enjoyed meeting me in person!

Nigel Farage remembers …

All in all, Alan has added to the gaiety of national life in a remarkable way. He's huge fun and a good friend. If anyone can't see the funny side of serious things, then I feel very sorry for them.

Long may it continue to flourish, and Alan with it.

Preparing for victory. (My private collection)

Who got most votes then, Nigel? (My private collection)

So that just leaves the times when David Cameron and Theresa May chose to stand against me.

CHAPTER 22

Cameron and May …

I stood against David Cameron in Witney in 2010. We had lots of fun there. We were good friends with Mr Cornish – landlord of the New Inn in Witney. He was the Conservative Association Chairman. We gave him loads of memorabilia to put up on the walls. David Cameron was often in there, so he must have seen it. When we had the Co-ALE-ition beer, the landlord put it on in his pub. It features David Cameron and me on the pump-clip. He must have seen that. Perhaps that's why he resigned. I probably had more interviews there than anywhere. I was there for ten days.

They read out the results in alphabetical order. So we're all lined up on the stage A to Z. I ended standing next to Cameron because of that. I didn't have to inveigle my way in. I was in all the camera shots. So when they announced: "Alan Howling Laud Hope (Monster Raving Loony Party) – 210." I just raised my arms in the air while we were shaking hands. He took it in good heart. He was shaking my hand and smiling. Perhaps he just had to. He couldn't have turned round and given me a left-hook, could he?

After the result was announced, and it was clear by then that David Cameron was not going to win a majority in the House, I gave him some advice on what to do next. "What you need to do now, David, is let Gordon Brown form a new government. It will be weak and fail. That will trigger another election and you'll sail home." If only he'd acted on my advice, he might have become a hero in the eyes of the public.

In those days, we were sponsored by William Hill, the bookmaker. They would pay the £500 deposits for us. They would also give prizes: £500 for the person who got most publicity; £250 for second;

and £100 for third. At Witney, they paid the deposit, and I won the prize for best publicity – simply because of that photo shot of me and Cameron. Nobody could beat that. Nobody at all. I think Dancing Ken, down in Cheltenham, got second; and Jason Chinnery in Chessington got third. That photo of me and Cameron made the Slovenian newspapers. I have a friend there and he sent me the cutting. I was going there anyway to visit him a couple of weeks later – for his birthday on June 25th. Most Slovenians don't know much about British politics, and there's me and David Cameron in their newspaper. They all thought I'd won.

Because of that I was invited as Guest of Honour to the new season wine tasting – up in the mountains somewhere. Thousands of people there and little old me as Guest of Honour. That weekend was the church carnival week as well. Three or four churches doing their own floats to go round town. I was made Guest of Honour to lead that. All because of this photograph in the newspaper. They all thought I'd won. I didn't tell them that I hadn't; but I didn't tell them that I had. The local winemaker, called Duchan, had a bit of a party in his garden – a proper wine garden. He wouldn't let me pay for anything. I got so drunk I had to stay away from him. But what good fun! I did go to the office of the newspaper, and I did manage to get six copies. I've still got some, but you can't understand a word of it, just 'Cameron' and 'Hope' and that's all. Alas, my friend, he lived in Fleet. His name was Geoff Andrews, he, sadly, fell down some steps and died. So I don't go there anymore.

That just leaves Theresa May. I thought it was a very crafty move when she called the general election. She was in a strong position, she could expect to pick up lots of seats, and come out with a hefty majority.

Well, how wrong I was, and how wrong she was! We all called it wrong.

Maidenhead was not the town I expected it to be. I thought it would be quite posh, but it's not at all.

But she decided to stand against me in Maidenhead, and as you know, she was not so much Theresa May as Theresa Dis-mayed. When she arrived at the count, I was right next to her. But she just whooshed straight past me. She wouldn't talk to the reporters, she wouldn't answer any questions, she didn't talk to anybody. There were all the cries of: "Prime Minister, are you going to resign?" and so forth. That didn't help her enjoyment of the evening did it?

Celebrating with David Cameron in 2010. (My private collection)

In discussion with Lord Buckethead. (My private collection)

We were all called together – all the candidates – and the Returning Officer tells us the result before we get on stage. I tried to give her a badge with her face on it and a speech balloon saying "Vote Loony." I said: "Go on. Take it. It's for you." She realised it was just a badge so she took it. She showed it to her minder chap, they both had a little smile, and she gave it back to me. I said: "No, no. It's yours. It's for you to keep." She said she couldn't as she had no pockets. So I took it back and said I would post it to her. "Oh," she said. "If you must." So I did!!

It was quite a boring count though. Election counts are normally much more fun than that. With 13 candidates, the Returning Officer didn't give us a right to reply. It's their call. Sometimes they allow everyone, sometimes just the first three, but 13 is a big number. It was all over pretty quickly on the night, and she was out the back door and away as soon as she'd made her acceptance speech. It wasn't an exciting night. I've been to much better. Generally the winner is glad to win, but in this case she was not in the best of moods.

I'm still standing! (My private collection)

My victory at Maidenhead. (My private collection)

Seeing red …

Apart from calling the election, I think the other big blunder she made was to walk into the count at Maidenhead dressed in red! Corbyn must have laughed himself all the way to bed.

Theresa May arriving at the count in Maidenhead. (My private collection)

They say Corbyn attracted a lot of the younger vote, partly through his policies, but especially through his use of social media like Facebook and Twitter. I don't think that was the key. It wasn't Corbyn attracting the younger vote, it was Theresa May and the Conservatives losing the older generation. I know at least six people in this town of Fleet – you meet all walks of life here in Wetherspoons – who are all staunch Conservatives, and they just wouldn't vote at all. They didn't want to vote for anyone else, but would not vote Conservative. If I knew six in Fleet, how many more people were there like that up and down the country? These are all people who are retired: they have their heating allowance; their bus passes; they don't want to be forced to sell their house.

It was just a terrible campaign. She wouldn't do any debates. She was supposed to be our leader, so people wanted to see her. It's no good hiding behind a wall.

And that phrase: "Strong and Stable". The only party you could describe as strong and stable is the OMRLP. I've been Leader for 20 years. If that's not strong and stable, I don't know what is.

I was invited to appear on The Last Leg the day after the election, but it was a bit of a disappointment. I was there all day, just for that walk-on part at the end. I can't say I know anything about the programme. I've never watched it. So many people watched all the way through that episode – it was a two-hour special. I got all these texts from people asking when I was coming on etc… I thought I'd get to say something. But Baroness Varsey was good. She was delighted to meet me. And Jamie Oliver was his usual amusing self.

I'm going to finish off this section with a quick reminder of my political achievements from 1983 to date. Wow. Is it really that long? I must be Loony!

- Setting up the Official Monster Raving Loony Party (OMRLP) with Screaming Lord David Sutch in June 1982. The Party has now been in existence for 37 years and I have been Leader for the last 20 years.
- I am the longest serving Leader of the OMRLP (20 years) and I am currently the longest serving Leader of any Political Party in Great Britain in over 100 years.
- Official Monster Raving Loony Party main policies which are now law include 24-hour all-day pub opening (1995), abolition of dog licences (1987), Passports for Pets (2001).
- I have represented the OMRLP in 9 General Elections from 1983 to 2019. In all 9 general election constituency seats which I have contested the Conservatives have gone on to win.

- I have represented the OMRLP in 18 by-elections from 1999-2019.
- I led the OMRLP into the Welsh Assembly elections in 2016. The OMRLP fielded a total of 25 candidates and were rewarded with their first ever TV election broadcast. I stood for the OMRLP in South Wales Central.
- I was elected Mayor of Ashburton (Devon) for two terms from 1998-2000 and still remembered in Ashburton to this day. I was invited back recently to open the annual Carnival.
- In 27 general and by-elections I have never been elected and have always lost my deposit, thereby maintaining the finest traditions of the OMRLP.
- My closest friends in politics are Nigel Farage and Sir Gerald Howarth.
- I have stood in elections against famous politicians including David Cameron in 2010 when he became PM, Theresa May in 2017 when she was the PM at the time, Boris Johnson, Sir Gerald Howarth, Michael Portillo, Douglas Carswell, Zac Goldsmith and George Galloway.
- In 1987 I became the first member of the OMRLP to be elected onto a Town Council – I served on Ashburton Town Council for a total of 13 years from 1987-2000.
- I was also elected Lord of the Borough and Chairman of the Town Council whilst representing the OMRLP and serving on Ashburton Town Council.
- I was first elected onto Fleet Town Council (FTC) in 2010 and then re-elected for 4 years in May 2018. I have served the local community for 9 consecutive years. I have served as Chairman and Deputy Chairman on several FTC committees. In total I have served my local communities for more than 20 years as a Local Councillor in Ashburton and Fleet.
- Hope Walk in Fleet has been so named in my honour.
- Under my leadership, the OMRLP is the only UK political party to have had their own commercial range of beers (13 in total)

which were successfully branded as Co-ALE-ition and went on to sell over 100,000 pints from 2013-2015 in 800 different pubs.

- I supported David Sutch at several high-profile by-elections e.g. Richmond (Yorkshire) when William Hague was first elected as an MP. In Bootle in May 1990 when the OMRLP received more votes than the continuing SDP party, a result which convinced David Owen to wind up the SDP a few weeks later. Bootle again in Nov 1990 when the OMRLP received more votes than the continuing Liberal party.
- In the 2019 General Election I achieved my personal best with 576 votes!

And I'm still going strong!

PART 6

BEER AND MORE …

In this Part:

CHAPTER 23

Having a Ball …

I have always loved beer … and parties. It was when I was running the Golden Lion that Alan Philips came into my life.

I used to run regular music quizzes at the Golden Lion – mainly based around my record collection. It would have been in 1986 when Alan turned up at one of my quizzes. He has a great knowledge of music, and we just got talking. Our record collections forged that initial bond, and we've stayed friends ever since. He worked at one of the other pubs in Ashburton, and he would sometimes drop by after-hours. We'd just sit up all night chatting and playing records.

Alan Phillips was a pretty good DJ too, and he was the DJ at a number of functions and parties at the Golden Lion, and sometimes we'd work as a 'double-act' trying to out-do each other. That was great fun.

Alan Phillips remembers …

I always made sure my record collection was properly catalogued, but Alan Hope's was always a right mess. He wasn't that careful with them either. He'd just leave them lying around. Alan talked too much when he was doing discos. I didn't do that. I think it stops people dancing. But he was always very entertaining when he was doing quizzes and the like. We were quite different in our approach.

So, it was Alan Phillips who first introduced me to the Bath Ball – a private party that happens every year. Sadly, Alan is no longer with us. Rest in Peace, my friend!

Alan Phillips explains …

The Bath Ball started in 1965 as a joint birthday party, and it just carried on. I got involved because I used to do the disco for them, and I was eventually asked to be one of the hosts. It's quite a good idea, but it's quite expensive if you go – about £2,000 per person. At first it was just a ball on the Friday, but people wanted to make it more of a weekend, so we did a disco on the Saturday. Then it extended to the Sunday. Some people start on a Thursday now. It was in the Assembly Rooms, but they fell out with us, so we went to the Pump Rooms a couple of times, but its current home is in the Pavilion at Bath. The disco always has a different fancy dress theme. It starts late after dinner, and can go on till mid-morning next day.

The Ball is big enough to attract some great musicians. Over the years, they've booked some great acts: Steve Gibbons, Mike Pender and the Searchers, Mud, Dave Berry and many others.

At the Bath Ball they always have fancy dress. For their 25th anniversary, the theme was 'Back to your school-days'. So we went down to see my friend Lionel in Torquay who has a costume hire business, and got ourselves kitted out with school uniforms (see photo). Short-trousers and all. That's me holding my crotch. That was all fun with girls dressed in gymslips or as headmistresses. There was one guy dressed as a headmaster in all his robes. I got some paper and wrote: 'Sir interfered with me behind the bike-shed', and I managed to clip this on the back of his mortar-board. He didn't know why everyone was laughing at him, and he wasn't too pleased when he found out. Our satchels were full of fake spiders, cars and marbles. We would try to run the cars up the girls' legs to see how far we could get: "Can I put my car in your garage?" But we never got past the thigh!

George and me at the Bath Ball. (Courtesy of George Stone)

But as I say. It's private party so you just can't turn up – strictly by invitation. It's a fun few days though, so if you ever do get the chance…

Due to my superstar status, I get invited to many fund-raising and charity events. I don't want to brag, so I'll just mention a couple. I open the Phyllis Tuckwell Garden Party every year, and I also support charities for MS. I've done some stuff for a dog rescue charity too. I have a secret job of turning on the Christmas lights in Fleet every year. The switch on the podium is a dummy. The real one is outside the pub. I have to make sure I get the timing right so it looks seamless.

CHAPTER 24

Wetherspoons …

As you know, I like a pint or two every now and then, and I like the Wetherspoons concept. Back in 2000 to 2005 when I had the Dog and Partridge in Yateley, a friend of mine visited and he had a Wetherspoons directory with him. It listed all the Wetherspoons pubs county by county – names, addresses, phone numbers. And each had a little box alongside that you could tick when you'd been there.

I was surprised. I hadn't realised that Wetherspoons had that many pubs at that time. I got myself one of those directories, and I started marking off the ones that I had been in. The first I ever went in was the London Inn at Torquay back when I was still living in Devon – but I didn't realise then it was a Wetherspoons. The first one I knowingly went into was in Winchester – called the Gaol House. So I started marking them off.

Then it just became an ambition. If I was, say, doing a by-election somewhere, I'd get to the hotel, park up, and do a little tour of the local Wetherspoons on the bus – using my bus-pass. It was fun. And I soon got to mark off 500.

I got in touch with Tim Martin who owns Wetherspoons, and lo and behold, they did a story on me. So I became not just the Leader of the OMRLP, but a recognised Wetherspoons Ambassador too. Later, of course, Tim Martin sponsored me for a by-election. Wetherspoons were very interested when we launched our Co-ALE-ition beers. Wetherspoon's publish four magazines a year, and I think that over the last six years or so, I've been in 12 of them, and there are more to come. I always use a local Wetherspoons as my HQ when I stand in an election, so it's good publicity all round.

I've been to most of their pubs now – I'll tell you just how many in a bit, but there's almost 900 operating as of 2019 and it's hard to keep up. At first it was easy, I could cover all the pubs in a county and feel pleased. But now new ones keep opening in counties I've done – so I have to keep going back to pick them off one at a time. I've done them all in Wales except two, but none in Scotland or Ireland. In places like Cumbria and Merseyside and Cheshire, I've done the whole lot. And most in the south, although there's a gap in Kent I need to fill – again I'll come back to that!

I was a VIP guest at the Opening Ceremony when The Queen Hotel in Aldershot, a pub I knew very well in my youth, reopened after a major refurbishment by Wetherspoons in April 2014. It was great to see that impressive old public house getting a new lease of life – thank you, Tim!

I admire Tim Martin and JD Wetherspoons for saving so many historic and loved High Street buildings for future generations to appreciate by converting them into pubs for the community whilst at the same time preserving and enhancing their internal and external features. There are hundreds of examples of former banks, post offices, cinemas and theatres which have been saved from demolition. I love visiting Wetherspoon pubs and learning about the history of the building and local area from the information Wetherspoons always display inside. My target for 2020 is to visit Wetherspoons' largest pub, the 'Royal Victoria Pavilion' which opened in 2017 on the beach at Ramsgate. This building was a dilapidated Grade 2 listed Pavilion, unoccupied for ten years, which Wetherspoons saved after investing £5M whilst at the same time retaining all of the main features.

Opening of the Queen Hotel in Aldershot with Terry Bridgeman, Mayor of Rushmoor. (My private collection)

In 2018, my 'local' Wetherspoons in Fleet, the Prince Arthur, celebrated its 20th birthday. Of course, I was Guest of Honour.

Celebrating at the Prince Arthur – Steve Lawson, me, James Norris-McCann (the manager) and Derrill Carr. (My private collection)

And just recently, I achieved a long-held goal to visit 700 Wetherspoons. It's rather fitting. My 700th was 'The Golden Hope' in Sittingbourne in Kent, and that's the gap I had to fill. It was great fun.

Two great pictures from The Golden Hope. (My private collection)

But it doesn't end there. JD Wetherspoon has just (December 2019) celebrated its 40th anniversary. Of course I was invited to be the VIP guest to this special anniversary event which took place in London, exactly 40 years to the very day after Tim Martin opened his very first pub, which was 'Martin's Free House' in Muswell Hill.

The Furlong – the original Martin's Free House, London. (My private collection)

I was dressed in my all-white suit and Stetson hat as I was performing the role of JD Boss Hogg from the Dukes of Hazzard cult TV series from the late 1970s. Boss Hogg was the origin of the JD part of the JD Wetherspoon name. My friend Steve Lawson was dressed for the part of Mr Wetherspoon, Tim Martin's geography teacher when he was at school in New Zealand.

There were 25 in the group and we all met up at Wetherspoons' 'Lord Moon of the Mall' in Whitehall where we had breakfast and a pint of Ruby Abbot Ale brewed by Greene King especially for this 40-year anniversary event. Tim Martin paid for our breakfasts and this first pint and Greene King provided specially inscribed 40-year anniversary glass tankards for us.

Two photos from the Lord Moon of the Mall. Even Boris Johnson showed up for the second one! (My private collection)

JD Wetherspoon's official photographer was with us as was a reporter/photographer from the Independent newspaper.

I then travelled to Tim's very first pub in Muswell Hill now called The Furlong. It was the very first Wetherspoon-branded free house, when he re-named it in 1980. The landlord of the Furlong had put on a buffet lunch for us, which was very kind.

I then visited two more North London Wetherspoon pubs – the Mossy Well and the Toll Gate before finishing the Tour at the Rochester Castle in Stoke Newington which is currently JD Wetherspoon's longest trading pub (36 years).

Lots of very good publicity in the full-page story which appeared in the Independent newspaper the next day, in the JD Wetherspoon quarterly magazine for Spring Quarter 2020, and also in The London Drinker February 2020 issue (CAMRA magazine).

But I need to tell you about another project I've been involved in over the last few years. That is the story of Co-ALE-ition Ales, and it follows in the next chapter.

CHAPTER 25

The remarkable story of Co-ALE-ition – the drinks are on me!!

(My sincere thanks to Derrill Carr for his help in writing this section.)

It has always been one of my long-term ambitions to have a beer named after the Official Monster Raving Loony Party. I discussed this with my friend, Derrill Carr, a CAMRA member, who I knew had very good micro-brewery contacts.

Between us, after many hours of discussion and lots of fun and laughs along the way, we eventually came up with an original idea for the Official Monster Raving Loony Party beer brand. This brand would feature a very special photograph of David Cameron and me taken together at the Witney General Election in 2010 as the centrepiece on the pump clips and labels. The photo of David Cameron and me was taken when Cameron stepped forward to make his winner's speech and I stepped forward and shook his hand and at the same time I lifted my own arm in triumph. This photo went viral worldwide and was on TV and in lots of national newspapers and magazines. It was a Loony thing to do at the time but this photo launched the Co-ALE-ition brand. The unique brand name we came up with was 'Co-ALE-ition'; this name could be linked to the Coalition Government operating in the UK at the time. The ALE letters in our Co-ALE-ition name represented 'Another Loony Experience' to reflect that no other UK political party had ever brewed their own ale before.

Derrill Carr remembers …

I enjoyed working with Alan on the Co-ALE-ition project and it was very different from what I had ever done before. I learnt for the first time what 100% delegation meant. As an accountant for 40 years I was used to working within a budget and keeping costs under control but none of this experience prepared me for working with Alan on Co-ALE-ition without any budget at all.

The first brewery we approached in June 2013 expressed interest but didn't follow this opportunity up. Then shortly afterwards, during a Meet the Brewer event at the Prince Arthur in Fleet, we spoke to the owner and head brewer of Longdog brewery based near Basingstoke. We told him that we wanted a local micro-brewery to brew a special ale to celebrate the 30-year anniversary that year (2013) of when the Official Monster Raving Loony Party was officially registered in 1983 as a UK political party. It was also 30 years in June 1983 when I stood in Teignbridge at my first general election for the Monster Raving Loony party. The Longdog owner and head brewer confirmed at the end of a long night that he was very interested. We then went along to his brewery for a tasting session the very next day and selected the first ever Official Monster Raving Loony Party ale which was a bitter we called 'Winning Co-ALE-ition'. When coming up with this name I was thinking at the time about David Cameron holding my hand up as the real winner at Witney on the photo we used for the pump clip and what could have been achieved if there had been a coalition between the Conservatives and the Official Monster Raving Loony Party with a high-priority role for myself as the Deputy Prime Minister. We spent a lot of time designing an eye-catching pump clip unique to the Loony Party in the Loony Party black and yellow colours.

Pump clip for Winning Co-ALE-ition. (My private collection)

Phil Robins of Longdog Brewery remembers …

When Alan Hope asked me to create a special brew for the Monster Raving Loony Party's 30-year anniversary my first reaction was to laugh but then I thought, *What a brilliant idea. David Cameron doesn't have his own ale.*

Winning Co-ALE-ition was officially launched in September 2013 at the Longdog brewery where the VIP guest was Pete Staples of the Troggs group from the 1960s who had many Top 10 hit records. This event at the brewery was attended by around 40 people and was followed the next day by a Launch Party at the Prince Arthur pub in Fleet attended by 350 people.

Derrill Carr remembers …

At the launch event at the Prince Arthur, Alan bought a cask of ale from the Longdog brewery and went around with a tray giving his 350 guests a sample of his ale. It was the smallest sample possible in the smallest glass available which made people laugh but nobody could have forecasted the number of people who turned up at this event.

Pete Staples of the Troggs. (My private collection)

Another launch photo with my grandson, Matt Seale, to the left.

(My private collection)

I gave a speech at the Prince Arthur event and then I was presented with a special anniversary cake by Colin Bex (Leader of the Wessex Regionalist Party) to celebrate 30 years of the Monster Raving Loony Party. Lots of my friends attended including Sir Gerald Howarth (Aldershot & Farnborough MP) who I was very surprised to see as he had been in France all day on government business, and Terry Bridgeman (Mayor of Rushmoor) together with 30 local councillors and both the leaders from Hart District Council and Fleet

Town Council, as well as several Loony Party members. It was a fabulous night and over 100 people were still there at midnight and this event is still remembered fondly by those who attended.

Dan Proctor, manager of the Prince Arthur in Fleet in 2013, recalls …

It was an unusual and memorable evening and the pub was packed out. Winning Co-ALE-ition will now become the locally brewed ale that is always available at the Prince Arthur and this will continue as long as there is sufficient demand from customers.

Sir Gerald Howarth remembers …

I received an invitation from Alan to go to the launch party there. I wasn't sure if I should go. Was I going to get labelled as a Loony in the local paper with whom I had a pretty ambivalent relationship? But in the end, my wife and I went along to the Prince Arthur, and when we opened the door, all my Conservative friends were there. The Chairman of Hart DC was there, the Leader of HDC, Stephen Parker was there, lots of my Councillors from Aldershot and Farnborough were there, and it was a great night.

Gerald Howarth (far left), and three local dignitaries. (My private collection)

Derrill and I managed to convince the JD Wetherspoon pub chain to stock Winning Co-ALE-ition in some of their pubs and very soon afterwards my beer became the best-selling ale (300 pints a week) in my local pub, the Prince Arthur in Fleet. It was great whenever I went in there to see my face on the pump clip and see people enjoying my beer which often prompted the start of many enjoyable conversations and friendships. People travelled from all over the UK to the Prince Arthur to drink Winning Co-ALE-ition and would often ask the bar staff if I was in and they would come over for a chat. Some of them even thought I had brewed the ale myself which was perhaps a step too far even for a Loony.

Derrill and I visited lots of local pubs and convinced many of them to stock our Winning Co-ALE-ition ale. I remember one country pub in a Tory heartland village in Hampshire refusing to stock our ale, their excuse being that Co-ALE-tion was a political ale which was a first for the OMRLP.

The great success and high profile of Winning Co-ALE-ition led to approaches from other micro-breweries and a decision was taken to expand the range of Loony Party beers and offer four more different styles of Co-ALE-ition ale. The first of which was 'Co-ALE-ition GOLD', a golden ale, brewed by Langham brewery in West Sussex. The GOLD name we chose was very topical at the time as it stood for 'George Osborne Lowers Duty' to celebrate the first time beer duty had ever been reduced by a Chancellor in living memory. We went to the launch event at the Langham brewery in December 2013 where I was introduced to Fanny the Fermenter who had played an important role in brewing our beer.

Tony Lea, CAMRA representative for locally brewed ales, comments …

The Co-ALE-ition range of ales boosted the turnover and profits of several local breweries through the free publicity they all received from Alan's visits to their breweries.

Very soon afterwards we launched my third Co-ALE-ition ale called 'Hope & Glory'. This was an IPA we converted to mean 'Insanity Prevents Austerity' which I am confident the Loony Party would have delivered if we had been the Conservatives' partner in the coalition.

The next two Co-ALE-ition launches, again in December 2013, were both in Somerset. Milk Street brewery in Frome produced a stout called 'Dark Side' and the same day we went on to the Cheddar brewery in Cheddar Gorge to launch a Porter called 'In the Black'. We stayed in Somerset overnight at my good friend Roger Bastable's Haslelbury Mill Hotel near Crewkerne. Roger invited us to have a few drinks in his Windy Miller bar and then to join him in the Tythe Barn for a Christmas dinner and a dance. A young lady asked to borrow my hat and I thought I was never going to see it again but I eventually caught up with her on the dance floor. By the end of 2013 and just three months after Winning Co-ALE-ition was launched, there were now five different Co-ALE-ition ales available and they were all proving to be very popular.

With Roger "Windy Miller" Bastable, and 5 co-ALE-ition beers on hand. (My private collection)

After a gap of three months we decided to further expand the range of Co-ALE-ition ales. In April 2014 we launched 'HowlinGale', an old-style ale, at the Wild Weather Brewery in Silchester (Berkshire). HowlinGale was a reference to my Loony Party name 'Howling Laud'. After the brewery we went to three pubs in Reading which all stocked Co-ALE-ition beers that night.

We then approached Mash brewery in East Stratton near Winchester to brew a Co-ALE-ition beer called 'Monster Mash'. They were delighted to be involved and we went to the Mash brewery for a tasting session. Up to now the previous six Co-ALE-ition ales had always used the photo of myself with David Cameron on the pump clip but on this occasion we decided to take a completely different approach and selected a photo of myself with the whole OMRLP cabinet for the Monster Mash pump clip. This created a lot of additional interest in the Co-ALE-ition brand.

Quintin Drake — Local CAMRA expert in dark ales – remarks …

I was very pleased that Alan selected two dark ales for his Co-ALE-ition range and because of the connection to the Loony Party, he got a lot more people drinking dark ales.

Howlin' Gale pump clip. (My private collection)

The Monster Mash launch in May 2014 was probably the best one of the lot because for the first and only time the whole of the OMRLP cabinet attended, probably because they were all on the pump clip!! The launch started off at the Mash brewery and then we went to the Fulflood Arms in Winchester; the landlord loved the Loony Party and was a big fan of Screaming Lord Sutch and he showed us some Lord Sutch memorabilia that he got Sutch to sign in 1997 when he was in Winchester for a by-election. Monster Mash was on sale, as was Winning Co-ALE-ition, and it was a very enjoyable party as all of the locals got involved.

A great photo was taken in the Fulflood Arms of the full OMRLP cabinet in exactly the same pose as the photo on the pump clip. We then all walked to the Albion pub near Winchester station which also had Monster Mash on sale along with two other Co-ALE-ition beers. The Monster Mash song was played in both pubs every half hour and everybody got up and danced but nobody could match my moves. The Albion pub was Screaming Lord Sutch's HQ, as confirmed by the blue plaque on the pub wall, when he stood for the OMRLP in the Winchester by election in Feb 1997. I was there myself supporting Screaming Lord Sutch for the whole week of his campaign and this proved to be the final time that Screaming Lord Sutch stood in an election.

Monster Mash triggered lots of other opportunities including a new record and a promotional video which I thoroughly enjoyed making at Stoke Newington Cemetery. This involved the original Monster Mash song from 1962 with the lyrics changed to reflect the Loony Party's beer of the same name. Loony Party member Knigel Knapp and his band The Big Fibbers recorded this new version of Monster Mash and sang it live at their concerts and at the OMRLP annual conference. The video also proved to be very popular and many copies were sold and downloaded, and this video is still available on YouTube today.

Cover for the Big Fibbers video. (My private collection)

Doing the 'Monster Mash'. (My private collection)

We ordered 1,000 bottles of Monster Mash from the brewery in June 2014 and these bottles completely sold out in less than a month because Monster Mash by then had quickly built up a cult following. I signed lots of empty Monster Mash bottles for friends and Loony Party supporters who wanted a souvenir and we still have a few unopened bottles left five years later, one of which we open every year on the anniversary of the launch date. Monster Mash bottles have been photographed around the world e.g. Sydney Harbour Bridge, Sydney Cricket ground, Home and Away film set at Summer Bay and the Marina Bay Sands hotel and the Long Bar in Raffles hotel in Singapore, and right to the top of Mount Kilimanjaro in Africa. Even the late, great Eric Morecambe was photographed holding a bottle of Monster Mash.

In June 2014 our first Co-ALE-ition beer was available at the Strangers Bar in the House of Commons; this was Winning Co-ALE-ition brewed by the Longdog brewery. A group of us went to the House of Commons where we were met by Sir Gerald Howarth (Aldershot & Farnborough MP) and taken to the Strangers Bar where we met up with three more MPs, Maria Miller (Basingstoke), James Arbuthnot (North East Hampshire) and Simon Hughes (Bermondsey).

I was delighted to meet Simon Hughes again. We had first met at the Bermondsey by-election in February 1983. That marked 30 years since the Monster Raving Loony Party first stood at an Election. Our Leader Screaming Lord Sutch represented the OMRLP but Simon Hughes won and became an MP for the first time and 30 years later in 2014 he was still the Bermondsey MP. We had a very enjoyable afternoon at the Strangers Bar sitting in the sun by the Thames, drinking our Winning Co-ALE-ition ale. I still kept thinking that somebody was going to take down the pump clip of myself with David Cameron holding up my arm on all of the hand pumps. I was delighted to hear that Winning Co-ALE-ition was very popular and all 360 pints were sold in a few days. I heard my beer was a great talking point amongst Parliamentarians and their guests and there was not a single complaint made.

In the Strangers Bar with Sir Gerald Howarth and James Arbuthnot.

(My private collection)

Sir Gerald Howarth comments …

I got involved with taking Co-ALE-ition beer to the House of Commons. In the Strangers Bar there is always a guest beer so it wasn't that hard. It's one of those things that people outside the House of Commons don't recognise. Yes, it's all very serious and there are massively important issues that are debated. However, people don't realise that although you might be at loggerheads on the floor of the House, you develop strong friendships across party lines. It was great to have Co-ALE-ition Ale in the Strangers Bar, and Alan was guest of honour at the launch party there.

In June 2014 my local pub the Prince Arthur in Fleet selected Ascot's Hope & Glory as their World Cup 2014 ale but unfortunately the England team was knocked out of the tournament early.

We started to encounter distribution and availability issues with the Co-ALE-ition Porter and Stout brewed by the two Somerset breweries and it was increasingly difficult to get these ales delivered to my local pubs in Hampshire, Surrey and Berkshire where demand for Co-ALE-ition ales was proving to be insatiable. We approached Ascot brewery who willingly agreed to brew a Co-ALE-ition Porter and Stout for the Monster Raving Loony Party. The Porter was called 'Monsters In the Dark', which we launched in July 2014 at Ascot brewery followed by a pub tour to three pubs in three different counties (Surrey, Berkshire and Hampshire) all of which had Monsters in the Dark available on hand pump. The Stout was called 'Ebony & Ivory' which we launched at the Ascot brewery at the end of October 2014. This was followed by a visit to a Halloween Ale Festival at the Rose & Crown in Sandhurst where both Monsters in the Dark Porter and Ebony & Ivory Stout were available by gravity feed straight from the cask. Both of these Co-ALE-ition beers proved to be very popular in my local area.

Chris Gill and me launching 'Monsters in the Dark'. (My private collection)

We had our first anniversary event in September 2014, which began with a lunch hosted by Susan Carr (Derrill's wife) where we ate fillet steak cooked slowly overnight in Monster Mash ale.

First anniversary … (My private collection)

Two great pump clips.

(My private collection)

In March 2015 we launched our tenth Co-ALE-ition ale with the Hogs Back brewery, this was our Best Bitter and we called it 'Hog in the Limelight' to celebrate that I was standing against Boris Johnson in the May 2015 General Election in Uxbridge where I was expected to be hogging the limelight in my Boss Hogg (Dukes of Hazzard fame) all white outfit.

The launch event took place at the Hogs Back brewery in Tongham (Surrey) followed by visits to three pubs in Farnham where Hog in the Limelight was available that night on the hand pumps.

Rupert Thompson of Hogs Back comments ...

We were flattered to be approached by Alan Hope to join their Co-ALE-ition. Linking a Hog character to the beer and the Loony Party's English eccentric character made this an attractive proposition for the Hogs Back brewery.

Hog in the Limelight pump clip. (My private collection)

Then a major breakthrough occurred in March 2015 when JD Wetherspoon agreed to supply one of our Co-ALE-ition ales to all of their pubs in the UK during the period of the 2015 General Election campaign. This was massive boost to our campaign. The ale supplied to Wetherspoon's pub was a mild from Wild Weather called 'Howlin' Gale'. It became the most popular ale across the UK during the months of April and May 2015. Mild stood for 'Monsters In Loony Dreamland' as this ale proved to be the pinnacle of the Co-ALE-ition brand achievement when total Co-ALE-ition sales across the whole of the UK went above 100,000 pints and a Co-ALE-ition beer was sold in more than 600 different pubs to 50,000 customers located across the whole of England, Scotland, Wales and Northern Ireland.

In March 2015 we heard that Wychwood brewery from Witney (in David Cameron's constituency) had brewed a special beer in a bottle to mark the end of the Coalition Government. Fifty bottles were produced for David Cameron to give to Coalition Government members. I was disappointed when I heard that Cameron's bottled IPA ale was called CO-ALE-ITION and spelt exactly the same as mine. In addition, IPA on Cameron's version was converted to Indispensable Political Ale, copying our Co-ALE-ition idea where IPA was converted to 'Insanity Prevents Austerity'.

The 'unofficial' Co-ALE-ition label. (My private collection)

I complained to Wychwood brewery who confirmed this was a limited edition of 50 bottles and the CO-ALE-ITION name would never be used again. The national newspapers soon picked up on this dispute and the following headlines appeared: "Did Cameron get his CO-ALE-ITION idea from the Monster Raving Loony Party?", and, "The Monster Raving Loony Party rules out any future coalition with the Tories after the arrogant theft of their Co-ALE-ition brand name by David Cameron". It was all great fun at the time and lots of additional publicity for the Loony Party, especially when the Daily Mirror ran a poll and asked its readers which Co-ALE-ition they preferred, David Cameron's or the Monster Raving Loony Party. Thousands of people voted online and 96% of the votes were for the Loony Party's version of Co-ALE-ition. This became the first and only time the Monster Raving Loony Party had beaten the Conservatives in any poll.

Straight after the general election in May 2015 it became clear there was no longer going to be a Coalition Government. At my post-election victory party at the Prince Arthur in Fleet where all of the Co-ALE-ition ales were available on hand pump, a decision was taken and announced to everybody there that no more Co-ALE-ition ale was going to be brewed. There was sadness in the room and I was very disappointed with this decision and I still am five years later as I didn't agree that the end of the Coalition Government should signal the end of my Co-ALE-ition ale.

Bart Longier (Manager of the Prince Arthur in Fleet in 2015) remembers …

A fantastic night, the six Co-ALE-ition ales are selling very well and I was sad to hear they will no longer be available.

In the weeks and months after this decision was taken, customers were still coming into the Prince Arthur asking for a pint of 'Winning Co-ALE-ition', and were being offered exactly the same beer brewed by the Longdog brewery but branded with a different name. Despite telling lots of customers it was exactly the same ale they refused to drink it and many of them said to me that this tastes nothing like 'Winning Co-ALE-ition'. That proves the power of branding and marketing. Interestingly within 12 months of the decision being taken not to brew Co-ALE-ition ales anymore, two Co-ALE-ition breweries ceased brewing their rebranded versions because the demand was not there for the alternative product.

At the 2015 victory party with Mad Max Bobetsky OMRLP candidate in 2015. (My private collection)

A month or so later in June 2015, I was going through all of the photographs taken at the Uxbridge by-election I came across a wonderful photograph of Boris Johnson and myself taken by Loony Party sympathiser and supporter, Steve Lawson from Fleet. Steve had uniquely captured a very special moment with me on the stage standing right next to Boris Johnson as I was gazing admiringly into Boris's eyes as he gave his winner's speech. After showing this photo to Derrill we decided with Steve's permission to use this photograph as the centrepiece of the pump clips for what was to become our final two Co-ALE-tion ales. We approached our two favourite Co-ALE-ition breweries, Ascot and Wild Weather, who readily agreed to produce a Boris Johnson themed Co-ALE-ition beer. Wild Weather's ale was called 'Monster Crush' and Ascot's ale was named 'Blonde Ambition'.

Mike Tempest of Wild Weather comments …

We have really enjoyed our Co-ALE-ition partnership with Alan Hope and the Monster Raving Loony Party which has had a positive effect on our business and has provided the Wild Weather brewery with considerable local and national exposure.

Me with Mike Tempest.
(My private collection)

The Wild Weather 'Monster Crush' launch party took place at the Prince Arthur in June 2015. We had invited Boris Johnson – but he didn't turn up. A few people came to the launch party wearing Boris Johnson face masks and we had a lot of fun.

Monster Crush launch. (My private collection)

Chris Gill (Ascot Ales Owner) comments …

It was a lot of extra work for us, but it shows you don't have to be mad to work here but being Loony helps.

The Ascot 'Blonde Ambition' launch party took place at the Ascot brewery in August 2015 and lots of people turned up as this was the final launch event for what became our 13th Co-ALE-ition beer, all of which were launched in a period of less than two years.

Blonde Ambition pump clip. (My private collection)

I was delighted when Ascot brewery were invited to supply Blonde Ambition to the Strangers Bar in the House of Commons in May 2016 right in the middle of the EU Referendum campaign. A group of us went along to the House of Commons, where Sir Gerald Howarth MP met us and hosted us in the Strangers Bar. We enjoyed a few pints of Blonde Ambition sitting outside by the Thames and toasted the final end of Co-ALE-ition. Our Blonde Ambition ale with a photo of Boris on the pump clip created a lot of interest and became a talking point amongst MPs and Cabinet members during a critical period of the EU Referendum campaign and debate. I was not surprised to hear that all 500 pints of Blonde Ambition had been drunk in just three days. I always wondered whether Boris had a pint of Blonde Ambition in the Strangers Bar; I would like to think he did. And in 2015 our Co-ALE-tion ales received Royal Approval when four of them were on sale at Royal Ascot and two were delivered to the Royal Military Academy at Sandhurst.

Two pictures of the Blonde Ambition launch in the Strangers' Bar.
(My private collection)

During the two-year period of Co-ALE-ition I was the VIP guest and MC at the Fleet Lions Ale Festival in 2015 where six Co-ALE-ition ales were available. I also opened Ale Festivals at Mytchett where I was born and also at East Stratton and Hartley Wintney.

With Jim Storey at the Fleet Lions Ale Fest. (My private collection)

Jim Storey of Fleet Lions remembers …

It was a masterstroke getting Alan Hope to be the VIP guest and MC at our 2015 Ale Festival. There were six Co-ALE-ition ales on sale and they created a lot of additional interest and we were able to donate a record amount to local charities.

I appeared on the BBC Politics Show twice in June 2014 and April 2015 with Andrew Neil and Jo Coburn and always got a mention for Co-ALE-ition. On the second occasion in April 2015, just before the general election, I had managed to sneak two bottles of Monster

Mash past BBC security and hid them inside my white jacket and to everybody's surprise I presented them on live TV to Andrew Neil and Jo Coburn. I also gave Nigel Farage two bottles of Monster Mash at the Clacton by-election.

Co-ALE-ition at the BBC. (Courtesy Steve Lawson)

Another highlight for me was visiting the best pubs in Reading, Winchester and London who were selling Co-ALE-ition ales. We also did a tour of Oxfordshire and stopped at pubs in Oxford, Witney and Wantage, all of which were selling Co-ALE-ition ales. We spent time in David Cameron's favourite local pub in his Witney constituency. This was a Tory Party local and I enjoyed drinking Co-ALE-ition ale with a photo of David Cameron and me on the hand pump and even getting the locals to drink it. I am sure David Cameron would have been told about this beforehand and given his approval especially as the landlord was the Chairman of the Local Conservative Society.

The Co-ALE-ition project was a great fit for the Loony Party and proved to be a fantastic experience and I enjoyed every moment of the whole journey. The Monster Raving Loony Party, directly through Co-ALE-ition, received lots of additional publicity on TV and from the hundreds of different articles and stories which appeared in newspapers and magazines. Over 100,000 pints of Co-ALE-ition ale were sold in 600 different pubs across the length and breadth of the UK which are all records for a beer produced by a UK political party. Just to get one Co-ALE-ition beer into the Strangers Bar in the House of Commons was amazing but to get two in there was unbelievable. No other political party has ever achieved that. I also became the first UK political party leader to have a beer named after me. During the 2015 General Election campaign this ale sold 43,000 pints in less than two months. To this day I still cannot believe how we got away with pump clips on the hand pumps in the Strangers Bar visibly displaying Prime Minister David Cameron and me in a Winning Co-ALE-ition, and Boris Johnson on the Blonde Ambition pump clip – that foretold the future, did it not? But as Leader of the Monster Raving Loony Party, I always knew anything was possible if you gave it a go.

I would like to give my personal thanks to Derrill Carr, the CAMRA Surrey and Hampshire Borders branch and Steve and Joy Lawson who attended every Co-ALE-ition event, plus every one of the eight micro-breweries who brewed a Co-ALE-ition beer for the Official Monster Raving Loony Party. I am especially grateful to Chris Gill from the Ascot brewery who brewed four different Co-ALE-ition ales and who arranged for our beer to go into the Strangers Bar in the House of Commons, and Mike Tempest from the Wild Weather brewery who brewed three different Co-ALE-ition ales. Mike also enabled one of our Co-ALE-ition ales to be available in 400 different Wetherspoon pubs across the whole of the UK during the 2015 General Election campaign. I am also very grateful to JD Wetherspoons and East West Ales, their real ale supplier, for all the support especially during the 2015 General Election campaign.

I have often been told as Leader of the Official Monster Raving Loony Party over the last 20 years that the Loony Party couldn't organise a piss-up in a brewery. Well, Co-ALE-ition has certainly proved everybody to be wrong as we have successfully organised 13 sessions in 8 micro-breweries and lots more great sessions elsewhere as well. We are the only political party to get Brexit right as in 2016 our "In Out, In Out, Shake It All About" prediction has proved to be spot on in the years of negotiations since the EU Referendum.

Who else other than the Official Monster Raving Loony Party would be crazy enough to try to get away with putting photos of me with two Prime Ministers on beer pump clips and then have the temerity to get both of these beers on sale at the Strangers Bar in the House of Commons?

We enjoyed a golden period of two to three years with our Co-ALE-ition brand of ales. We had lots of laughs and enjoyment on this journey as we proved once again that by refreshing all parts of the country the Monster Raving Loony Party does bring something very different and unique to the UK political scene.

Every year on the Co-ALE-ition anniversary date in September, a few of us get together and open up a bottle of Monster Mash, five years after its best-before date. Sounds Loony, I know, but the beer still tastes great and just like the Monster Raving Loony Party it is going to last a very long time.

PART 7

EPILOGUE

In this Part:

CHAPTER 26

Now I'm in Fleet

So now we approach the end of my story. But there's a gap I need to fill.

When I left the Dog and Partridge in Yateley in 2005 I was at a low ebb, but never low enough to contemplate suicide. I remember sitting on one of the benches on the green outside the pub, with tears in my eyes. I just didn't know what was going to happen. I was 'lost' for two or three years. It was the lowest point in my life. But I am naturally positive. I've always said that as long as you are not dead or in jail, nothing else matters.

I didn't really choose Fleet as the place to live, it chose me really. I was homeless when I had to leave the pub. It was a shock. I'd expected to stay there for the rest of my life. So at age 63 I was homeless, and out of work for the first time in my life, and my wife was dying. I needed somewhere to live, and quickly. I did have a small camper van, but that was no way to live.

I approached Camberley Council, but as I was out of their area, they wouldn't help me and told me to go to Farnborough – Rushmoor District Council. Again I was out of area, so I went to Hart District Council in Fleet. They agreed to help. Norma and I had often talked about retiring to Fleet, and all of a sudden, there I was. It was just by chance. They put me in a temporary flat in Albany Close first. I was there from July 2005 to Nov 2005, and then I moved to where I am now just in time for Christmas 2005. Been there ever since. I wanted a ground-floor flat and eventually got this one. It's worked out well.

I was visiting Norma about two or three times a week. She always wanted me to take her an Indian take-away – a Korma with all the trimmings (a Korma for Norma).

I've had no serious relationships since Norma died – plenty of lady friends, but no more than that.

I worked as a relief landlord on and off for a period of about three years. Various pubs. I particularly enjoyed the White Hart in Sevenoaks (twice) and the Three Mariners in Felixstowe. I thought that having the camper van would be helpful for that work, but it wasn't really as you are normally expected to 'live above the shop'. I eventually sold the camper van at quite a loss! I have retained my personal licence though, so I could step back in as relief landlord if needed.

Derrill Carr recalls …

When the manager left at the Prince Arthur in Fleet, we cooked up a story that Alan was going to step in. That put the wind up a few of the customers.

I normally go to Malta and Lanzarote every year – just for a week or so. I've made friends over there over time. Both islands have Loony Party branches now. Some of my friends from Yateley came with me to these places, and Portugal as well. I would like to go back to the USA, but it remains on my wish-list for now.

I now have 8 grandchildren and 13 great-grandchildren. Mark, my son, had two sons, Simon and Ryan, and a daughter. Simon has two children – Zackery and a daughter. Mark wanted Zac to be called Kerry, but he wouldn't have it.

Mark's wedding in Alton was a big family event. I gave a speech. I suppose I gave Mark away. Mark's step-brother was there with his family, which was nice. We are quite a family. Last Christmas there were 32 of us in the same room for Christmas evening.

My life is not as busy as it was when I had the hotel and pub, but it still has its high points. I still enjoy being on the Town Council on a Loony ticket, and I've made lots of great friends in Fleet.

I don't have a set routine for housework. I wash when the basket's full, and buy food when the cupboard's low. No set pattern. I don't use the washing machine. I wash everything by hand in the sink. I make food as I need it. Again, no set routine, but I'll have a decent meal every day. I don't drink at home, I never have. Obviously, I'd share a drink with regulars in the hotel or pub, but I was never one of those landlords who kept drink in their private rooms. I know that many do … but they die young. It's not a good idea.

I never get depressed or lonely, and I don't think I really have a 'serious' side in that sense. I am what I am – what you see is what you get. If I have a problem, I generally turn to myself. I have a discussion with myself in the mirror – Kerry and Al in conversation. I'm quite insular and rely on my own judgement. But I will 'suffer fools gladly' – I don't get nasty with people or turn my back on them.

The key thing is being amiable and getting on with people. There's many a time I would tell someone they'd had enough to drink. But rather than just throw them out, I would offer them a lift home, and promise to buy them their first drink next time they came in. They would usually accept the lift, but I was never reminded of the free drink offer.

I'm still driving and having a car is very important. The bus-stop is too far for me to walk now. I don't really have any hobbies. I regard the Prince Arthur in Fleet as 'my Club' – and that's where I meet people. It's a good life, and I don't want to change it in any way!

CHAPTER 27

Happy Birthday to me!

Well as it says on the tee-shirt: "I don't know how I got to 77, but I'm sure somebody somewhere lost a bet."

2019 has been quite a year: I turned 77; I've been Party Leader for 20 years, and it's 20 years since I first visited the Prince Arthur in Fleet. I've recently been given a portrait painted by Welsh artist Anna-Lisa Coleman.

Here's the portrait. (My private collection)

I combined my 77th birthday party with Father's Day and a celebration of being the Leader of the Official Monster Raving Loony Party for 20 years into one event.

There was a very good turnout at the Prince Arthur for a Sunday night; my four children and some grandchildren were there and a good number of Loony Party members and local friends. Lots of other people popped in during the night and came over to congratulate me. The party went on till closing time.

We all posed for a group photo outside. There were so many people milling around, we ended up stopping the traffic on the main road.

Wetherspoon's staff brought over a large birthday cake in Loony Party colours with a lit number 77 candle to my table. The cake was engraved and everybody in the pub sang Happy Birthday as I blew out the number 77 candle in one go.

Wetherspoons sent their official photographer and this event was later included in their September 2019 magazine. Wetherspoons do value the publicity I can get for them, and they really value my loyalty to their philosophy and approach. Stuart Merricks, the manager at the Prince Arthur, presented me with a specially inscribed glass tankard to commemorate the occasion on behalf of JD Wetherspoons.

I then stood up and thanked everybody and went on to tell them about my greatest achievement at the pub when I recommended my grandson, Matt Seale, to Dan Proctor, the Prince Arthur manager, over seven years ago. Dan interviewed Matt and offered him a job. Matt is currently the longest serving member of the staff at the Prince Arthur and I was delighted and very proud to hear that Matt had recently been promoted to kitchen manager.

Then it was time for a sing-song. I started with 'Mack the Knife', and followed up with several other songs. That brought even more people into the pub. We opened one of the last bottles of the Co-ALE-ition beer, Monster Mash. It still tasted great more than four years after its best-before date. Everyone agreed that the beer, the Party, and me, are still in great nick!

By the time we got to midnight, it was still busy and I was being cajoled to perform a very personal version of '77 Sunset Strip'. I have to say that I declined.

Here are some great pictures of the event.

Posing outside the Prince Arthur. (Courtesy Gill Evans)

I like cake! (Courtesy Gill Evans)

Entertaining the crowd while 'Boris' looks on. (Courtesy Gill Evans)

Monster Mash and Tankard. (Courtesy Gill Evans)

Dave Moore from Fleet remembers …

I attended Alan's 77th birthday party in June 2019 which was also a great celebration of his 20 years as the Leader of the Monster Raving Loony Party. I'm now retired and looking forward to going to Loony Party Conferences. and supporting Alan whenever he stands at an election.

CHAPTER 28

Looking forward …

The future …

I think the Official Monster Raving Loony Party will go on and on and on. During both the 2017 and 2019 elections, my phone never stopped with young people wanting to know who we are, what we are, can they join.

Over the last ten years or so, I've been asking the Party if they could find someone younger, who had the ambience, the time, and of course some money – you can't do this without some money in your pocket – if they could find somebody younger, maybe I could move over. Perhaps become the party president. I wouldn't mind doing that. Keeping an overview, while we nurture somebody else to take over fully as Leader. That's what we've got in mind. That's the future of the Party. I may be the future of the Party at the moment, but I know that in years to come, I won't be.

We need to build on this interest we're getting from younger people. It would be good to rejuvenate. But we're still here. I'm soldiering on. Things can only get better, as the song goes. But no-one in place to take over yet, so we'll keep going.

I don't really know how we could increase the OMRLP membership. We have quite a lot of members, and we are in the black financially. We are the Party that everybody loves; nobody hates us. But we do need to reach out to more sensible 'loonies'. We are the only sensible party. Our key principle is 'to have fun', and don't forget that we have had quite a few of our policies adopted. Leading politicians have often told me that they do read our manifesto, looking for good ideas they can 'steal'.

Mad Max Bobetsky comments …

Alan's problem is that he doesn't have an underlying philosophy to achieve power, or the money to fund it. It just seems to be about having a laugh and making people smile – there's not much politics. He's definitely a showman, although he is unique in politics.

I think the Party needs to get more serious and put a proper campaign together. The Leaders of our main parties all seem to be in a mess about who they are and who they identify with. We need to raise our game, field more candidates and do it properly, there's a gap in the market. Yes, we have to keep the humour, but we need to be serious too. There's a gap in the centre of politics and we should try to fill it. We just don't have enough candidates. We need to be up around 200 candidates to be taken seriously.

There isn't enough substance. That might have been there at the start, but it's gone now. We've got to get more serious. We need to really think about a new set of relevant policies – though the 99p coin is a great idea. It costs more than 1p to make 1p. It needs new policies to attract sponsorship, and then to field the candidates. We really should be targeting younger voters, many in the party are quite old. It needs to be a party of the young.

But Alan will be remembered by the Party. He's like a Founding Father. You could say he is the Lenin of the OMRLP.

Rumours of my death have been exaggerated …

I've had some health issues over the last few years, but those have been dealt with. I'm back to providing 'strong and stable' leadership again.

People just make stuff up. I've been written off more times than I've actually been unwell.

I know I said that I had that exploratory operation, and they found nothing wrong, and that's true. Some say I had a twisted bowel, but that's wrong. But there was a problem. I had a blocked bile duct as it turned out, but the operation didn't put that right. It was only afterwards that we realised what the problem was.

I'll admit to being in hospital a couple of times in recent years with fluid on the lung. That suggests a heart problem. But they checked that out and didn't find a problem. When I had the angiogram, the nurse said: "Mr Hope. Are you really 74 years old?" They said my heart looked years younger. I have got a bit of an enlarged heart, but it's not a problem, I'm just big-hearted!

And they treated me really well in hospital once they found out who I was – Party Leader and all.

The bile duct was about 15 years ago. The water in the lungs has been more recent – the last two or three years. I do have some oedema – which I take water tablets for – so I guess things just go out of balance a bit from time to time. I've had pneumonia a couple of times too – probably all connected. The last time was just a year or so ago, but I was in my 20s the first time I came down with it. I've had a pneumonia jab now, so I won't get it again!

I have gout as well now, and that causes the problems with walking. It's very painful. It comes and goes. Walking upstairs is hard – my ankles play up now – just wear and tear I think.

More recently I have had a pacemaker fitted, and that has made a difference. Perhaps I should start singing again – Kerry and his Pacemaker? After they fitted that state-of-the-art pacemaker, they told me I could live to 150, although I'd have to go back every ten years to have the battery replaced – not looking forward to doing that. It took a while to settle down, but it's working well now and has made a big difference. Less breathless, and no problems with water on the lungs.

What's important to me is just being alive – taking each day as it comes. I'd like to get to 150 – and I really enjoyed my 77th Birthday Party. I'm halfway there now.

Looking back, though, I don't think I would change my life. I'd do the same things in the same way.

So, I'm still here – alive and (almost) kicking. You can't write me off that easily.

Five years ago, John, my brother, was told he was dying, and I rushed down to see him. The priest had seen him and given his Last Rites, and John started to talk about all the regrets in his life. About how he hated his surname because he always got the micky taken – Hopey, Dopey, Ropey etc. I felt so sorry for him. I walked out of that hospital with tears in my eyes. And he's gone now. That's a great personal loss for me. And just recently, perhaps the friend I'd known for longest, Allan Phillips, has passed away. That's such a shame.

So to conclude. It has to be recognised that I won't be Party Leader forever, nor will my feet walk on England's mountains green, forever.

I'm too modest to talk about my legacy. That is for others to decide. But it has been tremendous fun. I've put a smile on people's faces, made them happy. And that makes me happy too! Have I changed people's lives? Well, some people. I have entertained lots of people, I made a difference to Ashburton, I've made a difference in Fleet.

I'm not a religious man. When it's time, it's time.

But whenever that time comes, I don't want to be buried; I don't want to be cremated.

I want to be wrapped in a shroud and placed in a cave, with a big boulder over the front.

If He can get out three days later, I'm damn sure I can!

WHERE'S MY EASTER EGG??????????????

Prince Rex reflects …

One night in March 2017, I'm chatting to my good friend Derrill Carr about this and that – just two guys in a pub over a pint. Our conversation turned to Alan, and from somewhere – and I can't honestly remember who said it first – we came up with the idea of writing his biography.

I was intrigued and slightly scared. I've written lots over the years, but I've never written a biography – never had to get inside someone else's head – never had to write in their voice. I really didn't know if it would work.

Inevitably, I've spent hours talking to Alan, his family and friends, and I thank them all for their time and their honesty. At the start of this project I'd never met Alan, so we did really start from zero.

I now think of Alan as a friend, and I hope he feels the same way, but for me, it's been a bit like a love affair. At first I was intrigued and interested in this entertaining man and the various 'lives' he has led. As we progressed and I learned some of the less nice things about him, I began to have some doubts. Was he really worth it? Did I really want to get into his head?

At times it felt like I was becoming Alan. I knew more about him that I know about myself. I was thinking about Alan when I woke up, then all day, and still when I went to bed – but I'm glad to say I never, ever dreamed about him!

But now we've come through that, and I'm back to liking him again. Perhaps we've just got used to each other – perhaps I just understand him better. But it has been fun.

Like Alan, I always like to have the last word, hence these thoughts.

But I don't think he'll let me …

Prince Rex of Fleet – 2019.

ACKNOWLEDGEMENTS …

No. I won't allow you that pleasure, Rex!

Lots of people have given up their time and their memories to make this book happen.

Alan Phillips	'Baron von Thunderclap'	Barry Toms
Bart Longier	Bob Burgos	Bob Hickson
Bob Potter OBE	Charlie Dennis	Charles Griffin
'Chinners'	Chris Bryant	Chris Gill
Chuck Pengilly	Dave Berry	Dave Brooks
Dave Moore	Derrill Carr	Dick Matthews
Don Proctor	Freddy Zapp	George Stone
Sir Gerald Howarth	Gill Evans	Jed Ford
Jeff Hinge	'The Jersey Flier'	Jim Storey
John Hope – my brother	Keith Smith	'Lady Muck'
Liz Riley	'Long Tall Sally'	'Lord Charles'
'Mad Max'	Mark Hope – my son	Mary Hands – my sister
Mike Carlin	Mike Tempest	My daughters – Angela, Gina and Helen
Nigel Farage	'Old Codgers' of the Dog and Partridge	Pete Webb
Peter Collins	Phil Robins	'Prince Rex of Fleet'
Quintin Drake	'R U Seerius'	Ron Stevenson
Rosemary Christophers	Rupert Thompson	Seb Gibley
'Sinbad'	Cllr. Steve Forster	Steve 'Lawd' Lawson
Sue Glover	Sylvia McMaster	Terry Twinn
Terry Wright	'The Flying Brick'	Tim Jenkinson
Tony Lea	Virginia Hill	Yvonne Elwood

I sincerely thank you all. And a very special vote of thanks to 'Prince Rex of Fleet' and Derrill Carr, both of whom worked so hard to make this book a reality.

And if I've forgotten anyone, I apologise and thank you too.

And that really IS the last word! (Until the next edition on my 100th birthday.)

Alan Hope, 2020

ABOUT THE AUTHOR

Alan Hope was born in Mytchett, Surrey, in 1942, and grew up in Hawley Estate in Hampshire. After his singing career, he bought a hotel in Devon and it was there in 1982 that he formed the Official Monster Raving Loony Party with his good friend Screaming Lord Sutch.

He moved back to Hampshire in 2000 and currently lives in Fleet.

In addition to being the Leader of the Official Monster Raving Loony Party, Alan serves as a Town Councillor for Fleet Town Council, and he has continued to stand in all general elections and most by-elections.

Alan has been married three times. He has four children and 20 grandchildren and great-grandchildren.

Printed in Poland
by Amazon Fulfillment
Poland Sp. z o.o., Wrocław

61740010R00186